THE ORPHANED ARIZONA STATE ROUTE 89

Historic SR 89 in Pima and Santa Cruz Counties

Dana Eker 2021 ©

ACKNOWLEDGEMENTS

In appreciation to my sister Paula Eker Riley, for her encouragement to move to Arizona. To my brother-in-law Dave Riley for loaning out my sister for adventures. Paula often stood watch at the car parked at gates while I slipped through barbed wire fences. "Leaving only foot prints and taking only photos."

The collection of history books amassed from the Green Valley Annex Bookstore in the Green Valley Village, thank you to all the Green Valley residents who donated books that were not in my budget to purchase.

Online information from the ARIZONA STATE MUSEUM was incredible for all the hours and dedication for preservation and filing of documents. This valuable tool saves me from allergens while perusing old books.

Find a grave.com, Legacy, Ancestry.com and Pima and Santa Cruz County Cemetery records, provides access to places that would be impossible to get to.

The National Park Service has no comparison in digging up the past and presenting facts clearly and orderly.

Early miners sketched out the landscape for brochures to promote real estate speculation. We get the benefit of their artistic talents.

Much of Arizona history is in Spanish, the online translator program was very helpful.

TABLE OF CONTENTS

INTRODUCTION

EXPANSION of the UNITED STATES 1783–1853 — 1

INDIGENOUS TRIBES — 2

US STATE ROUTE 89 — 3

OVERVIEW OF ROUTE 89 — 4

TOURING THE SANTA CRUZ VALLEY — 7

ROUTE #1 — 7

SAN XAVIER DEL BAC — 8

SILVER LAKE and THE SANTA CRUZ RIVER — 9

THE SANTA CRUZ RIVER — 9

ROUTE #1 CUTOFF PIMA MINE RD. — 10

THE TUCSON – NOGALES RAILROAD — 12

ROUTE #2   OLD NOGALES HIGHWAY — 13

THE SAHUARITA REGION — 14

SAHUARITA AIR FORCE RANGE — 17

HELVETIA MINE AND HISTORIC RUINS — 19

THE GREEN VALLEY PECAN COMPANY — 21

I-19 BUSINESS AND DUVAL MINE ROAD — 22

QUAIL CREEK RESORT — 24

CAMP CONTINENTAL — 25

CONTINENTAL — 26

THE SANTA RITA MOUNTAINS and MADERA CANY — 27

LA POSADA — 28

SANTA RITA EXPERIMENTAL RANGE — 30

MADERA CANYON — 31

GREEN VALLEY — 32

SANTA RITA MOUNTAIN PEAKS — 36

SAN IGNACIO de la CANOA LAND GRANT — 39

AMADO	41
REVANTON RANCH	44
AGUA LINDA	46
PAJARITO RANCH / SHANKLE	48
APACHE WARS GAVE WAY TO MEXICAN DRUG WARS	52
ANOTHER WAY TO CROSS THE BORDER	55
MISSION SAN JOSE DE TUMACACORI	56
CAMPS AND FORTIFICATIONS IN THE SANTA CRUZ VALLEY	58
U.S. ARMY HELIOGRAPH STATIONS	63
GERONIMO	65
RAILS MAKE NOGALES	67
NOGALES	72
BIOGRAPHIES of PEOPLE and PLACES	74
EUSEBIO FRANCISCO KINO	75
JUAN BAUTISTA de ANZA II	76
MARTINEZ HILL	77
SAHUARITO	78
CYRUS S. RICE	79
ALBERT C. BENEDICT	82
ELIAS BREVOORT	84
JAMES KILROY BROWN	89
WILLIAM A. HARTT	95
JAMES B. BULL	90
WILLIAM B. ROODS /RHOADES	93
FREDERICK MAISH, THOMAS DRISCOLL and THE CANOA RANCH	98
ANTONIO FERRER AMADO	101
SABINO OTERO	104
CARMEN CELAYA ZEPEDA	106

TERESA CELAYA, LA DOÑA DE ARIVACA	108
Col CHARLES PATTERSON SYKES	110
CALABASAS	117
HISTORIC YERBA BUENA RANCH	118
PETER KITCHEN	122
JOHN ROSS BROWNE	126
RAPHAEL PUMPELLY	128
HUMAN BURIALS, SACRED OBJECTS, and YOU	129
CEMETERIES ALONG THE WAY	130
LOS REALES CEMETERY	133
AGUILAR RANCH CEMETERY	137
HELVETIA CEMETERY	138
MORENO RANCH CEMETERY	140
TWIN BUTTES CEMETERY	142
SOPORI RANCH CEMETERY	155
AMADO CEMETERY	160
MISSION LOS SANTOS ANGELES de GUEVAVI	174
OTERO CEMETERY	181
SALERO RANCH CEMETERY	182
TELLOS-RAMOS-ESPINOSA-LOPEZ BURIAL SITE	184
TUBAC CEMETERY	185
SAINT JOSEPHS CEMETERY	186
TUMACACORI MISSION CEMETERY	194
WHITEHOUSE GRAVESITE MADERA CANYON	197
MORALES FAMILY CEMETERY	199
CONCLUSION	
INDEX	

INTRODUCTION

Visualizing over 478 years of history along route 89 through the Santa Cruz Valley, using modern interpretation that stimulates tourism with colorful brochures, requires hard labor to pry away layers of land grants, ranching, wars, and migration.

The original Nogales Road diverts from Summit, southwest of the Tucson airport, heading south and it once intersected with the south and east Santa Rita Roads towards Helvetia.

From Helvetia, the Helvetia road followed the mountains south to Madera Canyon, to Proctor Ranch, then towards Elephant Head and once connecting with Canoa Ranch. A Canoa Road exits in Santa Cruz County that intersects with Stage Lane at Santa Gertrudis Lane. An unnamed irregular road follows the east side of the railroad tracks, across private property that intersects with Pendleton Drive around Rio Rico. Crossing over the Rio Rico Drive, this dusty dirt road connects with Willow Drive. **EXIT 17** Off of Rio Rico Drive east, is a small road named Stable Lane.

The original State Highway 89 was designated in the late 1920s as part of the Federal Highway System, the most important road in Arizona between all major cities and smaller towns from Mexico to Canada. Construction of the new Interstate Highway system began in the late 1950's and by the end of the 1970's, the distance from Nogales to Flagstaff was covered by three Interstates highways: 19, 10 and 17.

In 1992, US Route 89 was decommissioned, abandoned as a federal highway. Expanding of Interstate Highway 19 will have more travelers whisked north or south in comfort without having the privilege to explore the dusty, rutted original roads that Spanish explorers trekked from Mexico into the Arizona territory. Layers of history continue to be buried as progress encroaches on the area.

Presented here are personal struggles, migrations, failures and successes of the early pioneers, mostly unknown, who developed the area with shovels and picks. Travelers today are safe from the terrors of Apache wars, malaria deaths, ranch wars, and the biggest worry is tee-off reservations. Not all there is to relate is in this work, especially since many south of the border, believe Arizona is still Mexican Territory. Please enjoy some of the obscure and enlightening history of the southern US route 89.

Dana Eker 2021

Expansion of the United States, 1783–1853

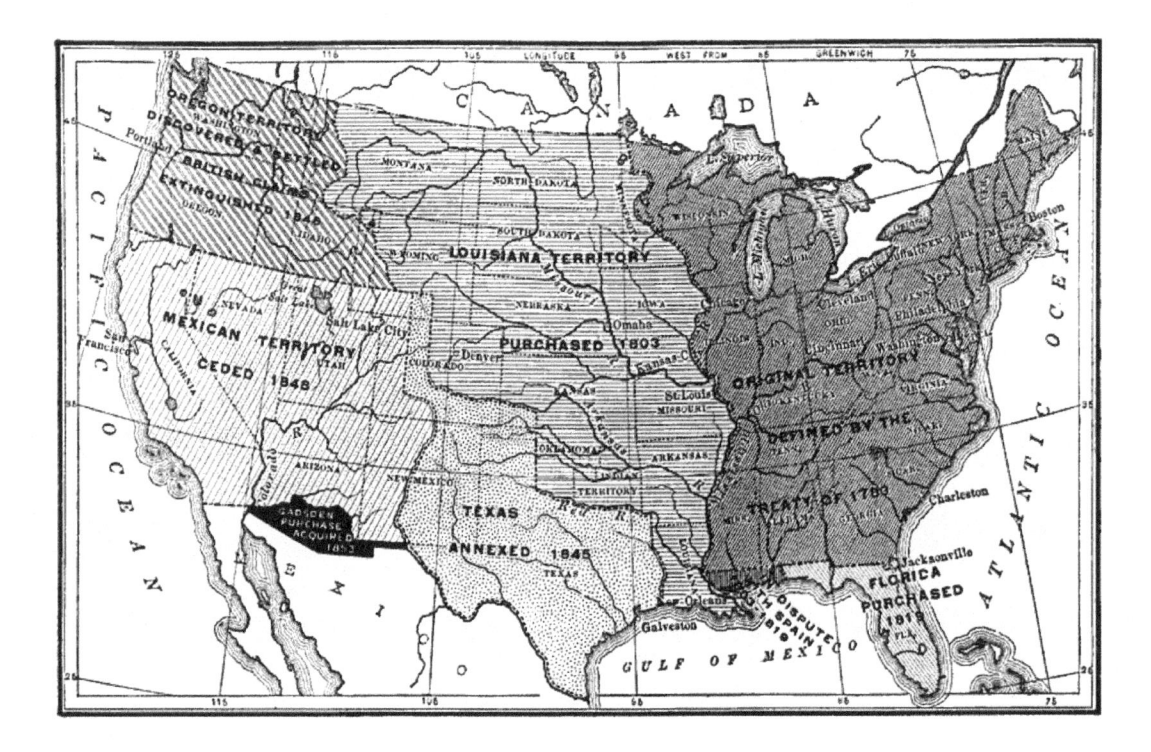

A brief review will add to the landscape of Arizona history, starting with early European holdings here in this country.

Mexico was a colony of **Spain**, known as 'New Spain.' The colonial period lasted 1521 until 1810, when Mexico revolted and was unofficially independent of Spain.

The Treaty of Paris of 1783, passed the Northwest Territory from **Great Britain** to the new United States.

The Louisiana Purchase of 1803, passed 828,000 square miles of territory from **France** to the United States doubling the size of the expanding nation.

Annexation of Texas of 1845 came after the **Republic of Texas** declared independence from the Republic of Mexico in 1836.

The Oregon Treaty of 1846, also known as the Washington Treaty, was signed between **Great Britain** and the United States.

The Treaty of Guadalupe Hidalgo of 1848, brought an official end to the Mexican-American War (1846-1848), **Mexico** passed 55 percent of its territory, including parts of present-day Arizona, California, New Mexico, Texas, Colorado, Nevada, and Utah, to the United States.

The Gadsden Purchase of 1853, **Mexico** sold another 38,000 sq miles of desert for $15 million to the United States securing a railroad linking Southern California and the East.

Who can rightfully make a claim of ownership on native land? Have they been better stewards of the land?

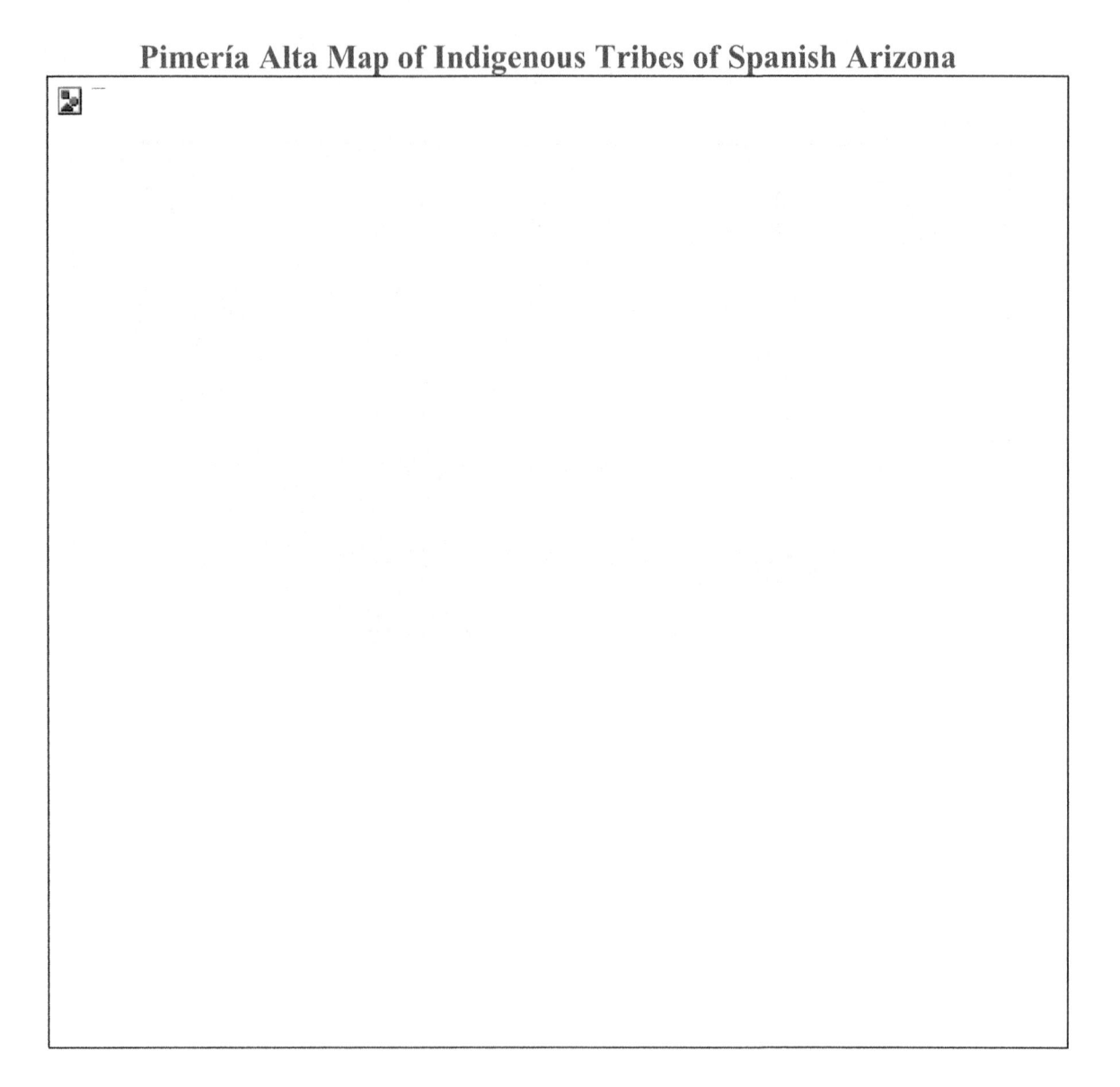

Pimería Alta Map of Indigenous Tribes of Spanish Arizona

PIMERIA ALTA / UPPER LAND OF THE PIMA

Conquests of indigenous people who are not party to any treaties or purchases that severely affect their way of life result in warfare, migration or assimilation. Many people in Arizona and Mexico are still connected by lineage and tradition, they deserve respect.

It's very uninformed to require Latinos to automatically speak English when entering their former country. Yet the lines are long when enjoying a fabulous meal in a favorite Mexican restaurant and being served by a bi-lingual waitperson. A few kind phrases in Spanish will open doors for you. Kindness and courtesy on reservations is welcomed also. Language optional.

Another quick review: Early people in the Santa Cruz Valley:

2,000 years ago lived the **Hohokam** ancient people known for the canals, terraces and dams to control water from meager rain fall to grow their crops. Evidence of these people are found around the community of Continental. Their descendants include the Pima people. **Upper Pimean** are the **Tohono O'odam** who lived along central rivers, raising corn, beans, and squash using flood irrigation by 1600 when the Spanish arrived. (more later)

"Papago" is the Spanish word for "tepary-bean eaters." By the late 20th century, the Papago tired of being referred to as bean-eaters, their name was officially changed to *Tohono O'odham*, meaning Desert People.

The **Sobaipuri** (soh-BY-per-ee or soh-by-poorh-ee) people were an Upper Piman group who occupied southern Arizona and northern Sonora in the1400s to the 1800s. Ruins are found at the village of Santa Cruz de Gaybanipitea near the San Pedro River.

Source: The Battle of Santa Cruz de Gaybanipitea: Historical Narratives and Archaeological Insights. Old Pueblo Archaeology Center Bulletin 64:1-11. Deni Seymour

The **Apache** people arrived in 1300's -1400's from Canada and Alaska. Apache were many small bands of migrating hunters and gatherers living in mountain forest, canyons, and deserts. Then, enters European influences exaggerated by Hollywood.

The **Yaqui** tribe dwelt on reservations in Sonora Mexico. When Mexico was independence from Spain, the Yaqui retained their individuality and considered themselves as self-governing, then revolted in the year 1825. They were granted 817,000 sq. meters of lands by the government of the United States in 1964, some are in the southwestern part of Tucson in Arizona. The Pascua Yaqui Tribe a division of the Yaqui community has gained federal recognition. As farmers, they grew crops such as beans, corn and squash. While women gathered herbs, nuts and fruits, the men rabbits, deer and small games. (Yaqui have much more history. *Pascua* means Easter to honor the date of the settling of the village.)

Source: Yaqui Indians Facts, History and Culture | Only Tribal

In 1971 a group in San Xavier formed a cooperative of landowners in order to piece some of the lands back together and find a way to farm it as a whole. The **San Xavier Cooperative Farm** considers the following aspects (and others) of the Tohono O'odham Himdag, or Way of Life, to ensure that decisions in the farm's rehabilitation project are consistent with the culture. The San Xavier Cooperative Association is committed to healthy farming practices and growing traditional crops to support the cultural and environmental values, as well as support economic development within the community. Online shopping.!!1

Source: About Our Cooperative | San Xavier Co-Op Farm (sanxaviercoop.org)

US State Route 89

The original trading route that became **US State Route 89**, ran 1800 miles from the Mexican border at Nogales to the Canadian border near Babb, Montana. In Arizona it travels from Nogales through Tucson, Florence, Phoenix, Wickenburg, Prescott, Ash Fork, Flagstaff, to Page.

During the 1920's, SR 89 was considered Arizona's Main Street. The new highway system starting in the 1950's and through the 1970's, constructed Interstate Highways 10, 17 and 19.

In 1992, Highway 89 was no longer used as a federal highway. Parts of the original route still exists in Pima and Santa Cruz County, running through Tucson and along Highway 19, used for local traffic. (see map US 89society.org.)

The original route had traffic flow through Tucson from Stone Ave. southward, connecting with the Old Nogales Highway or US 89/ BUS 19. A variety of roads is used for this tour to see the history.

The following chart from usroute89.org, shows the mileage of Highway 19 from Tucson to Nogales, with side roads noted. The kilometers and miles start from Nogales to Tucson.

Mileage and roads to follow in this writing will aid you in your travels according to modern roads. Included in this work are historical maps for comparison.

OVERVIEW OF ROUTE 89
US 89society.org

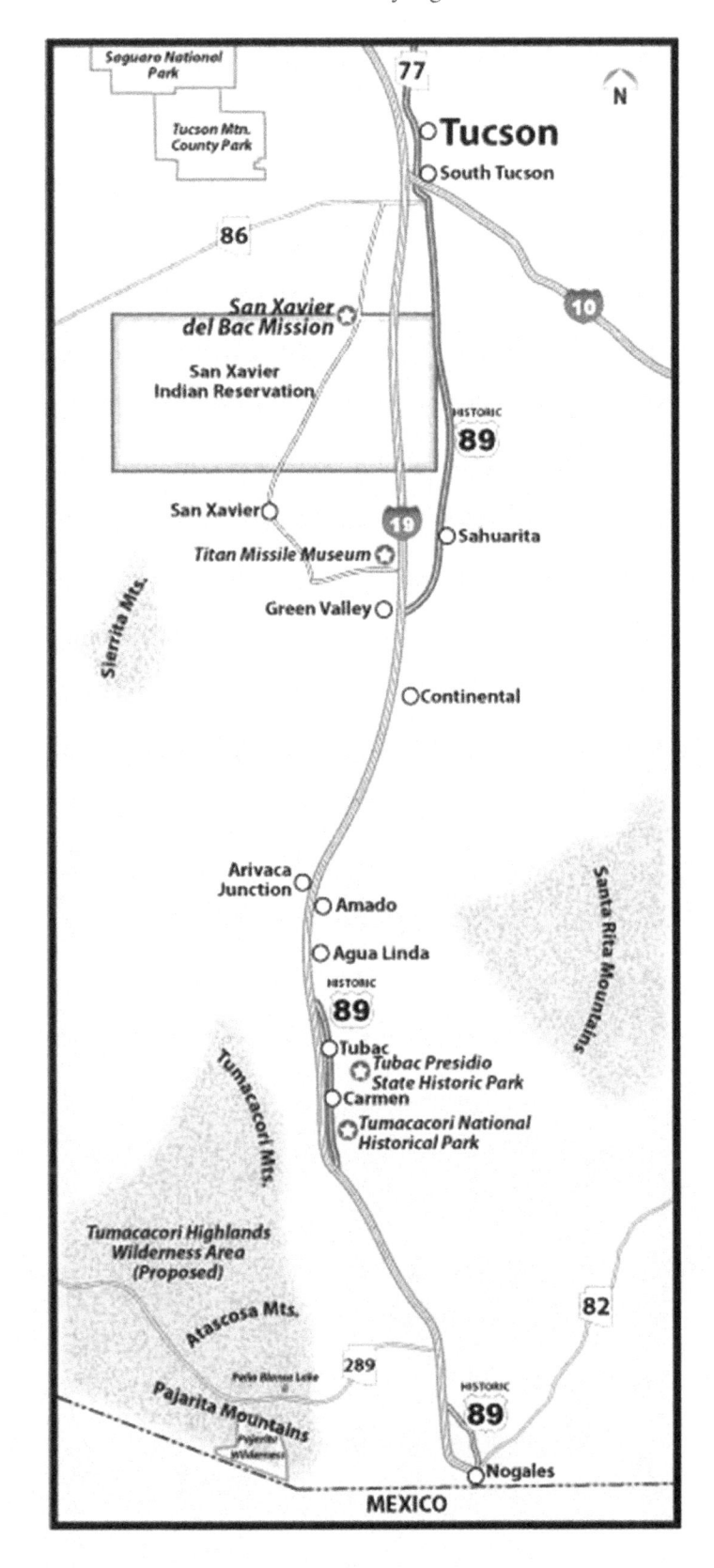

TUCSON SOUTH

County	Location	km	mi	Exit	Destinations	Notes
Pima	Tucson	101.84	63.28	102	29th Street, 22nd Street, Silverlake Road, Starr Pass Boulevard	Continuation beyond I-10, leads to westbound I-10 frontage road.
		101.63	63.15	101	I-10 Phoenix, El Paso	Northern terminus. I-10 exit 260
		99.97	62.12	99	SR 89 (Ajo Way)	
		98.35	61.11	98	Irvington Road	
		95.10	59.09	95	Valencia Road – Tucson	Tucson International Airport
		92.04	57.19	92	San Xavier Road	Los Reales Cemetery (defunct)
		87.98	54.67	87	Papago Road	Dead end, U-Turn only
		80.32	49.91	80	Pima Mine Road	Desert Diamond Casino, Tohono O'odham Nation
	Sahuarita	75.48	46.90	75	Sahuarita Road	
		69.72	43.32	69	Duval Mine Road	I-19 BL Shopping, Gas
	Green Valley	65.74	40.85	65	Esperanza Boulevard	Dining, Drug store, Banking
		63.63	39.54	63	Continental Road	Shopping, Banking, Dining, Gas
		56.26	34.96	56	Canoa Road	History
		48.39	30.07	48	Arivaca Road	Dining
		42.84	26.62	42	Agua Linda Road	
		40.10	24.92	40	Chavez Siding Road	
		34.94	21.71	34	Tubac	History, Tourism
		29.34	18.23	29	Tumacacori-Carmen	Tumacacori National Historical Park
		25.17	15.64	25	Palo Parado Road	
Santa Cruz	Nogales	22.45	13.95	22	Peck Canyon Road	
		17.53	10.89	17	Rio Rico Drive, Yavapai Drive	Dining, Gas, Shopping, Gas
		12.42	7.72	12	SR 289 (Ruby Road)	
		8.55	5.31	8	Grand Avenue	I-19 BL; southbound exit and northbound entrance
		4.76	2.96	4	SR 189 (Mariposa Road)	Shopping, Dining, Gas
		1.90	1.18	1	Western Avenue (Target Range Road)	Signed as Exit 1B southbound
		0.71	0.44	1A	West International Street	Southbound exit only, to cross border, park on US side and walk over.

0.28	0.17	North West Avenue	Begin freeway
0.16	0.10	North Sonoita Avenue at West Compound Street	At-grade intersection
0.06	0.04	West Bradford Street	At-grade intersection, northbound is not signed
0.05	0.03	West Mix Street	At-grade intersection
0.00	0.00	West Crawford Street at North Sonoita Avenue	Southern terminus, Downtown

Sources: www.arizonaroads.com/us/us89.htm
http://usroute89.com/where-is-us-route-89-in-arizonas

TOURING THE SANTA CRUZ VALLEY TODAY

Today's travelers ride in comfort while exploring the Santa Cruz Valley. The first improvement is dressing comfortably. A Conquistador's suit of armor, complete with a skeleton in it, part of the collection of General George Cook was found in the desert, (ON THE BORDER WITH COOK by John G. Bourke). We know the rapid rise of temperature in a car with summer heat shining through the windshield, but what the temperature would be in a suit of armor in this dry desert heat, is uncomfortable to consider.

Starting at the southernmost part of Tucson are two routes. ROUTE #1 - From Highway 10 at Hwy 19 with the Nogales turnoff, ROUTE #2 - from Stone Ave. in Tucson to the Hwy 89 Old Nogales Highway.

ROUTE #1

If the I-19 route from Tucson is used all the way to the Mexico border it is an easy 63-mile trip to Nogales, Sonora, Mexico. A trip in the 1800's took several days on dusty roads by horse, wagon train or stagecoach, hindered by Apache raids, floods, mud, and broken wheels. Many historic sights on the Old Nogales Highway from Tucson to Continental are not visible from the I-19 Freeway.

The present day communities of Sahuarita and Green Valley did not exist until the late 1900's. The Santa Cruz valley was first written about by explorers from Spain and Mexico, the U.S. Army, Indian wars, cattle ranching, and people migrating from back east. The population in Tucson was newly developed in the 1700's, the majority of the population in the Nogales area. Natives dwelt along the Santa Cruz River a year-round flowing river watering forests of green trees.

SAN XAVIER DEL BAC   [San HAH - vee – air del bac]

Leaving Tucson on Highway 19 with the Santa Cruz River on the right or west side, is the 'White Dove of the Desert' - the San Xavier del Bac Mission built in 1700 by Padre Kino, a Jesuit Priest from Spain. The 2 square mile Pascua Yaqui Indian Reservation is located on the west side of Highway 19 and is surrounded by the Tohono O'odham Indian Reservation.

The **Pascua Yaqui** people of Arizona are descendants of the ancient Toltecs who occupied a large area of the Southwest and Mexico. Today, they have eight communities in Southern Arizona.

The **Tohono O'odham** (desert people) are a nation with a population of more than 24,000 people, on 2.7 million acres. They are closely related to the Pima Tribe. Once thought by explorers to be non-enterprising people because they were not making the most out of the fertile and well-watered land, it was learned that what the peaceful Pima cultivated was raided by the Apaches from the east. The Pima grew it, and the Apache took it. Apache raids and wars were the cause of much conflict and death in Arizona's early history.

Source: www.sanxaviermission.org/Tohono.html

As in most societies the **Tohono O'odham** men did most of the farming, hunting, and protecting the village. The women took care of the domestic duties. Both men and women took part in passing on historical culture with storytelling, music, artwork, and traditional medicine. **Tohono O'odham** are famous for beautiful Indian baskets, red pottery and beaded jewelry.

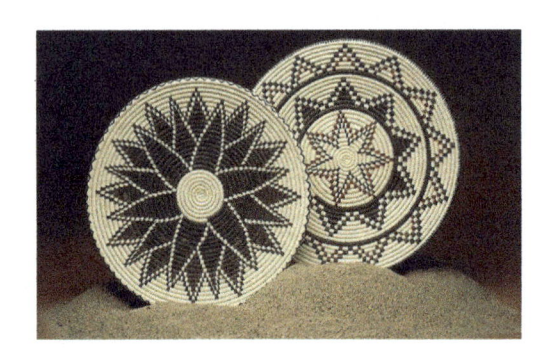

These native **Tohono O'odham** historically built shelters; **Wickiups**, simple small round or cone-shaped houses made with a wood frame covered with brush and dirt, used primarily to sleep in. Their diet consisted of corn, beans, squash, deer, javelinas (peccaries, like large rodents), small game like rabbits, nuts, fruits, and herbs.

Source: Tohono O'odham artists. www.bigorrin.org/papago_kids.htm

THE SANTA CRUZ RIVER (Holy Cross River)

The Santa Cruz River flows south from its origin in eastern Santa Cruz County then flows south into, and northward out of Mexico. From the Mexican border the Santa Cruz continues north near Nogales and on to Tucson. From Tucson the river would normally finish its journey to Phoenix where it joined the western flowing Salt River.

Historically the **Santa Cruz River** naturally flowed yearly above ground before mining interests lowered the water table. In this modern era the river flows only during rainy seasons, often at flood stage. From Tubac the Santa Cruz River historically entered a deep valley fill of millenniums of gravel, then reappeared as a marsh or Spanish 'Cienega' [syey-nay-gah], south of the black volcanic rock **Martinez Hill** on the east side of Highway 19 north of the Mission. (See Biographies)

Note: Martinez Hill is on the San Xavier District and access is restricted.

South of Martinez Hill and the often dry riverbed of the Santa Cruz River is a former marsh (cienega) now dry with withered **ironwood trees.** This area was a much larger marsh when the river ran normally for the ancient people. Ironwood trees are now protected in the county. The land was scoured by severe flooding in 1983 and 1993, then a barrier was created with the help of the Bureau of Reclamation to protect the restoration site from a 10-year flood event. Funded through a variety of grants the Tohono O'odham Nation has 10 acres located on the west side of the Santa Cruz River, south of Martinez Hill as restoration work for the Santa Cruz River.

Source: Tohono O'odham Nation Hikdañ Riparian Restoration Project Site

Further south on the west of I-19 is the view of several mining concerns. The Sierrita Mine is the large copper mine located west of Green Valley and Sahuarita in the Sierrita Mountains. The deposit had estimated reserves in 2006 of 907 million metric tons of ore grading 0.26% copper and 0.03% molybdenum.

Source: Minerals Yearbook, 2006, V. 2, Area Reports, Domestic; U. S. Department of the Interior, p. 5-2.

According to a 2007 report by Pima County, 76,000-acre feet (94,000,000 m^3) of water was pumped from the aquifer in the Upper Santa Cruz Valley in 2006, with 85 percent of that water being used for mining and agriculture. The remaining 15 percent was split between water used for golf courses and residential/commercial water use. The **Central Arizona Project** (CAP) is Arizona's single largest resource for renewable water supplies. CAP is designed to pump about 1.5 million acre-feet of water from the Colorado River to Central and Southern Arizona every year. If water is available from Lake Mead on the Colorado River.

Source: www.pima.gov/pdf/Long-Term%20Green%20Valley%20Water%20Supply%20.pdf

In 2021 Lake Mead is 200 ft above the 'dead zone' level, the point where no water passes through Hoover Dam. RED ALERT!

Source:Smithsonian.org

Continuing south on I-19 you will see much of what is covered in this writing parallels historic Old Nogales Highway / SR89 crosses over along the way to give you glimpses of the entire upper Santa Cruz River Valley.

EXIT 80 From I-19, take the Pima mine road east to join the **Old Nogales Highway** / historic SR-89; the subject of this work. The scenic route is going to change due to water depletion in the aquifer, removal of the pecan orchards, development of cultural activities, and residential areas by the city of Sahuarita and Sahuarita Farms.

See Biographies for history of Jesuit priest Eusebio Francisco Kino (1645-1711) who founded missions in Arizona and Mexico.

See Biographies for history of Spanish explorer Juan Bautista de Anza and his Conquistadors in 1759 and their 1,210-mile trip to San Francisco, California.

ROUTE #1 CUTOFF

Old Nogales Highway - Historic SR89 / Old 19
[Nogales is pronounced 'No-gal-as'] (walnuts)

Desert Diamond Casino at 1100 W Pima Mine Rd, Sahuarita is owned and operated by the Tohono O'odham Nation, providing resources for vital community services both on and off the Nation and generating millions of dollars in state tax revenue.

EXIT 80 On **Pima Mine Rd**. the north side borders the San Xavier Reservation. The south side borders Rancho Sahuarita Community where families live. The town of Sahuarita sits between the reservation on the north and Green Valley on the south.

The **Rancho Sahuarita Community** began in the 1980s with a dream of creating a place that thousands of families would one day call home, with amenities creating a self-contained community

On this leg of the tour, imagine the year 1687 with Jesuit priest Eusebio Francisco Kino and strings of horses passing by with cattle in tow, or Spanish explorer Juan Bautista de Anza in 1774 traveling with his armored conquistadors along the Santa Cruz River.

Ahead in the eastern Empire Mountains, might be **Apache** smoke signals; making plans to raid the **Army Troops of Colonel George Cook** as he commanded the Mormon Battalion in 1846. **Gold miners of 1848** traveling through the mountain pass on their way to California, herds of cattle grazing in the valley of tall grass waiting for the rains to provide forage in the desert ahead, allowing the herds to get to the west to feed gold miners. Many wagon trains made the journey, although some families got no further than this valley due to illness and their only choice was to settle where water was found.

The **Railroad Survey Expedition in 1855** and the **Butterfield Stage** delivering mail in 1857, will complete the image all coming through the gap between the northern Rincon Mountains and the low Empire Mountains on the south.

This historic entourage traveled what was the **Gila Trail**, the **Southern Emigrant Trail** or the **Kearny Trail** from Missouri to California. These early travelers survived on poor water, little food, heat, dust, and the will to survive. Yes indeed, it was not an easy drive with air conditioning on paved roads through the arid Sonoran desert.

Pecan trees from **Pima Mine Road**. Turn south onto the **Old Nogales Highway** / Historic SR-89, these orchards are due for removal for the Sahuarita Farms Project.

East of this Pima Mine Road / Old Nogales Highway intersection was the **Union Pacific Railroad**, built in 1909-1934, connecting the Nogales, and Guaymas, Sonora, Mexico line built in 1879 to October 25, 1882.

THE TUCSON – NOGALES RAILROAD

After the Spanish conquest of Pimeria Alta, the road from Tucson south became an important economic link for the pueblos, missions and ranchos in the Santa Cruz River valley. The road to Guaymas left the Santa Cruz River at Calabasas and followed Potrero Creek to a walnut grove (los nogales) in a pass through the hills. Following the 1853 Gadsden Purchase from Mexico, of Tucson and all the surrounding country south of the Gila River, the boundary survey party placed a monument marking the border at Los Nogales in 1855.

Twenty years later, as two transcontinental railroads prepared to cross the Territory of Arizona, the **Atchison, Topeka & Santa Fe** made plans for a rail connection with Guaymas. William Ray Morley surveyed a route through Los Nogales in 1878 and the following year the **Sonoran Railway** was formed in Mexico as a subsidiary of the **ATSF**. In 1880, San Francisco merchant Jacob Issacson built a trading post in Nogales pass. It was the first rail line linking the US and Mexico. A Post Office was established in the Issacson store for the community of Issacson, sometimes also called Line City, right on the border. But when the railroad built its depot there it chose to name the stop Nogales.

Source: Train town page: Nogales, AZ (up.com)

Pima County maps from 1893 to 1922, show the various ranches and communities along the Old Nogales Highway from Stone Avenue leaving Tucson southward towards Nogales, this indicates ranches were bought out for various reasons, a few small concerns became large profitable ranches. The Tucson International Airport bought parcels, the Davis Monthan Air Field acquired others, so slowly small ranches dissappeared; leaving family names in around the Tucson area.

Shown on the map below is one such large cattle ranch and farm of Jesus and Andrea Felix with beans, corn, chilies, squash, tomatoes, onions, potatoes, herbs and a flower garden. Cheese was made and sold along with the vegetables in Tucson according to Granddaughter Socorro Felix Delgado. She also recalls living on her grandparents' ranch in the area of the pecan groves of Sahuarita and Continental. The ranch and farm was so large that it was registered at the post office.

Source: SONGS MY MOTHER SANG TO ME, An Oral History of Mexican American Women by Patricia Preciado Martin.

JESUS FELIX

BIRTH   1860 Pitiquito, Pitiquito Municipality, Sonora, Mexico

DEATH   17 Jul 1925, Tucson, Pima County, Arizona
s/o of Apolonia Corrales and Francisco De Felix

APOLONIA CORRALES De FELIX

BIRTH   1827, Tucson, Pima County, Arizona

DEATH   10 Jun 1935 (aged 107–108), Tucson, Pima County, Arizona
d/o Jose & Andrea IRIGOYIA CORRALES of Spain. Widow of Francisco FELIX.

ROUTE #2   OLD NOGALES HIGHWAY

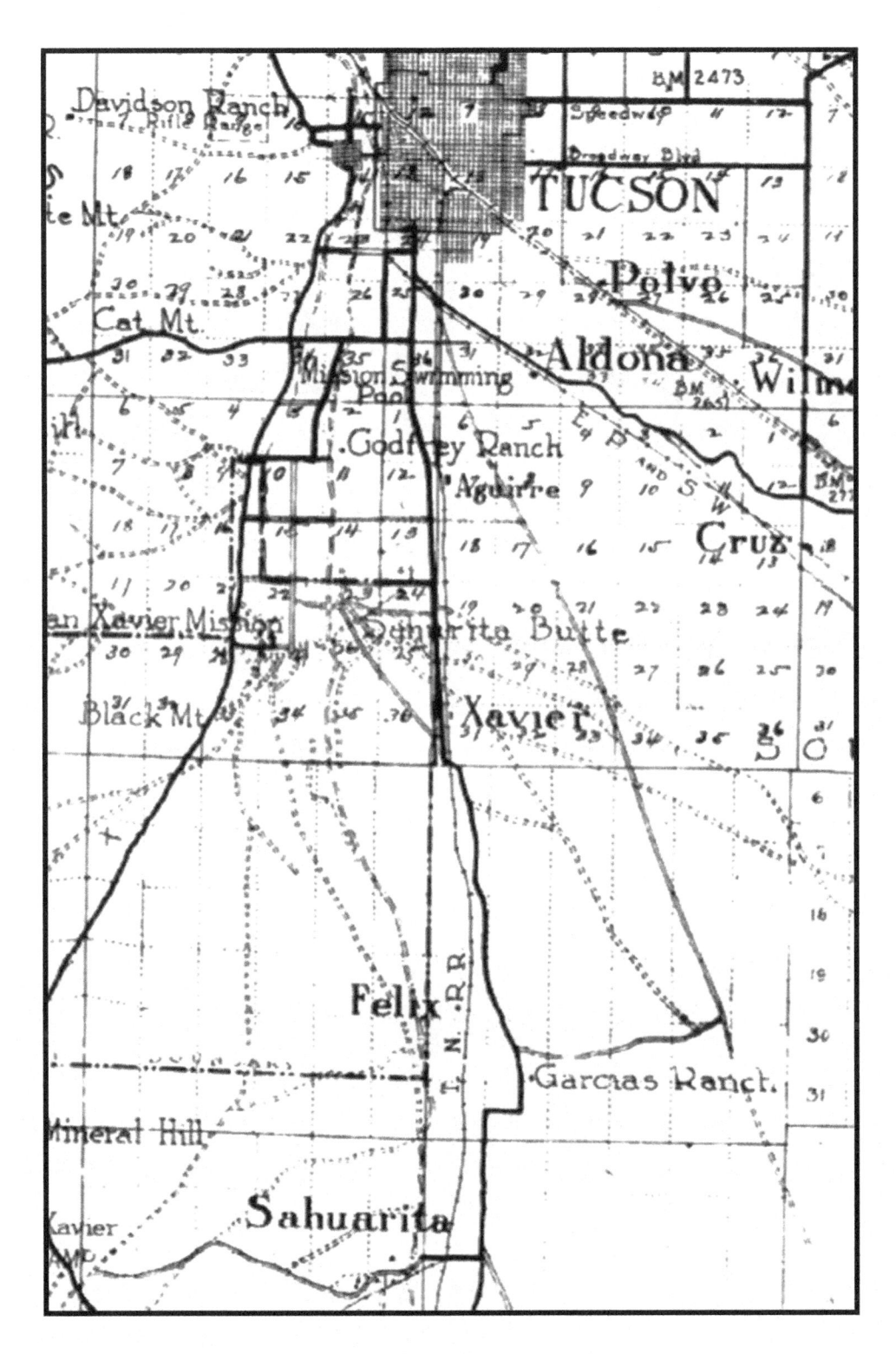

1922 PIMA COUNTY MAP

THE SAHUARITA REGION

The prehistoric Hohokam people were the first inhabitants of the Santa Cruz Valley during (200-1450). The peaceful people are known for their extensive use of irrigation, and extensive trade routes into Mesoamerica. The Pima people considered to be the descendants of the Hohokam, occupied the area with extensive farming making larger villages possible. Native lands extended to Central Arizona: to Sonora, Mexico: east to the San Pedro River: and west to the Gulf of California. The Pima now live with the Tohono O'odham Nation, and the Maricopa Tribe on the Salt and Gila rivers.

The Rancho Sahuarita Survey (Stephen and others of 1997) located 25 sites in the area of 2800 acres near the Helmet Peak / Pima Mine Road to the west side of the Santa Cruz River.

These archaeological sites may never have been discovered if it were not for the mining concerns and the expansion of residential subdivisions which are required to have archaeological surveys before construction starts.

SAHUARITA [in Spanish "Saw-wa-ree-ta"' (Little Saguaro)

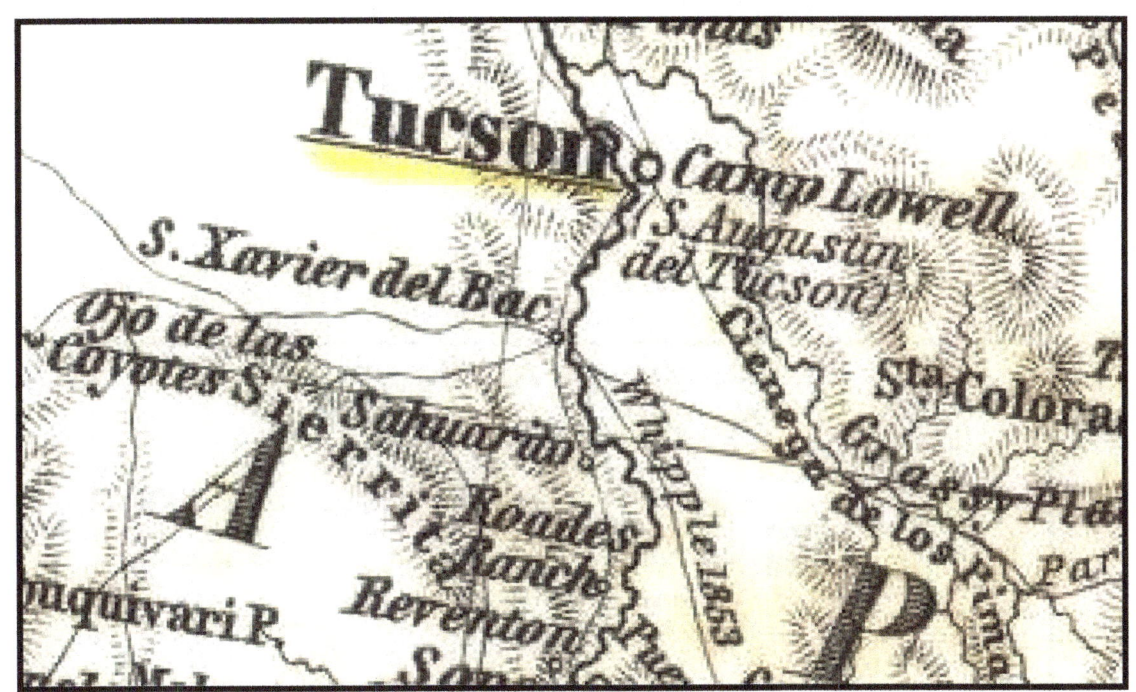

"1875-Sahuarito" David Rumsey Collection

In 1879 the Sahuarita Ranch was created by **James Kilroy Brown** (and partner who died) and named after the saguaros (sa_gwär-ōs) (tall green column cactus that dominate the scenery) in the area. The Brown cattle ranch was a small community with a stage stop and post office. Pioneer rancher at **Sahuarita Ranch** and Pima County Sheriff, Brown and family left this hospitable ranch in 1890 due to the danger to his family because of Apache raids. (see Biographies as to earlier owners)

Early in the new century, when the Twin Buttes Railroad was being built from Tucson to the mining camp called Twin Buttes, Brown granted the railroad right of way through his property with the agreement that the train station be called Sahuarito (little Sahuarito). In 1886 Brown sold off his ranch and holdings and moved to Tucson. (see bio)

EXIT 75 The hub of original Sahuarita commerce was at the intersection of **Sahuarita Road and Nogales Highway**, in the building of the **One Stop Market** and **Sahuarita Bar and Grill**. These and a 130-year-old building were demolished for a road expansion: "While some have said the '1 Stop' and the shuttered 'Sahuarita Bar' on the north side of Sahuarita Road were long-time fixtures that might deserve historic recognition, the longest-serving council member, Charles Oldham, and the council member who lives closest, Marty Moreno, both said the convenience store should make way for needed road improvements.

(Further research reveals that it was for our safety, tank related leaks and spills underground and above ground storage tanks may pose risk to human health and/or the environment. The pecan orchards water usage was creating a subsidence feature with ground slumping close to the road.) de

The **Sahuarita Bar and Grill** built in 1926, according to the county assessor's records, was popular as the only establishment open at night between Tucson and Amado, with a huge wooden bar and two pool tables. There was live music on weekends. **The One Stop** was built in 1967.

Source:

http://tucson.com/news/blogs/streetsmarts/street-smarts-sahuarita-s-name-may-be-misspelling/article_08a0bf43-890f-5be1-bc24-a718f6fdcdb2.html

(see bio)

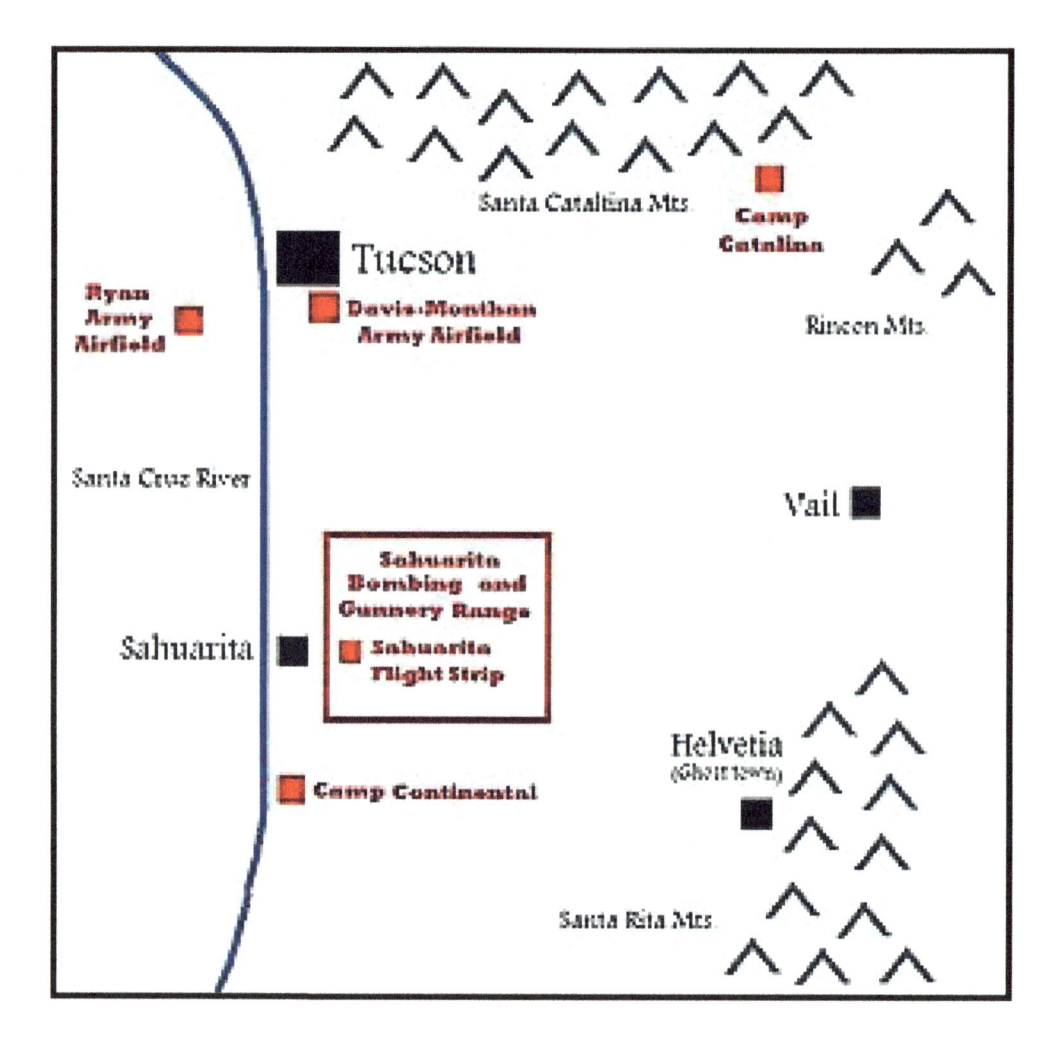

Military installations in the Tucson area during war time for training grounds.

SAHUARITA AIR FORCE RANGE

The Davis-Monthan Landing Field, originally on what is now the Tucson Rodeo site, was the first municipally owned airfield in the United States. Established in 1919, the municipal airport was soon moved to a site large enough to accommodate increased air traffic. The new airfield was completed in February 1927, just in time for a famous visitor to land his Spirit of Saint Louis on the new runway.

"Lindberg landed at Davis-Monthan," says Larry D. "Doug" Herndon, Chief of History, and 355th Fighter Wing at Davis-Monthan Air Force Base.

Lindberg, the first aviator to cross the Atlantic Ocean solo, visited Tucson in 1927 as part of a three-month tour of the United States, a tour meant to generate interest in building airstrips and other infrastructure for the burgeoning aviation industry.

On Dec. 7, 1941, Pearl Harbor was attacked by air. American aviation would play a major role in WWII. Soon another new facility, the Sahuarita Bombing and Gunnery Range, became an important supporting player on the war's aerial stage.

Bombardiers, aerial gunners, and anti-aircraft gunners must be trained, and places to practice the essential skills were critical to the war effort. The deserts of the American Southwest soon became some of the best proving grounds for the trainees.

Parcel by parcel, the U.S. Army Air Corps, forerunner of the U.S. Air Force, accumulated land south of Tucson for the bombing and gunnery range until the Air Corps had 27,046 acres.

The range eventually included circular bombing targets made of stone (remnants of which were still visible from the air as recently as 2005), 12 buildings, observation towers, utilities, a radio-controlled range, four bomb targets and air to ground targets. Most of the bombardiers in training came from Davis-Monthan Field, but military personnel from other locations also used the range.

The 5540-foot airstrip was completed in 1943, and the air-to-ground gunnery range was closed shortly thereafter because the range was too close to the runway.

After the Cold War ended and Sahuarita began developing and expanding, enthusiasm for the old range and airstrip diminished. Although much of the facility was in mothballs, portions of the installation were still used as a training site for Tucson's 650-man 8th Battalion, 40th Armor U.S. Army Reserve.

In 1972, the 8th Battalion, 40th Armor decided to move its operation to Fort Huachuca

.

Source:
Article is in part to conserve space
By Susan E. Swanberg Special to the Sahuarita Sun - Sep 24, 2014

SAGUARO

Saguaros are very slow growing cacti that reach adult stage at about 125 years.

Saguaro can grow to be between 40-60 feet tall (12-18m) and live to be as much as 150-200 years old. When swollen with rainwater, the saguaro is fully hydrated and could weigh between 3,200-4,800 pounds

The brilliant white waxy flower of the Saguaro is Arizona's state flower. The fragrant flowers bloom at night on the saguaro when the cactus is 35 years old. An arm of the plant begins to grow when it is about 70 years old. Red fruit that is produced is relished by all the native inhabitants, human or not.

Holes in the Saguaro are cut out by birds to build nests in. These holes "or boots" were used by native Americans as water containers, and prized possessions even today by collectors and used as planters.

Even after the saguaro has died, its woody ribs can be used to build roofs, fences, and furniture. Truly a recyclable plant.

The contortions of the saguaro arms often keep travelers amused creating stories to match the shape. "Stick 'em up" or "they went that'a way". Old and corny but you get the idea.

Saguaros sometimes grow in odd or misshapen forms. The growing tip occasionally produces a fan-like form referred to as crested. The reason is unknown.

Protected by the Saguaro National Park.

Crested top of a Saguaro

HELVETIA MINE AND HISTORIC RUINS [hel-vee-shuh]

Towards the east is a blotch of white Paleozoic limestone on the Empire Mountains. Off the East Sahuarita Rd. is the dusty Santa Rita Road that goes out to the Helvetia Mine.

Helvetia was named by a miner, Ben Hefti, in honor of his native Switzerland. It is a word comparable to the English "liberty." Copper mining began in 1875. The first mine, Old Frijoli, was located in 1880 by Bill Hart and John Weigle. By 1883 twenty claims had been recorded in what became known as Helvetia Copper Group. Early major developers were the Omega Copper Co. (owners included Tully and Ochoa, Fred Hughes, and T.J. Jeffords) and the Columbia Mining and Smelting Co.

In 1898, twenty-seven claims were owned by the company. Helvetia included several permanent company buildings and a line of tents to house workers. Two Tucson stage lines traveled the old Santa Rita Road and carried passengers to and from Helvetia. In 12 years, the settlement became Pima County's largest and most important mining camp.

Ruins of Helvetia are all that remain.

In 1890 and 1900 about 350 men were employed. About 550 to 650 people made up the Helvetia Camp described as a motley collection of tents and adobe and grass shanties. There were four saloons; a Chinese laundry; Schroutz barbershop; meat market (Casky and Korb); J. R. Glenn, shoemaker; Dorsett's Helvetia House, restaurant/boarding house. Workers, organized by the Western federation of Miners, were paid $1.25 to $1.50 a day for surface work and $3.00 a day to work underground. It was the merchants, however, who made money, grossing $10,000 a month at the peak of mining activity.

A post office that remained in service until 1921 and school were established in 1900. Helvetia became the third largest school district in Pima County. At one point 101 pupils were enrolled in the school. Between 1912 and 1914 the school had steady enrollment. In late 1923 the school was shut down for good. At that time there were 10 or 12 students, children of Mexicans working on the neighboring ranches.

Mine workings included fifty or more small to medium-sized mines and prospects that have been opened and worked since the early 1880's. Total estimated and reported production through 1972 would be some 430,000 tons of ore containing about 17,500 tons of copper, 350,000 oz. of silver, 680 tons of zinc, 260 tons of lead and a minor amount of gold, molybdenum and tungsten. An indefinite amount of limestone and marble have been produced.

Source: www.mindat.org/loc-31252.html

It is estimated that up to 1950 the Helvetia district had produced about 17,000,000 pounds of copper worth $4,000,000. Back in the 1960's Helvetia was occupied by hippies. When the company that owned the property could not get them to leave, the old structures were bulldozed down. That is why we do not see more signs of the community.

Material was collected and edited by Charlie Del Becq, Bill Fritz, Harry Frye, Chuck Rogers and Peggy Smith.
Source: www.gvrhc.org/Library/Helvetia.pdf

Photographer: Mike Conway Photo Date: 2017

On the Geologic Map of Arizona, this quarry is lumped with Paleozoic sedimentary rock units - limestone, dolostone, quartzite and shales. It is Mississippian in age. Image courtesy of Google Earth. From Mindat: 'Mineralization is a contact metamorphism deposit of marmolized Paleozoic Escabrosa Limestone altered to marble.'

THE GREEN VALLEY PECAN COMPANY

Along both sides of the Old Nogales Highway or County Road 19 are pecan orchards and for more than six decades, the Walden family has owned and operated Farmers Investment Co. (FICO) and the Green Valley Pecan Company. FICO is the world's largest grower and processor of quality pecans. (read more at Continental)

Keith Walden founded his agricultural company in 1937, and it was incorporated as FICO in 1946. In 1948, Keith negotiated to buy the Continental Farm from Queen Wilhelmina of the Netherlands. The cotton farm Keith bought had been a guayule plantation (for making rubber during World War I). At the time of the purchase, the Crown family joined Keith as investors in FICO, beginning a partnership and friendship that has spanned three generations.

With approximately 7,000 acres of agricultural land in the Sahuarita area — 6,000 acres in the Town of Sahuarita (Specific Plan area) and 1,000 acres in unincorporated Pima County — FICO is a vital community partner to the Town of Sahuarita and surrounding communities. Over the years, FICO has donated land for employee housing, a church, and a high school. FICO has also reserved land for a future middle school and hospital.

As farmers, the Walden's have always emphasized stewardship of land and water resources for the region and the state. Leaders of the effort to bring the Central Arizona Project (CAP) to southern Arizona, the Walden's continue to work to extend the CAP pipeline to the Santa Cruz Valley to recharge groundwater and offset pumping of groundwater. For many years, FICO has utilized state-of-the-art irrigation and water conservation technologies to conserve water and reduce its use. Years ago, FICO voluntarily applied to the Arizona Department of Water Resources to designate its farm to be a Groundwater Savings Facility (GSF) and has led local efforts among water companies and users to devise a plan to return to aquifer balance.

In 1948, R. Keith Walden relocated his Farmers Investment Company (FICO) from California to Arizona and purchased the Continental Farm to use as his headquarters.

In the 1950s, Keith grew concerned that competition from synthetic fibers would threaten the cotton market and in 1965 he transitioned his farming operation to pecans as an alternative crop. Keith chose pecans because of their compatibility with the climate of the Sonoran Desert. FICO is still owned by the Walden family and their orchards combine to form the largest pecan grove in the world.

EXIT 75 The Green Valley Pecan Store and Gift Shop are located on 1625 East Sahuarita Road.

Source: www.sahuaritafarms.com/about/

The **West Sahuarita Road** goes to the shopping center, gasoline, post office, schools, and Highway 19. Then it turns onto Hemet Peak Road, intersects with Mission Road and goes back towards Tucson.

The **East Sahuarita Road** goes to Carona de Tucson and Highway 83.

I-19 BUSINESS AND DUVAL MINE ROAD

Northbound to Tucson

Southbound from Tucson

EXIT 69 Duval Mine Road continues right towards Green Valley, Abrego Drive, La Canada Road, I-19, Walmart, Restaurants, Safeway, and other shopping venues. **Duval Mine Road** continues west to the mines and intersects with **Mission Road** back towards Tucson.

Take the left turn towards the historic community of Continental.

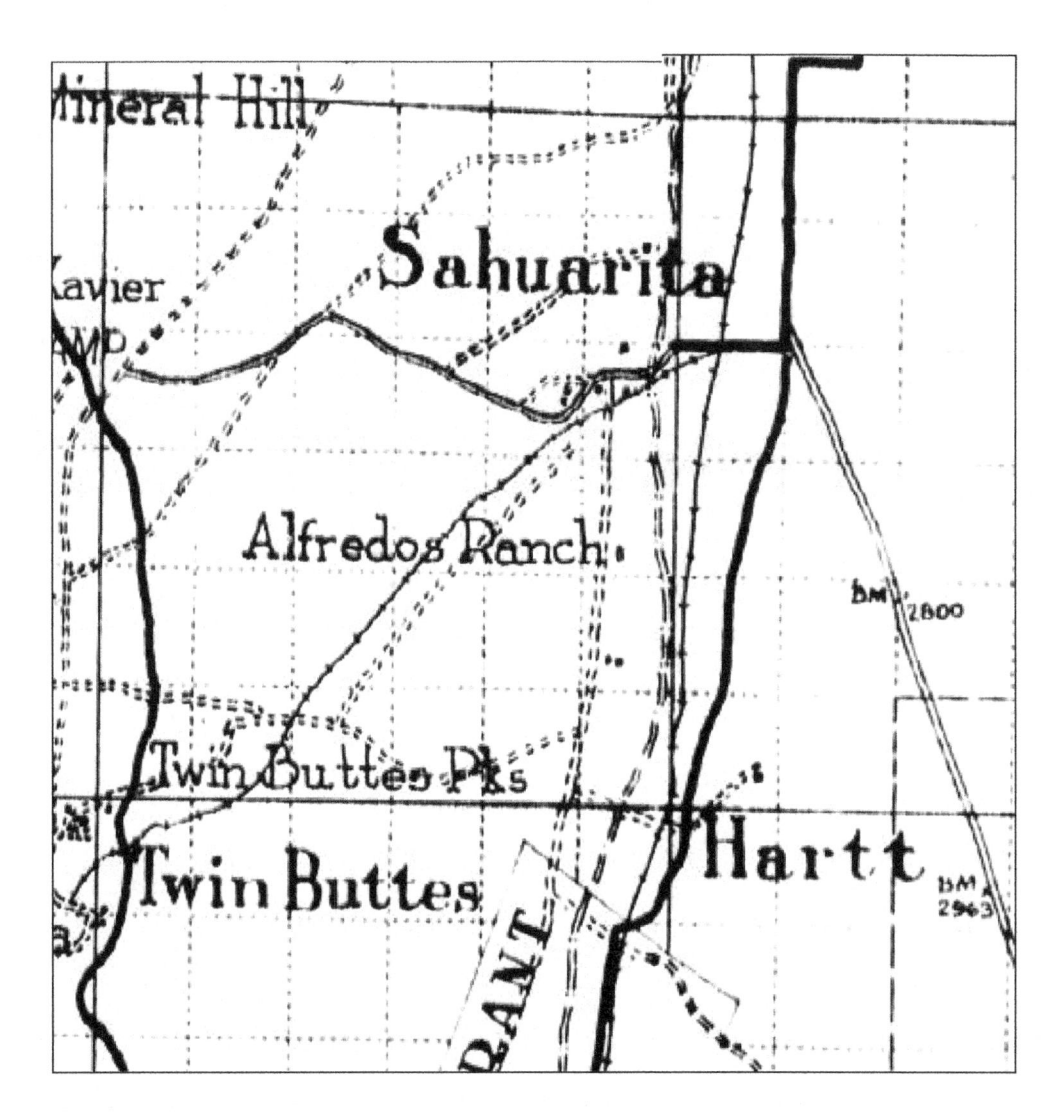

1937 PIMA COUNTY MAP

Today's heavy traffic benefits from the 2015 road expansion for school buses going east and west and commuters going north and south. One would never know the old buildings were ever there as the roads and railroad tracks were also removed.

Source: medlibrary.org/medwiki/Sahuarita, Arizona

www.sahuaritasun.com/news/historic-one-stop-market-nearby-bar-come-down-in-sahuarita/article_75f90546-54cd-5fe5-b891-b1fa9abfb8e4.html

W. A. Hartt **1876**, took out a land patent to sell lots and provide water using compound duplex pump engines. He wrote a pamphlet to sell his idea and Hartt's name is connected to John V. Weigel in 1882 concerning the Helvetia Mining District.

In 1926, Arkansas farmer James B. Bull acquired a 160-acre plot naming it the Bull Farm, growing alfalfa, vegetables, and grains until **1927**. At its peak, Bull Farm was one of the largest in the area with its 6,150 acres. After the sale of Bull Farm, Quail Creek was established as a retirement community in 1989 by Robson Resorts,

QUAIL CREEK RESORT

A far cry from the depredations of pioneer life and Apache raids is Quail Creek, located in southern Arizona. Quail Creek sums up for itself their products, amenities, and activities, including 27 holes of championship golf, a luxurious clubhouse, restaurant, indoor and outdoor sports facilities showcasing 16 Pickleball courts and a Creative Arts and Tech Center.

'The Anza Athletic Club expanded the fitness facilities with cardio and fitness machines, multi-purpose fitness studios, and a wellness room. A Pickleball complex featuring 16 courts, ramada and restrooms. An impressive Creative Arts and Technology Center, spanning 12,348 sq. ft., featuring a variety of rooms catering to the homeowners' artistic aspirations. A resident favorite, the Grill nearly 4,000 square foot expansion included an expanded outdoor covered patio, a new u-shaped bar with ample seating, boardroom, and a private dining room.

'Amidst the natural beauty of the rugged Santa Rita Mountains, you can step outside and right into the scenic vistas of Madera Canyon – a wonderland for bird watchers, outdoor lovers and nature enthusiasts. Located only 25 miles south of Tucson, Quail Creek is a world of its own within the friendly town of Sahuarita in the Green Valley area.

'One of the most interesting aspects of the Quail Creek community is the amount of giving back that the residents do. There are a number of different groups that do volunteer work to serve the community, including the Blanket Brigade, the Care and Share Lending Closet, the Community Emergency Response Team, the Critters Club, and the Memorial Committee.'

SOURCE: quailcreekhoa.org/web/quail-creek-hoa

CAMP CONTINENTAL

Camp Continental was the southernmost of at least 21 smaller "branch camps" built around Arizona during World War II, according to "PW: First-Person Accounts of German Prisoners of War in Arizona," by Tempe author and Arizona Historical Society member Steve Hoza.

Camp Continental was built on the west side of Old Nogales Highway, on a ranch owned by James Bull. It sat across the highway from where Quail Creek Crossing Boulevard is currently.

A note attached to an undated photo of Camp Continental in the Arizona Historical Society's archives states that between Sept. 17, **1945**, and Feb. 10, **1946**, prisoners picked 1.86 million pounds of cotton, cleaned irrigation canals, hoed fields, and helped harvest crops on nearby farms or worked in warehouses. The POWs provided desperately needed labor while most of the country's work force was involved with the war. Nothing remains of the camp and many locals are surprised to hear about it.

POW Camp Continental

The family of Armando Felix, born in 1948, lived along Old Nogales Highway north of Quail Creek for generations, said the tall fences, mobile trailers on wheels and a corrugated steel building with barbed wire on top were still in place 13 years after the camp closed.

The camp is near the dog park

CONTINENTAL

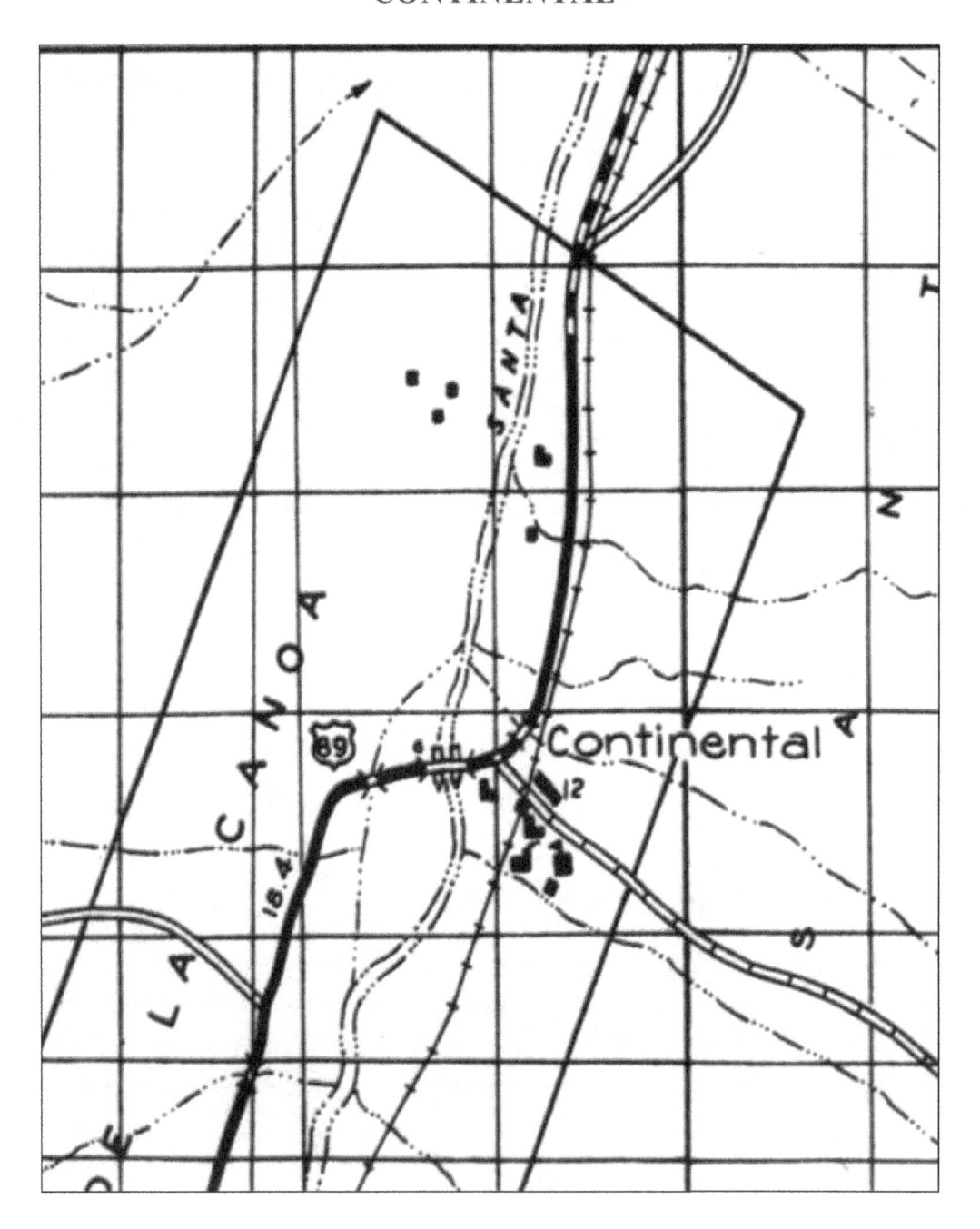

1937 PIMA COUNTY MAP

Continental was founded during World War I in 1916, after President Woodrow Wilson asked the **Intercontinental Rubber Company** of Bernard Baruch, Joseph Kennedy, and J. P. Morgan to grow guayule. Guayule is a plant that produces latex and can be used to make rubber if, as many Americans feared, the German navy were to cut off shipping lanes and imports of rubber from the Far East.

In **1916**, **Intercontinental Rubber Company** established the **Continental Farm** seven miles south of Sahuarita and east of the present-day Green Valley, along the eastern banks of the Santa Cruz River and the Southern Pacific Railroad. Over the next few years, a small town was built to accommodate the workers at the farm. In addition to several large adobe homes that were built for the farmers around 1918, the fields and the processing facility built for the guayule, the town of Continental had a post office that opened in 1917, a schoolhouse built in 1918, a church, a general store, and its own cemetery. The guayule project was abandoned after the end of World War I. In 1922, Queen Wilhelmina of the Netherlands bought the farm and rented the fields to cotton farmers until 1949.

THE SANTA RITA MOUNTAINS and MADERA CANYON

From this point the view of **Madera Canyon** in the **Santa Rita Mountains** provides a good reason to pull over for a look.

The **Santa Rita Mountains** in Pima and Santa Cruz Counties is a multi-vented volcanic complex. The highest point is Mt. Wrightson at 9,453 ft. with an age of 245 million years. This complex consists of Pre-Cambrian granodiorite core, Paleozoic marine deposits of limestone and dolomite, Triassic rhyodacite volcanics, Jurassic intrusions of monzonite and granite, Cretaceous limestone beds, thrust faulting, folding, and intruded by granitoid stocks of diorite. On 3 May 1887, a magnitude 7.2 earthquake rippled across Sonora, Mexico, and southern Arizona. The earthquake killed dozens of people and damaged or destroyed several hundred structures. A false story was sent out that the Santa Rita's were erupting. People still refer to the non-event as fact. Some had to live with the title of THE BENSON LIAR.

From October 1, 1866 to March 7, 1867 The California Volunteers troops posted at Tubac were overtaken with malaria and established Camp Cameron at Madera Canyon. there are no remains of the camp named in history as Camp Cameron, located about 16 miles northeast of Fort Mason at Calabasas near Nogales.

The large alluvial fan extends from Madera Canyon invites exploration. The early O'odham people inhabited the canyon. Prior to the Gadsden Purchase in 1853, the Spanish mined this region for silver. Apaches made raids from there and Madera Canyon was seen by Europeans as a resource for mining, lumber and grazing of cattle. Focus is now on tourism with the Chuparosa Bed and Breakfast Inn, the Santa Rita Lodge, camping, where birding, and hiking awaiting you. (Chuparosa is Spanish for hummingbird.)

Source: www.friendsofmaderacanyon.org

The Old Nogales Highway turns west towards I-19, there is a four-way stop sign at the intersection of Continental Rd. and White House Canyon Rd.

On the right-hand side or looking north you find *La Posada.*

The entrance to La Posada retirement Community pre-2017, looking north

LA POSADA [La Paw-sah-th ah] (The Hotel or Inn)

La Posada is one of the reasons that people do not wait for God in Green Valley. A premier retirement community in the country, with a fitness center, classrooms and indoor pool, a large outdoor pool, an art studio, and several unique dining venues. La Posada was built for resort-style living with amenities that enhance seniors' well-being.

Source: posadalife.org/

Welcome to The Shoppes at La Posada!

"**Posada Java** is a place for great coffee, light lunches and treats including baked goods and ice cream. The **Vensel Treasure Shoppe** is filled with quality consignment items at great prices. Need a haircut? We even have a **Barber Shoppe**. In the beautiful courtyard you can enjoy frequent concerts, sit near our calming fountain, or sit in the sun with your laptop or tablet logged on to our free Wi-Fi."

The intersection of **Old Nogales Highway**: west into **Continental Road** and **White House Canyon Road.**

A left / south turn on **White House Canyon Road** up the long, gently sloping alluvial fan to **Madera Canyon**.

Today, several of the old adobe homes in Continental are still in use. The old Continental School was replaced in the 1990s by a new facility located about one mile to the east. The old school was refurbished and now serves as the Continental Community Center. The is the **Continental Medical Center** on the left towards **Madera Canyon.**

The **Continental Cemetery** is located northeast of the old school and completely surrounded by the **Madera Reserve Subdivision**. Considered to be a holy site by local Native Americans, the cemetery has been in use since 1903, and the oldest marked grave is from 1918. This area has been found to be one of the sites for the prehistoric **Hohokam** people (200-1450) known for their extensive use of irrigation, and extensive trade routes into Mesoamerica. There are 26 known digs in the area does not open to the public.

In the northeast end of the Santa Rita Mountains the **Rosemont Anamax Project** (Debowski 1980) is located in the foothills. Rosemont is a new mining area where over 600 archaeological sites were located in 30 square miles of the survey area. The sites of habitation were generally found near the headwaters of larger drainages, revealing 102 Ceramic period sites, pit houses with roasting pits, along with ground stone tools. (Huckell 1984)

Approximately 30 historic sites in the Rosemont area were primarily mining activities from the 1870s-1920s. the plan is to blast a mile-wide, half-mile-deep pit and dump toxic mine tailings and waste rock in the Davidson Canyon/Cienega Creek watershed, a source of Tucson's groundwater supply. The mine also would destroy thousands of acres of federally protected jaguar critical habitat that's been formally designated as essential to the survival and recovery of jaguars in the United States. Thousands of acres of prime jaguar habitat, a scenic highway and critically important springs and streams are at immediate risk of irreparable harm."

Tohono O'odham, Pascua Yaqui and Hopi tribes have made their voices heard concerning this proposed destruction.

SANTA RITA EXPERIMENTAL RANGE

The drive on the Whitehouse Canyon Rd. will pass through the Santa Rita Experimental Range (SRER), founded in 1903. It is the oldest research area, a principal site for pioneer range research on the improvement and management of semiarid grasslands in the Southwest. SRER was administered by the United States Forest Service until 1987 when the University Of Arizona College Of Agriculture took over administration of the site. The Santa Rita Experimental Range's http://cals.arizona.edu/general/departments/santarita.html 50,000 acres have served as an outdoor laboratory for researchers to investigate sustainable grazing practices.

The Desert Grassland edited by Mitchel P. McClaran and Thomas R. Van Devender writes about thousands of horses, cattle, and sheep that were living on private ranches in southeastern Arizona between 1831 till 1855. Population varied due to Apaches raiding and a cholera epidemic of 1855. (p. 237)

1846 to 1854 War between the United States and Mexico ended with the Gadsden Purchase; the United States purchased the Arizona Territory and the U.S. Army moved in to contain the Apaches. Most of the wild cattle had disappeared in the Santa Cruz Valley by 1854. (p.239)

Information on the grasslands of southeastern Arizona are kept in records before the Gadsden Purchase by the Spanish and Mexican records of the eighteenth and early nineteenth centuries. (p.240)

From 1870's to 1880's the Anglo-American settlers with their herds moved into southern Arizona. Cattle numbered nearly 400,000 by 1891 causing overstocking and overgrazing followed by a severe drought of 1892 – 1893.

1890 is the year channel erosion began with damage to Tucson, 1891 was channeling of the river and damage to farmlands.

In 1902 conservation was established in the Santa Rita Mountains and elsewhere. (p.240)

Source: 1938 -www.fcd.maricopa.gov/pub/docs/scanfcdlibrary/A105_904

Overgrazing reducing the ground cover, therefore surface run-off and erosion resulted with massive loss of livestock and financial ruin for cattlemen. Historic grazing lands were further impacted with changes of the native desert plants; the decline of tall grasses and the increasing dominance of woody plants like mesquite, acacia, burroweed, and snakeweed. By 1900 the focus was on raising superior animals instead of feeding large herds.

MADERA CANYON [Lumber Canyon in Spanish]

Madera Canyon offered respite from the heat of the Santa Cruz Valley to ancient ones just as it does today to the local residents. Madera Canyon is not the focus of this writing but obviously the Santa Rita Mountains are too large not to mention. Mount Wrightson is 9,452 feet in elevation. Mount Hopkins near the middle of the range is home to the Smithsonian's Whipple Observatory. Information about the canyon is thoroughly discussed in THE NATURE OF MADERA CANYON by Douglas W. Moore and published by the FRIENDS OF MADERA CANYON TUCSON ARIZONA. This extensive publication covers geology, plants, animals, native people, minerals, and recent history.

Madera Canyon was the site of extensive logging that provided lumber to the growing town of early Tucson and frequent Apache attacks for miners and inhabitants of Santa Cruz County. Later as the country developed the great forest of timber was cut down for fuel and to clear lands for farms since Tucson and all the nearby mining camps were supplied from this source. It once seemed there was enough wood in the forests to last Tucson for a hundred years, with no thought to reforestation.

Currently Madera Canyon is famous for bird watching and a resting place for migration species. The limited campground, picnic areas and hiking trails system is popular. Be a friend of the canyon and take care of it. Whipple Observatory is accessed from Elephant Head Road from I-19 south of Green Valley.

GREEN VALLEY [Valle Verde in Spanish]

EXIT 63 Continuing from the 4-way stop at **La Posada** the **Continental Road** will cross over the **Santa Cruz riverbed**, which is probably dry because the water moves underground at this point through the 'deep valley fill of millennium of gravel'. Flooding brings the water to the surface. Notice the concrete channel built to control flooding and erosion. Flooding is the dominant reason for stream migration and channel widening.

After crossing the bridge over the riverbed, notice the Fire Department on the left side before the first traffic light and the Post Office on the left side before the 2nd traffic light.

In case this area is feeling too civilized, where the local Post Office is located now was the location of a rancher named on the 1875 map the Santa Cruz Valley as **William B. Roods/ Rhodes**. Spelling was iffy in those early days and the accurate location of the ranch is based on the "1875-sahuarito" map in the David Rumsey Collection, and others.

SKETCH BY J. ROSS BROWNE (see biographies)

At the overpass, you may choose to continue south on Old Nogales Hwy. by turning left before the overpass towards the **hospital** or drive under the overpass to a shopping center, Chamber of Commerce, restaurants, banks, drug stores, gasoline, etc.

At the far west end of **Continental Road** are the mine tailings on **Mission Road** and the road returns back to **Tucson** by way of the mines. An enjoyable excursion, with good views of the Empire and Santa Rita Mountains from Continental Road and to **Duval Mine Road**.

EXIT 63 WEST GREEN VALLEY was originally a retirement Community envisioned in 1953 by Chicago developer Donald and Norman Maxon, using the 1959 amendment to the Federal Housing Administration to build subsidized housing for the elderly. Population in 2014 was 22,050.

It has been said that people move to Green Valley, Arizona to "wait for God" and one may have the 'Green Valley Grin'. Life in Green Valley is much slower than in Tucson, here La Canada and Abrego Drives are used to avoid the north and south traffic on highway 19 between Tucson and the Mexico border. However, locals here are very busy people even in their golf carts, and they wait for no one.

Part time residents come from all over to spend winter here. The term "Snowbird" is now "Winter Visitor". The first question one might be asked is, "Are you fulltime in Green Valley?" Meaning; is it your home year round, the heat and monsoons, the mild winters, pollen and dust in the spring, and with sensational clouds and sunsets during the monsoons.

One cannot say enough about Green Valley if you are ready to retire and it would take pages to do so; therefore, here is the promo from:

www.topretirements.com/reviews/Arizona/Green_Valley.

"Green Valley is in a basin below the Santa Rita Mountains located in the southwest United States. The average year-round temperature is 68.9 degrees Fahrenheit. The area is known as a haven for snowbirds during the winter months as a result of its warmer temperatures. The dry warmer climate is also a popular for those seeking relief from arthritis."

The ancient Hohokam lived here, ruins have been found, giving us the idea that Green Valley was a great place to live, plant, and a ball game court has been found, No large protective dwellings have been found so far to indicate severe winter weather.

Provided is a 2015 map of Continental Road intersecting with Highway 19 headed south. The side roads of La Canada and Abrego Drive. help locals to get around town while avoiding the big trucks coming from Mexico on Highway 19 traffic at 65 mph. By the way, in Green Valley the speed limit is 35 mph. People use golf carts for golfing and driving on the public streets; using the bike lane on the right edge of the road. Do not be afraid to pass them because you risk holding up traffic.

Some golf carts are enclosed to keep out the wind and rain; people love to talk about their carts so ask away. Some fancy ones look like scaled down trucks and roadsters. It is amazing how much you can carry with the aid of two plastic buckets in place of golf bags. It is a real hoot to drive around in a golf cart, with the surround mirrors in front you can see everything without turning your head like in a car or truck. Golf carts are often for sale and parked on busy streets. Winter visitors rent them for the winter.

Keep in mind residency in Green Valley is for 55 plus and many seniors have eyesight problems. So, drive defensively as always.

Another saying in Green Valley, referring to "cocktail hour, is "When the mountains turn pink, it's time to drink." And when the mountains are gray we drink all day. Arthritis is surely responsible for this adage.

RITA MOUNTAIN PEAKS

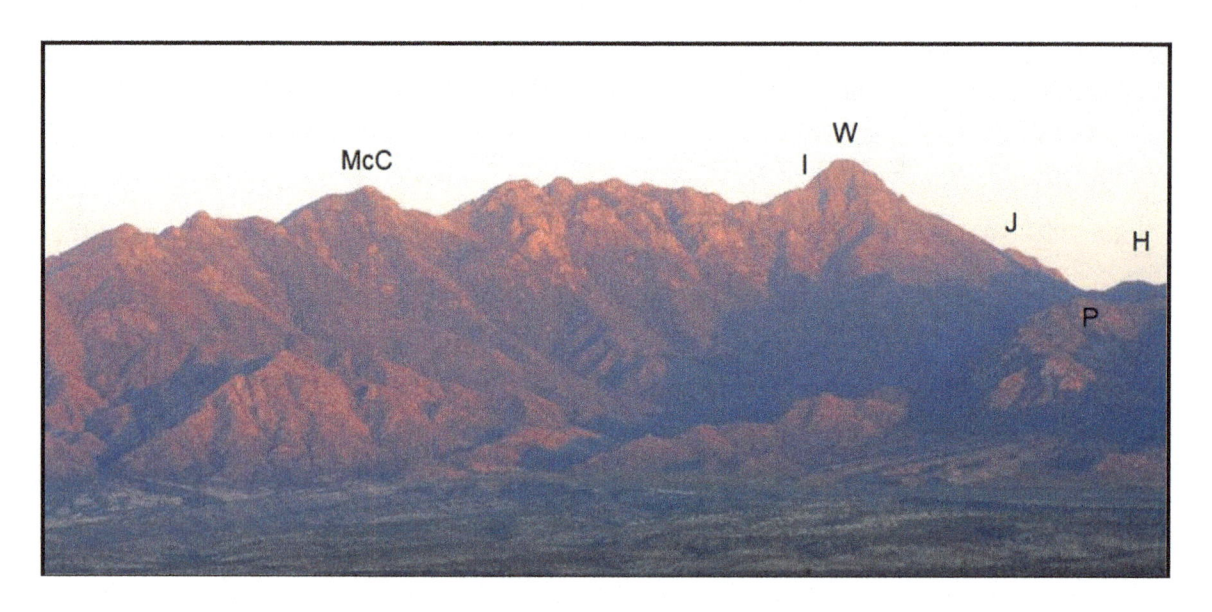

Mount McCleary 8,357 ft. Named by the U.S. Forest Service for William B. McCleary, b. 13 Oct 1849 Maryland, d. 29 Sep 1932 Tucson, Pima County, Arizona. An early cattleman, miner and pioneer, who located a ranch in this area about 1879. Forming the nucleus of what became known as the Rosemont Mining Camp at Wasp Canyon on the east slope of the Santa Ritas. Killed by Apaches Feb 17, 1865, during the Battle of Fort Buchanan.

Mount Ian 9,146 ft. Unofficial name. Just north of Mt. Wrightson.

Mount Wrightson 9,453 ft. Named after: William Wrightson published the first Arizona newspaper *The Weekly Arizonian* from Tubac. Superintendent of the Santa Rita Mining Company. Killed by Apaches Feb 17, 1865. The peak was named after Gilbert Hopkins, who was killed nearby during the Battle of Fort Buchanan in 1865.

Josephine Peak 8,478 ft. The peak was given its name by George Roskruge who surveyed Southern Arizona in the early 1890s. He also named Josephine Saddle and Josephine Canyon for Josephine Gardner, daughter of Tom Gardner, who died as a child. **Arizona Place Names**, Will C. Barnes.. Roskruge never gave a reason why he named the Peak

Pete Mountain 7,661 ft. Roskruge map 1893, named after Old Pete Gabriel A prominent lawman in Pinal County, Arizona . Died on July 30, 1898, from drinking poisonous water at his mine in the Dripping Springs Mountains.

Mount Hopkins 8,560 ft. Named after: Gilbert A. Hopkins, mining engineer for the Salero Silver Mine. Killed by Apaches Feb 17, 1865, during the Battle of Fort Buchanan.

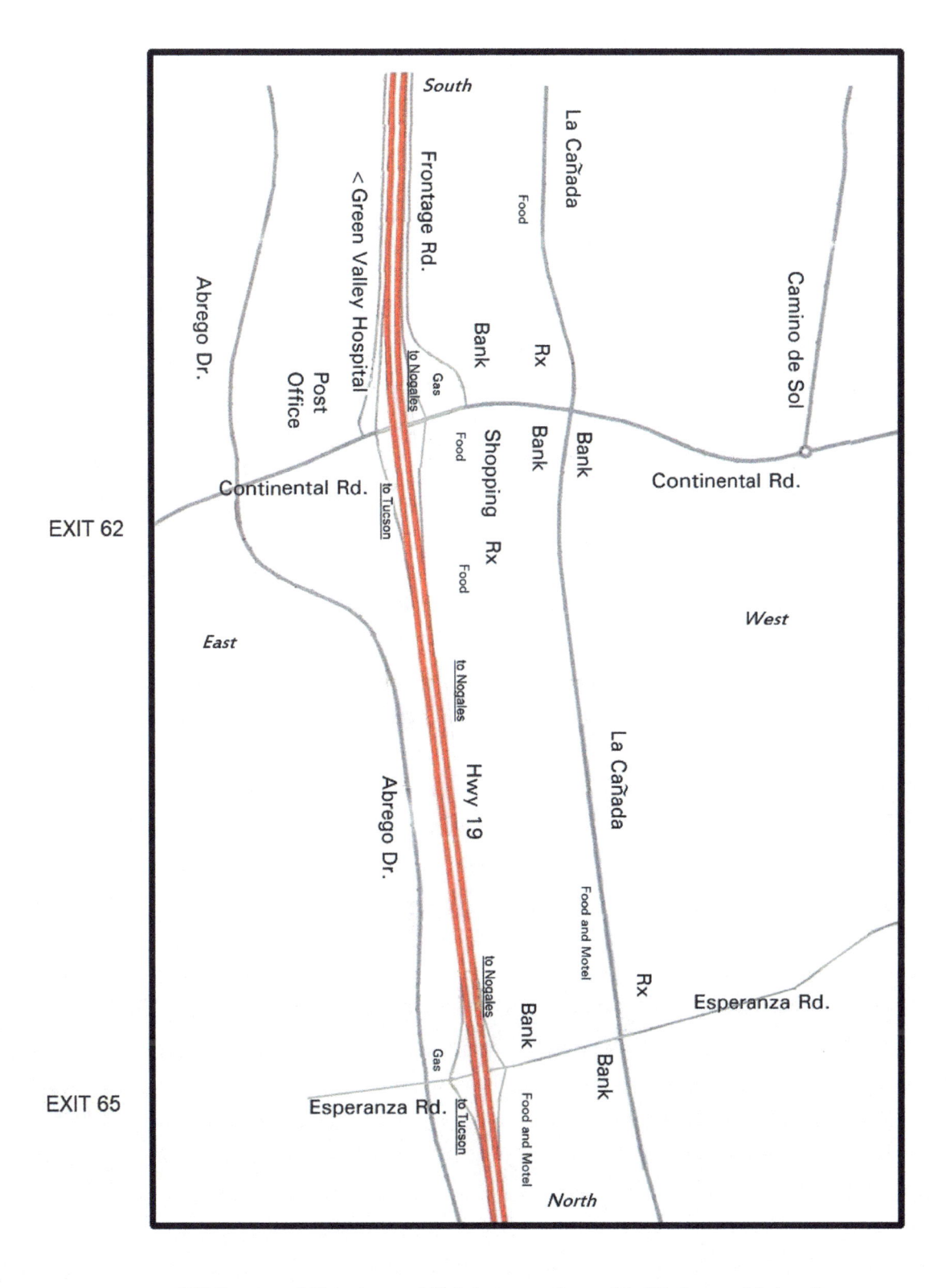

2015 map of Continental Rd. intersecting with Highway 19 / author

Green Valley is one of the larger active adult communities in the world. It is actually a collection of developments and communities located in extreme southern Arizona. The population is over 21,000 and growing. Surrounded by copper mines, hiking and birding areas of the Santa Rita Mountains, Green Valley is an unincorporated retirement community composed of 59 Homeowner Associations.

Green Valley offers good value for the money in terms of the housing and amenities offered. It also has a moderate winter climate, although periods of hard freeze can occur. Because of its size the range of its activities and the range of people to meet are more extensive than most other active adult communities. The non-profit Green Valley Recreation is quite extraordinary, operating 13 different recreation centers with golf courses, swimming pools, fitness centers, etc. It also provides many opportunities for the arts and entertainment. One of its attractions is that its facilities and programs allow people from different communities to mix.

More than 80% of Green Valley is age restricted, so if you do not meet the age requirements this may not be the place for you. Green Valley is below average in walk ability when compared to other communities, though golf carts are legal to be driven in the street and are a common alternative to walking. Golfers, group activity enthusiasts, and people who like the outdoors will feel at home here.

While there are many medical offices and facilities in Green Valley, Tucson offers a number of major hospitals along with the University of Arizona "teaching" hospital. Green Valley Hospital is just off I-19, south of Green Valley

Interstate 19 runs through the middle of the community. Tucson International Airport is 23 miles. There is a local bus service." http://suntran.com

For more information read, Images of America - Green Valley Arizona by Philip Goorian 2002

Green Valley can be really "green", not just from the pecan orchards but also around the golf courses. Join a club or move into a community with its own golf course right out your back door. Some greens are private and others are public. There have been water issues for some years, thoroughly research this before buying a home here.

Choices have included:
- Canoa Hills Golf Club
- Canoa Ranch Golf Club
- Country Club of Green Valley
- Desert Hills Golf Club
- Haven Public Golf Club
- Quail Creek Country Club
- San Ignacio Golf Club
- Torres Blancas Golf Club

The GREEN VALLEY RECREATION DISTRICT / GVR provides the community with many activities. Most homes are legally subject to GVR but the fees rise every year, even if the property owner does not use the facilities. Same with some golf courses.

Green Valley and the San Ignacio de la Canoa land grant

San Ignacio de la Canoa [san / ig-NAH-see-oh / de la / _ca·noa] (Canoa - a sloop-rigged fishing boat)

Green Valley is at the north end of the 17,000-acre San Ignacio de la Canoa land grant issued by the king of Spain in 1820. It was presented to brothers Tomas and Ignacio Ortiz. At its peak, the ranch controlled more than 100,000 acres.

By 1859 this working cattle ranch included a stage stop at the Canoa Hotel, Crossroads Tavern and a lumber sales operation are believed to have been briefly located in the southeast corner of the current 4,800 acres. Frederick Maish and Thomas Driscoll began running cattle on the Canoa Grant in 1875. (see bio Maish and Driscoll)

In 1887 the Canoa Canal Company was initiated.

THE CANOA, AN IMPORTANT STATION IN EARLY DAYS, THE SCENE OF MANY TRAGEDIES.

http://genealogytrails.com/ariz/bios-pioneers.html

EXIT 56 Canoa Ranch includes historical and pre-historical archaeological resources, historic buildings and structures, and historic landscapes. The preservation and restoration of historic buildings, as well as efforts to protect important habitat and restore natural systems are well underway for public use.

A free walking tour of the Canoa Ranch headquarters shows how people lived and worked on the ranch. Tours are seasonal and reservations are required. Please call 520-877-6004 or email canoaranch@pima.gov for reservations and more information.

The railroad between Tucson and Nogales was completed in 1911 and Amado was the new passenger freight station. Mail was then delivered to Arivaca by mule-drawn buckboard

Arivaca is home to some 700 residents including descendants of the area's pioneer families, and became a town during 1876-1881, with a short-lived mining boom. The **Arivaca Mining District** encompasses the Guijas Mountains. By 1896, the population of Arivaca reached 236 people. The drive from Amado at the **Arivaca Junction** is 25 miles on a paved road.

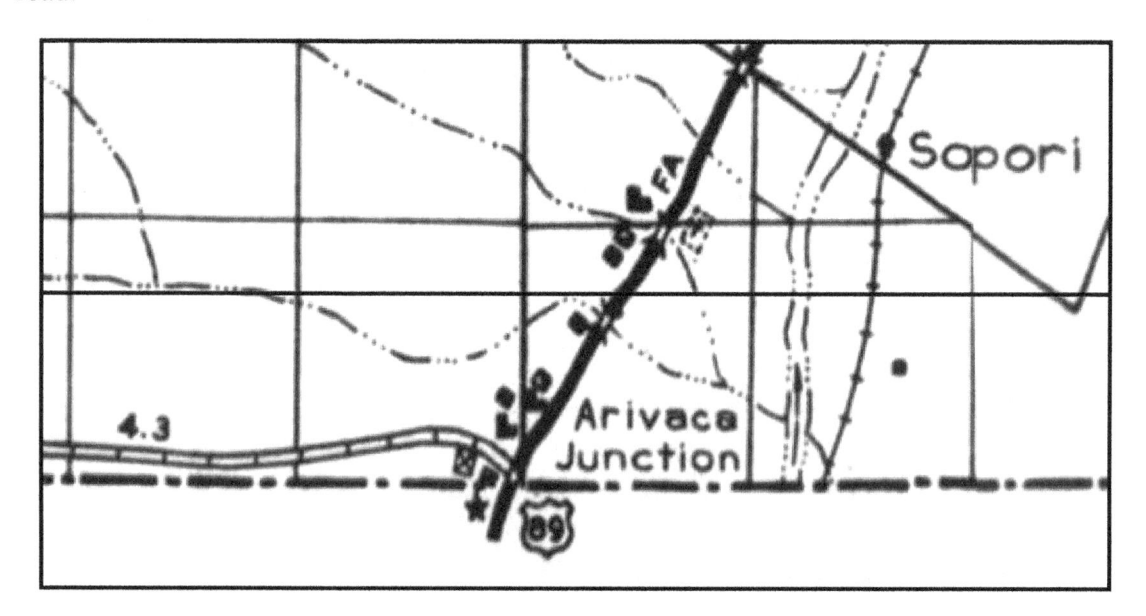

The Court of Private Land Claims had been asked to approve a land grant for which no title had ever been issued by Mexico. El Sopori had no written foundation and its claimants, the Sopori Land and Mining Co. had submitted forged title documents.

The Spanish Grants of Arizona
Written by Fred Roeder, LS Tuesday, 17 March 2009

Now leaving Pima County that was created in 1894 and entering Santa Cruz County created in 1899. Be prepared to be stopped North bound by Customs and Border Protection on Hwy 19. Great guys doing their job to stop illegal immigration, human and drug trafficking. More on that later.

There is much to learn about Santa Cruz County, or as rancher Pete Kitchen said of the dangerous road, he took between Nogales to Tucson from selling produce in Tucson and back to his Potrero Ranch near Nogales, "Tucson, Tubac, Tumacacori to Hell." His home was a stronghold against Apaches and a welcome spot for travelers. (see his bio)

AMADO [Spanish for 'beloved']

EXIT 48 The town was named for Spanish pioneer family of Manuel H. Amado. The Amado Family has been in the area since 1852, with an extensive ranch when the railroad station opened about 1910. The Post Office was established as Amadoville on June 17, 1919, with Manuel H. Amado as Postmaster.

"The Amado family of Southern Arizona can be traced to four brothers who left Spain sometime during the **1790s** to serve as **presidio soldiers**. Three of these brothers settled in the Tucson and Sonora areas. The other brother is said to have settled in California.

"During the **1850s** my great-great-grandfather, **Manuel Amado**, was involved in freighting cattle and goods from Mexico to California. Manuel did very well with his freighting business and was able to diversify his business interests to include ranches, a dairy farm and a butcher shop. In the **1880s** the U.S. government established the San Xavier Indian Reservation and confiscated the dairy farm and family home belonging to Manuel and his wife, Ismael Ferrer de Amado. Manuel and Ismael moved their ranching interests further south and established **Amadoville**, Arizona. In 1920 Demetrio, their son and my great-grandfather, was the postmaster and formally changed the name of the town to Amado."

Source: Melissa Amado/ Bloom Southwest Jewish Archives (jewishgen.org)

The next Amado generation; **Gustavo Elias Amado and Elvira Hidalgo Amado** raised cattle and grew cotton, grain crops and hay. A son, Gus Amado was born in Tucson in 1932, attended Sopori School in Amado, later graduated from Tucson High and the University of Arizona before returning to Rancho Nuevo in Amado in 1956. Gus talks of his childhood on the ranch in Amado and his businesses ranching and farming. An oral history was conducted in 1989 and 1990 for the Tubac Historical Society's "Voices of the Valley" which talks of life on the ranch in Amado and going to rodeos, cattle round ups and Otho Kinsley's store and dance hall.

The next owner, **Otho Kinsley** was born in 1899 on a California ranch and moved to Arizona where he established a 420-acre ranch in **1920**, on which he supplied stock for the Tucson Rodeo. **Kinsley's Ranch Resort and Lake** was once located east of the Old Nogales Highway at the Arivaca Junction. For over 30 years, Otho Kinsley owned a mini-western-theme-park at Arivaca Junction, with a restaurant, bar, dance hall, rodeo arena, service station, air strip, swimming pool, lake, cotton farm, a jail guarded by African lions, and a greyhound race track. A favorite stop for travelers before Interstate 19 was built.

Source: Meandering the Mesquite: AT THE KINSLEY RANCH-Heydays in Amado/Sun Life/sahauritasun.com

Source: us89history.blogspot.com/2018/01/kinsley-ranch-resort.html

The community of Amado has always been ranching. It had been a **"Halfway Station"** for a **stagecoach route** between Nogales, Arivaca, and Tucson. A 1905 stagecoach schedule details the buckboard stagecoach leaving Tucson three days a week for Arivaca, Oro Blanco village, and mining camps of gold, silver, and tungsten. The stage departed at 6:00 a.m., traveled south to Arivaca Junction (passing right through what would become Green Valley), turning west to reach Arivaca by 2:00 p.m. The mines were two additional hours to the south. The horse or mule teams that pulled the stagecoach had to be changed seven times to keep up the pace.

Frederico Jose Maria upon his first trip from Mexico in 1882 recalls in his autobiography, *"a Chinese cook at the line changing station for the Aguierre stage at the Arivaca Junction, who dressed like a cowboy with a 45 Colt on his belt."*

Hardy Cowman Recalls Days Of Apache Raids
The Arizona Daily Star 1-31-1965

"The Amado ranch was a stopping place for the Nogales stage for many years. In 1910 the town of Amado came into being when the railroad track from Tucson to Nogales was laid. When the Nogales Highway. was built the town was moved west to its present location."

MANUEL AMADO
Born: 1832
Died: 20 Jan 1904
Buried: Holy Hope Cemetery, Tucson, Arizona

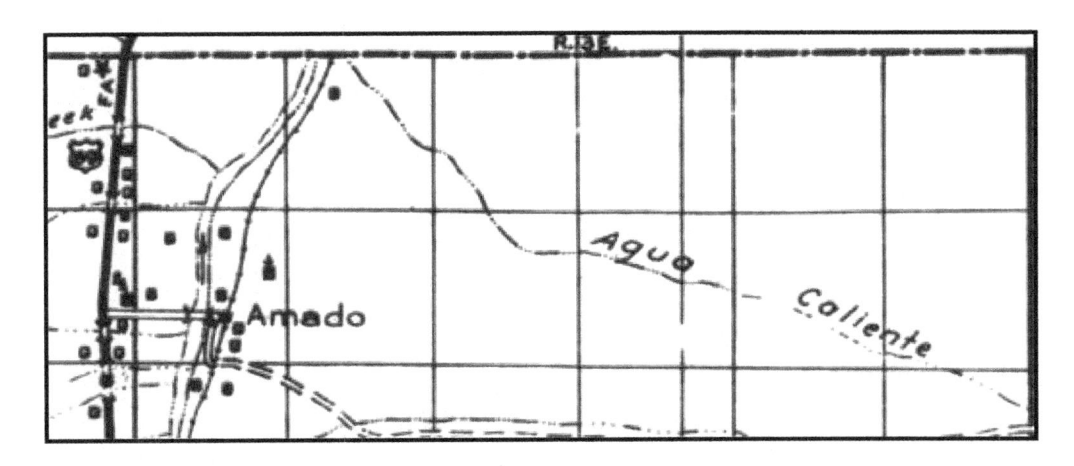

The old Railroad Survey map shows Amado on the east side of the Santa Cruz River.

Bob Ring has a great website explaining events and recollections around Tucson. He has much to say about the stagecoach lines.

Source: www.ringbrothershistory.com

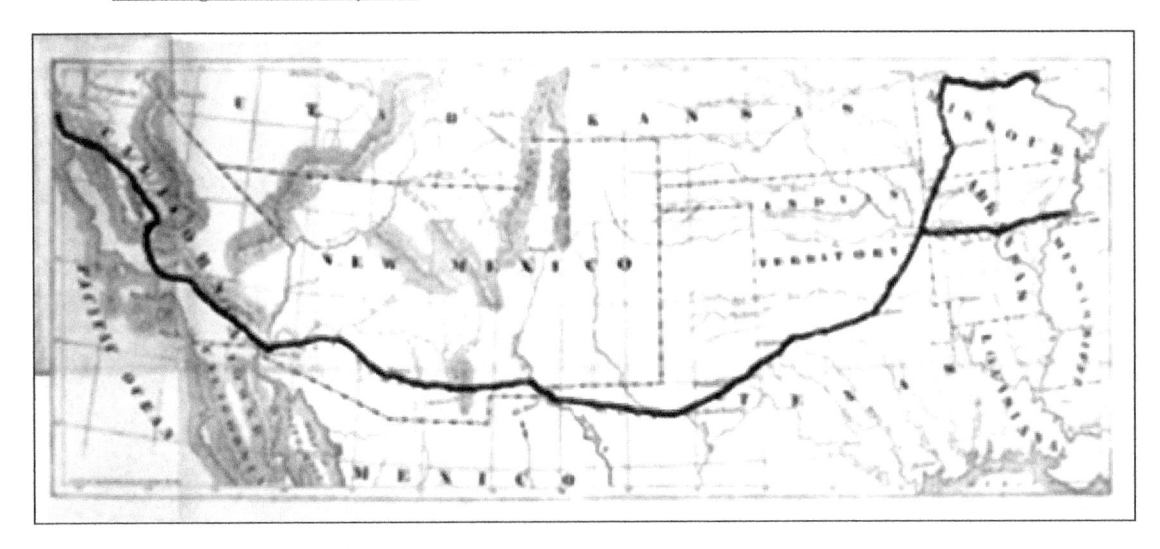

The first Butterfield overland stagecoach reached Tucson in 1858

"1870, experienced freighter **Pedro Aguirre** started the Arizona and Sonora Stage Line in Tucson to carry mail and passengers between Tucson and Altar, Sonora, Mexico, with connections southward to the Sonoran capitol of Hermosillo and the important Gulf of California port at Guaymas.

In **1873 gold** was discovered south of Arivaca, near the border with Mexico, setting off an American mining boom and the development of the Oro Blanco mining camp. This strike, along with successful silver mining around Arivaca, led Aguirre in 1877 to start regular stagecoach service to Arivaca, south to Oro Blanco, with continuing service to Altar, Sonora.

In 1889, (Aguirre) sold his company and retired to his Buenos Aires ranch west of Arivaca.

From 1892-1908 stagecoach service to Arivaca and Oro Blanco was provided by Mariano Samaniego, a Sonoran-born freighter, cattle rancher, and merchant.

Regular stagecoach service from Tucson to the Oro Blanco mines began soon after the completion of the transcontinental railroad through Tucson in 1880. The stagecoach trip was 70 miles over rough dirt roads.

Source: www.ringbrothershistory.com

When we reached the "Junction," a stage rest stop at the turnoff for Arivaca and the borderland mining country….. The Junction was a settlement of the stage station and a few ranches."

"Old Smith" had been running the station for ages."

"The Handbook to Arizona: Its Resources, History, Towns, Mines, Ruins, and Scenery. By Richard J **Johnston**.

PAYOT, UPHAM and CO., SAN FRANCISCO. AMERICAN NEWS CO., NEW YORK. 1878.

Prof. John Davis, of the Aztec Mine, tells of his journey from California across the Gila Valley and down the Santa Cruz into Sonora. The San Xavier Mission Church at that time was occupied by a Mexican, and the ranches at Canoa, Revanton, Sopori, Calabasas and Arivaca were under cultivation to a limited extent.

The distances from Tubac by the road are as follows:

Revanton, 9 miles
Sopori, 5
Cerro Colorado, 11
a total of 25 miles.

REVANTON RANCH

Among the most important settlements formed after the **Gadsden Purchase** was that known as the **Revanton Ranch**, about nine miles north of Tubac, and forty south of Tucson. It is thus described in Browne's "Adventures in the Apache Country," under date of 1803: "It was at one time clanned and occupied by **Elias Brevoort**, who built upon it a fine adobe house, with a large corral and garden, at the crossing of the river, here the road takes off to Sopori and the Cerro Colorado. This palatial edifice occupies a square of several hundred feet and is perhaps the largest and most imposing private residence in Arizona, sixteen thousand dollars were expended in the building of the house and improvement of the premises.

The Revanton is now a ruin; the house is deserted - a deathlike silence reigns over the premises. The grass is crisped, the trees are withered, the bed of the river is dry; the sap of life seems to have deserted the place of its inhabitants and left nothing but ruin and desolated spot. Yet a more beautiful region of country than that occupied by this ranch it would be hard to find anywhere. It is naturally rich in vegetation; the climate is unsurpassed; and during the season of rain, when the earth is clothed in verdure, it must be one of the loveliest spots in the world."

Santa Fe, New Mexico, November 8th, 1877, Mr. Brevoort, who has resided there for some years, writes as follows:

"I went from here in 1856 as sutler (a person who followed an army or maintained a store on an army post to sell provisions to the soldiers) for the United States troops who were ordered to establish a military post upon the so-called Gadsden Purchase. About 1859 I sold out my sutlership and went to reside at Revanton.

About 1860 or 61 the troops were withdrawn from the territory, leaving many exposed settlements to the mercy of the Indians. This movement compelled many of us to break up, abandon our improvements, and leave the country. The Hacienda del Revanton was not covered by a Spanish grant, or in other words settled and claimed under a grant but was held by pre-emption under the United States laws. In those days, a Lieutenant **Mowry** (afterwards delegate) was reported as owning a Spanish grant which included Sopori and extended down the Santa Cruz some miles towards Tucson. In those unsettled days but few if any gave their attention to land grants in Arizona."

The Hacienda del Revanton, a fine home at crossing of the river. - J Ross Browne 1893.

(see Elias Brevoort, third owner of Sahuarito)

Another of the Santa Cruz Valley's historic ranches is the **Baboquivari Cattle Co.'s Agua Linda Ranch**, owned by Carlos Ronstadt. It was founded in 1787 by Toribio de Otero, who was sent to Tubac by the Spanish government at Arizpe, Sonora, to establish a school. As for the small Otero Grant, **Toribio Otero** had received title in 1789 to a house-lot and four suertes (suerte: an area of 276 x 552 varas, or about 26.4 acres) of farming land. The grant had been made by the commander of Tubac under a 1772 Spanish regulation that allowed him to grant up to four leagues (17,354 acres) of land near the presidio to attract settlers. Under the terms of the grant, Otero had to keep arms and horses for defensive purposes, but by 1838 he had abandoned his land because of the hostilities of the Apaches.

Otero equipped his ranch with brush dams and irrigation ditches carrying water from the Santa Cruz. The ranch remained in the Otero family until 1941.

AGUA LINDA

EXIT 42 The **Agua Linda Farm** is 60 acres with an adobe home was built by rancher and farmer **Carlos Ronstadt** in the '40's. Carlos sold the property in the '50's to movie producer, Arthur Loew Jr. whose family had founded **Paramount** and **MGM pictures**. After retiring from the cattle business, Arthur's son, Stewart Loew began an organic vegetable and beef farm with his wife, Laurel.

Weddings and Music Events have become the focus!

Source: www.agualindafarm.com

CARLOS RONSTADT
BORN: August 25, 1903
DEATH: March 1972, Tucson, Pima County, Arizona
Rancher of the Santa Margarita Ranch at the base of Baboquivari Peak and the Aqua Linda Farm in Amado.

In-depth history of the Ronstadt family can be located at: The Ronstadt Family Album / Through Our Parents' Eyes.

SHANKLE RANCH FIELD

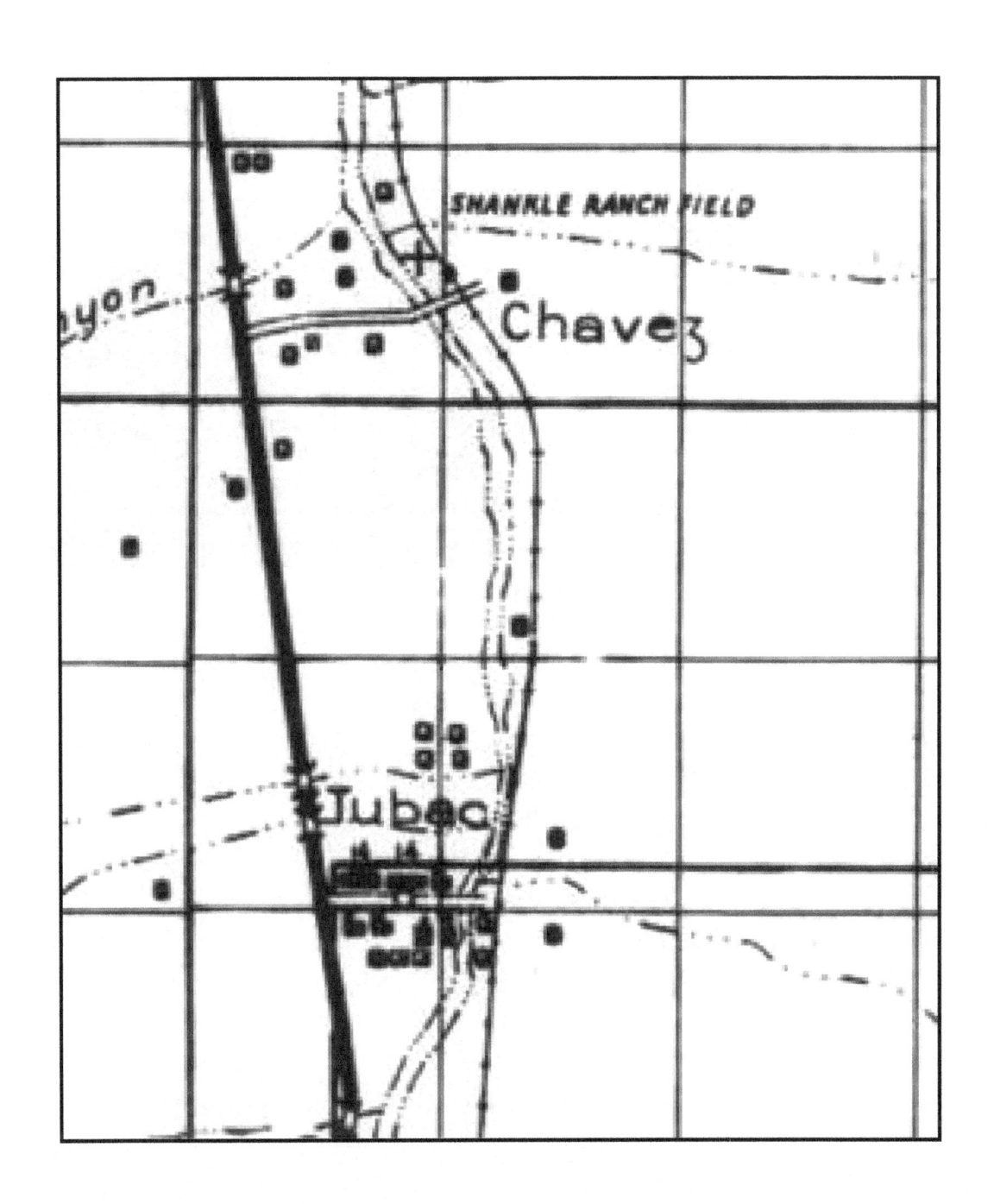

Chavez

Tubac

CLARENCE E. "DUTCH" & JOAN FAY SHANKLE

Arizona Aviation Hall of Fame, *Enshrined 1999*

Clarence E. "Dutch" Shankle was trained as a US Army pilot during the closing days of WWI. After the war ended, "Dutch" became the flying instructor for the Aviation Unit, 26th Division, US Army based in Boston, MA. "Dutch" and Joan Fay were married in Boston. Soon after the wedding, "Dutch" began giving Joan Fay flying lessons.

In 1929, Joan Fay became the first woman in Massachusetts to earn a private pilot's license.

In 1930, Joan Fay became the first woman to be issued a limited commercial pilot's license.

In 1931, Captain "Dutch" Shankle resigned his commission and the Shankles purchased the **500-acre Pajarito ranch north of Tubac, Arizona**. Their first addition to the ranch was a runway and hanger. They flew a "Stearman" J-5 and a Lockheed Sirius from their ranch runway. From 1931 through 1941, both Shankles were prominent in national aviation events.

In 1931, Joan Fay was the first woman to fly from Boston to Miami. She was also the first woman to fly solo from the West coast to the East coast. She was the only woman to compete in the National Air Race. She competed in the 2400-mile Women's Speed Classic, finishing third in the field of 16.

From 1929 to 1938, Joan Fay logged over 1300 flying hours. She earned her instrument rating in 1937.

In 1933, both Shankles entered the Air Race at the First Annual Tucson Air Show. "Dutch" took first place and Joan Fay third in the "Pathe Movie News" filmed race. Captain Clarence E. "Dutch" Shankle was recalled to active duty during WWII. He served his country well and retired as a Colonel.

Source: pimaair.org/hall-of-fame/clarence-e-dutch-joan-fay-shankle/

EXIT 40 Chavez Siding Road does not appear to look like more than ranches but is now 1,233 acres of the **Pajaros Migratorios Guest Ranch** built in 1930. Translation from Spanish is; migrating birds. Mission style main house, 2 detached guest houses, tennis court, private pond, and views of Mt. Wrightson in the Santa Rita Mountains.

Photo by author.

"Just miles south of Tubac is Tumacacori National Park. We were disappointed to find that the park was undergoing restoration and that some features were closed. As we were leaving, we noticed the Old Tumacacori Bar ... a kitschy 1930's cowboy bar and hangout. It is said that the current owner holds the oldest liquor license in Arizona."

Source: www.trailergypsies.com/Arizona/Tubac%202.htm

Abe Trujillo came from tough ranching stock. His father, Tirso, first built a store and gas station on the Old Nogales Highway. He then built the bar when Prohibition ended but died when Abe was just 12. His mother, Guadalupe, then had to take over bar duties. Her son taught her to mix drinks and tend bar, while he took care of administrative duties such as inventory and beer and liquor orders, according to Dolores Riggan, his daughter. When Abe turned 21, he took over the bar.

To all readers,

I am the great-grand daughter of "Tirso Trujillo" whom built the Old Tumacacori Bar back in the 1920's. My grandfather is Abraham T. Trujillo who is Tirso's 1st born son, who still owns, runs and maintains the bar to this date. Abraham just celebrated his 59th year bartending since his 19 yr. birthday to which his mother, "Guadalupe T. Trujillo" gave to Abraham after his father passed away at the yearly age of 29. Abraham just turned 78yr. old and you can still catch him serving you a drink of your choice if you are lucky.

Respectfully, Kelly Ann Trujillo

P.S. if you are in the neighborhood, stop by and we'll be happy to share more history with you.

Source: tucson.com/lifestyles/bonnie-henry-mission-only-one-reason-to-visit/article_2dbb461e-2959-506d-b511-db1372177a97.html

Movie Actor John Wayne owned a number of ranches in Arizona when he was alive. One ranch that was previously owned by John Wayne and his neighbor Ralph Wingfield included 74 acres of beautiful ranch land in the Nogales area between Kino Springs and the Nogales International Airport. It was not developed in his lifetime.

The Stage Stop Inn was originally built in 1969 by local ranchers Anne and Floyd Stradling. It stands near the site of the Patagonia stop on a branch of the famous Butterfield Stage Line. In 1882 the old stage line was replaced by the New Mexico and Arizona rail line, which connected Nogales, Mexico with the main Southern Pacific line in Benson, Arizona. (Visiting Patagonia, Arizona and stopping for a meal at The Stage Stop Inn, a staircase in the lobby shown to us by the hostess, was used by Wayne to fall off during filming.)

Anne and Floyd were friends of John Wayne, and they built the Inn in part to accommodate cast and crew filming in the high desert around Patagonia. Many Westerns were filmed in this region. Among them are Red River, Rio Lobo, Rio Bravo, Young Guns and Tombstone. The San Rafael Valley located just 11 miles away served as a location in the filming of Oklahoma.

Source: stagestoppatagonia.com

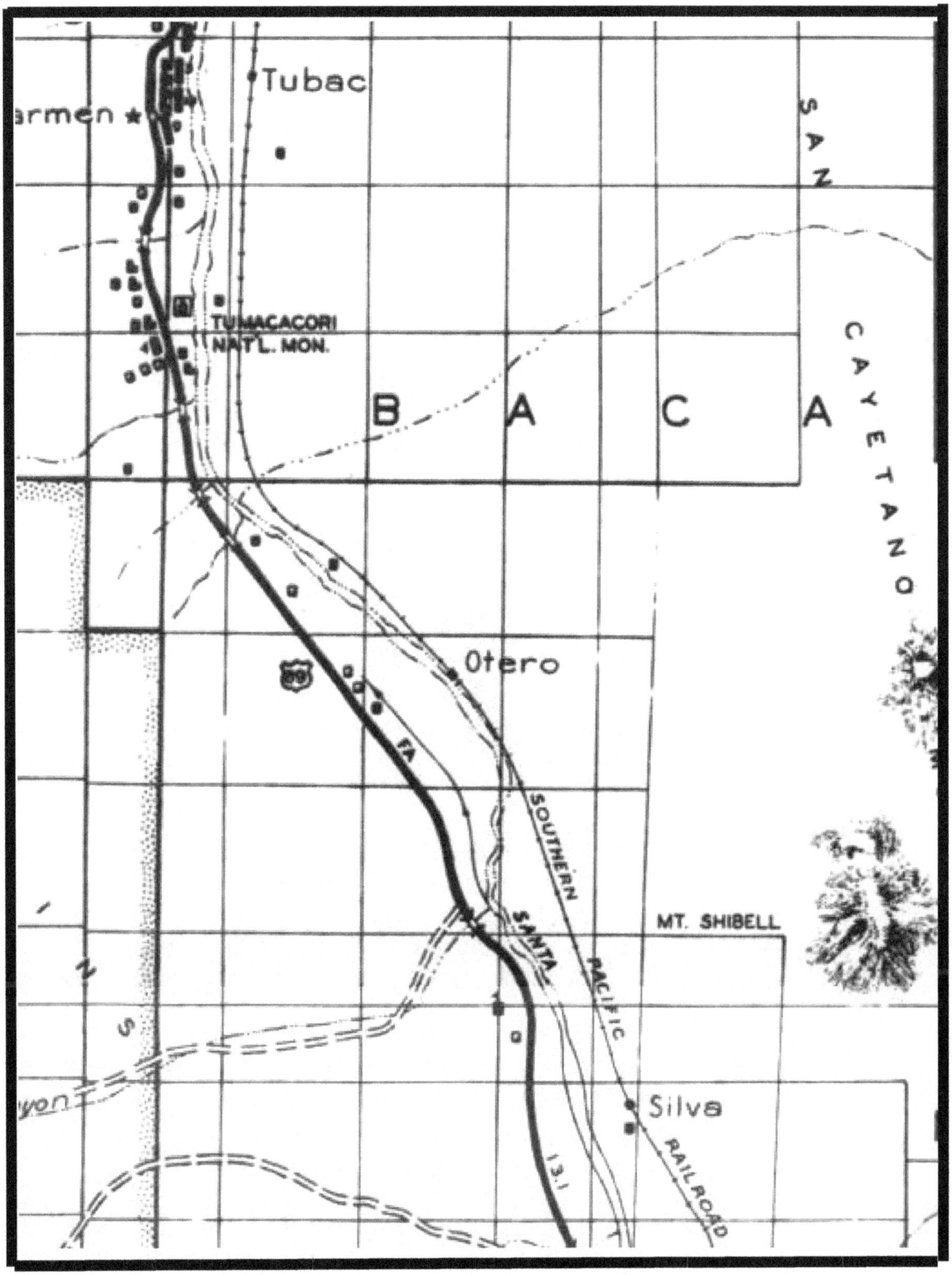

Tubac
armen
SAN
TUMACACORI
NAT'L. MON.
B A C A
CAYETANO
Otero
89
FA
SOUTHERN
SANTA
PACIFIC
MT. SHIBELL
Silva
13.1
RAILROAD
yon

APACHE WARS GAVE WAY TO MEXICAN DRUG WARS

The Arizona 'borderlands' surrounding Nogales have always been wild, similar to the 1800's Apache Wars against local inhabitants and the U.S. Army trying to protect the newly gained land from Mexico. The area today continues to be remote and largely unpopulated. Smuggling trails crisscross the area, many leading through the mountains. Law enforcement have been dropped by helicopter into isolated areas due to lack of roads among the Sonoran desert growth of chaparral, shrub live oak, mesquite, catclaw acacia, prickly pear cacti, and the dreaded cholla cacti to rip clothing and skin making their job insurmountable. Why? Drug smugglers are growing more aggressive and retaliate against ranch owners who try to close the drug routes across their land.

EXIT 22 The Peck Canyon Corridor is one such route beginning west of Nogales, through the remote borderlands and follow 2-foot-wide trails down into Peck Canyon, between the Atascosa and the Tumacacori Mountains. This is part of the Coronado National Forest land, dedicated for camping and recreation. The Peck Canyon entrance from the Atascosa mountains to Interstate 19, is only three miles east of Rio Rico the former wild town of Calabasas.

Peck Canyon is named after rancher Al Peck. His wife, daughter and a ranch hand were brutally murdered by Geronimo and his band of Apache during a raid in 1886. Today the Pecks would be borderland residents living among Mexican drug smugglers. What are the warning signs? Gunfire coming from the Coronado National Forest on a regular basis could be hunters, unless they are the sounds of fully-automatic weapon firing followed by returning fire. What about ultra-light airplanes over the mountains at night dropping bundles? While hiking have you found a body in a shallow grave that has been shot multiple times? If you find hidden backpacks, leave them alone. Smugglers hide in caves and bushes to ambush anyone. If you see a group that doesn't look like a gold mining or hiking club, **leave the area**. Even gold prospectors carry arms these days.

The border is more secure in some areas—such as right behind the new fencing east and west of Nogales, where most of the new agents have been placed. 50 borderland robberies, assaults and shootings including nearly a dozen people shot and three killed were recorded during early 2008. April use to be the prime season for illegal immigrants to migrate northward, now it's escalating in size, with human and drug trafficking. Some comfort lies in the knowledge that Nogales is home to hundreds of working federal agents, with the Drug Enforcement Administration, Border Patrol, Immigration, Customs Enforcement and others. The average person visiting Nogales is safer than in Tucson. Yet, in the remote borderlands, assault and ambush training are given to law enforcement who are advised to wear bulletproof vests on the job.

Then there are crimes of opportunity committed by competing drug dealers who find it easier to help themselves to what has been brought across the border, rather than risking it themselves. These bandits or *'bajadores'* are essentially "rip-off crews" that steal illegal immigrants from as far as Central America from other smugglers along the US-Mexico border, to extort payments from the immigrants' families. Working close to the border *'bajadores'* can "slip over the line" easily back into Mexico without having to worry about law enforcement response time to a tip off. Empty handed *'mules'* were captured in 2016 at a mine in Pima County and deported, only to return again. It's a way of life, drop off the merchandise, allow capture, eat at Mc Donald's, get treated for medical issues and get a free ride home.

Even a good hearted person trying to do the humanitarian and crime free gesture of offering water to passing illegals is a target. Using a cell phone in the open could be misconstrued and one could be shot at. Drug scouts set up observation posts on hilltops to assist smugglers; they carry rifles, infrared binoculars and satellite radios. The Apache used similar tactics observing from hilltops but arrows don't compare with today's electronics.

We were once assured that illegals move through areas quickly and stay away from campsites. A personal experience related to this writer was that one large group camping on Mt Lemon had a line of immigrants quietly walk through their camp at night. Immigrants using '*coyotes*' or guides have infiltrated the forest and know the trails.

Shootings by ambush are very chilling and regularly clearing suspicious thick brush along your road might deter migrant traffic. Snipers dressed in black, fire at illegals in Peck Canyon with automatic weapons, multiple shots were fired at Border Patrol agents north of Peña Blanca Lake. A "green" area suspected of growing marijuana. Border Patrol on horseback encountered illegals two miles northwest of Peña Blanca Lake. On the "flip-side", the National Parks Service offers this description of the area:

> *"This medium-sized lake fills 49 acres of Pena Blanca Canyon in the Pajarito Mountain foothills. It is surrounded by grassy, oak-dotted hills, some of which are topped with bluffs of limestone. Pena Blanca Lake is a popular recreation spot for visitors from neighboring Nogales, Arizona and nearby communities in Mexico. On weekends, and some weekdays, during the peak summer season, this area can be quite crowded. On holidays, especially Easter, it becomes extremely crowded. Pena Blanca Lake was created in 1957 when the Arizona Game and Fish Department constructed a dam. This is a mountain lake located at 4,000 feet elevation. The area offers a boat ramp, fishing piers, a lakeshore trail, and picnic areas."*

People from many countries, including Central and Latin Americans illegally enter the United States with great efforts to escape extreme violence, poverty, and political instability. Crossing the Arizona-Sonora borderlands is like entering an unmarked graveyard. Thousands of bodies have been discovered along the border in the past twenty years. A human rights group have over 3,500 missing person cases, people have disappeared and their bodies left to the elements. Specifically, after animals have feasted, the torrential monsoons scatter the remains to be buried under mud, rock and debris. Make good choices.

Source: In part by the *Nogales International* newspaper

Once known as "Polack Canyon" after resident Joseph Piskorski, also "Palaco Canyon" until officially re-named "Peck Canyon" 1930. **Arizona Place Names**, Will C. Barnes.

THE STATE OF ARIZONA IN AND FOR THE COUNTY OF SANTA CRUZ JACOB ROCHLIN and ANNIE ROCHLIN, Russian husband and wife. Plaintiffs, vs. JOSEPH PISKOSKI; JOSEPH PISKORSKI, *Nogales international*. (Nogales, Ariz.) 18 Feb. 1944.

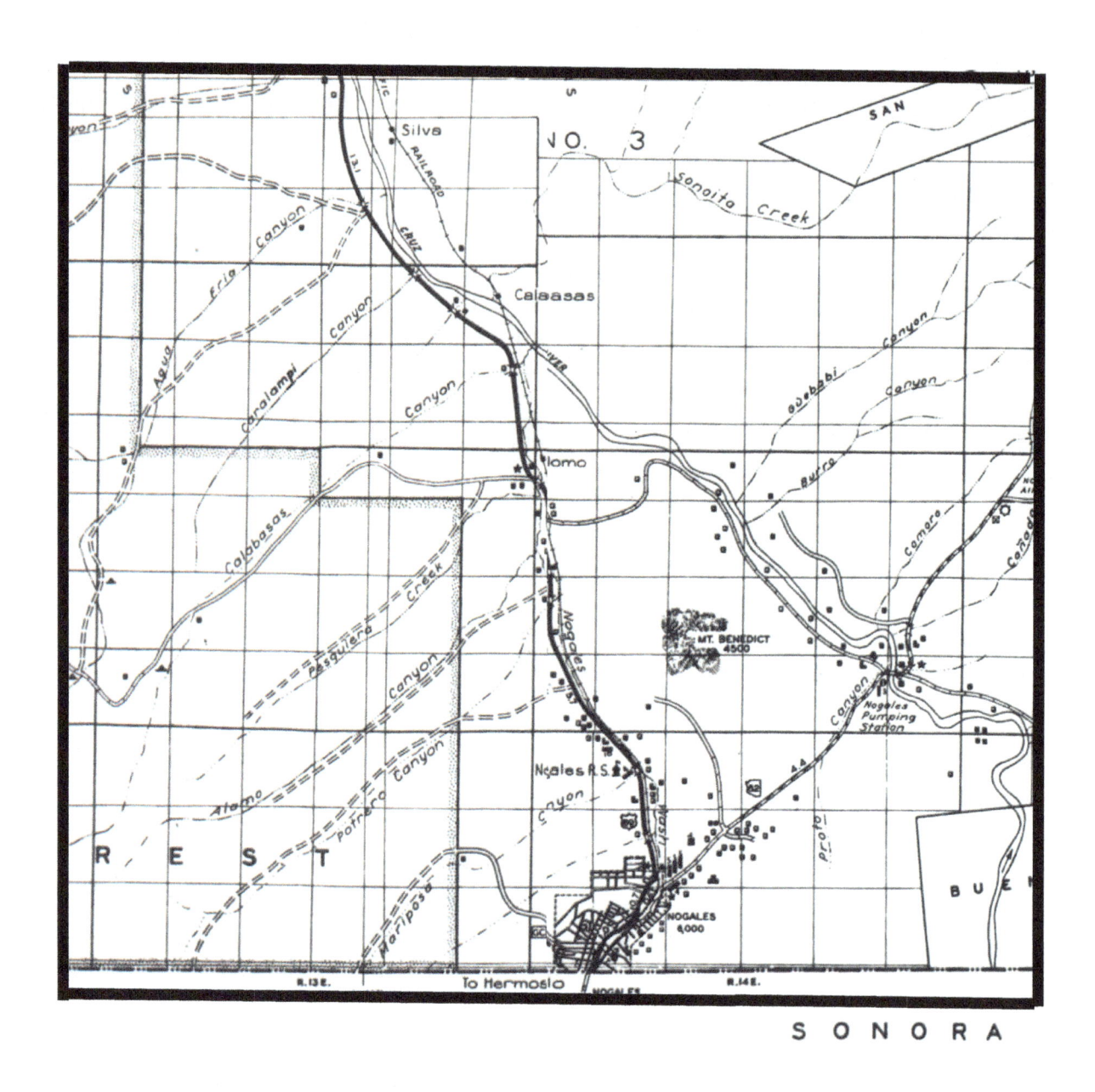

Notice the numerous canyons west of I-19 that were available for Apache raids against the immigrants trying to cultivate the well-watered region or used by today's drug smugglers.

ANOTHER WAY TO CROSS THE BORDER

It's been mentioned that daily thousands of people try to cross the border illegally between the United States and Mexico, led by smugglers under cover of night, on foot, or hidden in vehicles while trying to elude the border guards. But there is another way to cross the border: under it. A maze of tunnels connect the two countries at Nogales and children orphaned or with partial families, have made these tunnels their home.

Decades ago two large drainage tunnels were built to drain water during the summer monsoon floods from the Mexican side, out to the Arizona side in the same direction that the Santa Cruz River runs, northward. Nogales Arizona, is smaller in size, quieter, whereas the Nogales Sonoran side is cramped with people and buildings. In these conditions children not only live in, but also make a living out of these tunnels that connect Mexico and the US, essentially as tour guides and thieves. Think of the book OLIVER TWIST by Charles Dickens for an example.

Entrances to the tunnels exude a noxious smell from brownish water contaminated by the factories south of the border, illegal dumping, human waste, anything that can flow downstream. Besides the children already mentioned, there are other people in the tunnels with drugs and weapons waiting for immigrants being led through the tunnels by *'coyotes'* or human traffickers.

There are children living in Tucson who hang around in the Malls as *'mall rats'*. In Nogales they are known as *'tunnel rats'*, and without Mall Security to run them off they know the tunnels like a home. It's a fact that they can move from one country to another without being caught, a form of freedom; but they choose chaotic Mexico where immigrants need a guide.

Source: "Tunnel Kids" by Lawrence Taylor and Maeve Hickey spent two summers documenting the life of these children under the border.

Secret Tunnels That Lead To Strange Places (grunge.com) John Moore/ Getty Images

SPANISH MISSION IN THE SANTA CRUZ VALLEY

MISSION SAN JOSE DE TUMACACORI

EXIT 29 **Mission San José de Tumacácori** (O'odham: **Cemagĭ Gakolig**) is a historic Spanish mission preserved in its present form by Franciscans in 1828.

Mission San Cayetano del Tumacácori was established by Jesuits in 1691 in a different location, as has been discussed by Seymour (2007) who has documented and excavated this original native site and mission location.

After the O'odham rebellion of 1751 the mission was renamed and relocated to the present site on the west side of the Santa Cruz River, where this first church structure was erected for the mission. The architectural style of the church is Spanish Colonial.

Jesuit missionaries Kino and Salvaterra in 1691 as **La Misión de San Gabriel de Guevavi**, a district headquarters in what is now Arizona, near Tumacácori. Subsequent missionaries called it San Rafael and San Miguel, resulting in the common historical name of Los Santos Ángeles de Guevavi.

History

Missionary Juan de San Martin was assigned as the first resident priest until he left in 1703, with construction of a small chapel in 1701. Guevavi was designated as *cabecera* (headquarters) that same year. The ruins of the mission church are situated amidst a native Sobaipuri or O'odham (Upper Pima) settlement.

Agustín de Campos and Luis Xavier Velarde visited occasionally after that.

1732, Grazhoffer reestablished a second church in Guevavi.

In 1751, Garrucho contracted the building of a new and larger 15 foot by 50 foot church, the ruins of which still exist today. The mother of Juan Bautista de Anza is buried in front of the altar. (See biography of Juan Bautista de Anza)

By the late 1690s, the Mission consisted of a church, a carpentry shop, and a blacksmith's area.

By the 1770s, the settlement had been abandoned.

The first Franciscan priest, Juan Crisóstomo Gil de Bernabé, arrived in 1768 and took up residency at the Mission with about fifty families.

The Apaches attacked in 1769 and killed all but two of the few Spanish soldiers guarding the Mission;

In 1770 and 1771 the natives continued their attacks and the *cabecera* was relocated to Tumacácori.

Mission Los Santos Ángeles de Guevavi was abandoned for the last time in 1775.

Archaeology

The convento and church have been excavated by the Arizona Archaeological and Historical Society and the National Park Service. Historian John Kessell has written a comprehensive history of Guevavi. Archaeologist Deni Seymour has excavated a portion of the indigenous Sobaipuri-O'odham settlement of Guevavi and Kino's "neat little house and church."

The Mission's ruins were incorporated into Tumacácori National Historical Park in 1990.

CAMPS and FORTIFICATIONS in the SANTA CRUZ VALLEY

Today, The Anglos have had their Land Grants settled, Ranches bought and sold; Apaches, Yaqui, Tohono O'Odam have their Reservations, Casinos, Websites and legal representatives. The current need for law enforcement is urban, highway or border patrol. This has been accomplished by previous military camps and fortifications, primarily of the Union Army of the USA. Battles were won and lives were lost, many bodies shipped back home and many others lost to the desert elements, Military records were kept and we have an idea who is where and it's interesting to know who they were. These partial records and those in the cemeteries fill in the details of people who lived during the Conquistador, Spanish Colonial Period, Mexican and Civil War eras.

Please show respect to these historical treasures and follow all regulations, these historic places are delicate, and an increasing number of tourists impact the grounds and buildings.

Mission de los Santos Ángeles de Guevavi (Tumacácori National Historical Park)
(1701 - 1775)

Tumacácori is the oldest mission in Arizona, established by Kino Jesuit missionary in 1691 among the O'odham native people. The mission was originally founded as **Mission de San Gabriel de Guevavi**, also later known as **San Rafael** and **San Miguel**, resulting in the common historical name. The **Pima revolt of 1751**, later Apache raids, disease, and the **removal of the Jesuits in 1767** caused much disruption to mission life. The first Franciscan, Juan Crisóstomo Gil de Bernabé, arrived in 1768 and began the mission with about 50 families. The ruins of **Guevavi** which remain today are from a 1751 church that once measured 15 by 50 feet. Guevavi was abandoned due to Apaches attacks for the last time in 1775

Guevavi ruins were added to Tumacácori National Historical Park in 1990. Access to site only by NPS (National Park Service) ranger-led guided tour.

Tubac Presidio (Tubac Presidio State Historic Park)
(1752 - 1776, 1787 - 1821, 1848)

The **Tubac Presidio** has the distinction of being the first fort in Arizona, the first European settlement in Arizona, the first American mining community in Arizona, the first printing of a newspaper in Arizona, the first Arizona State Park with 2,000 years of history including native peoples, Spanish, Mexicans, and United States pioneers. (A delightful Village to accommodate the modern visitor.)

Source: www.tubacpresidio.org

1753 **San Ignacio de Tubac** was constructed. The **Tumacácori Mission** was afforded protection of nearby soldiers until the garrison was moved north to Tucson in 1776.

1782, the Spanish government raised a company of hard-fighting O'odham soldiers who wore Spanish uniforms. In 1787 the **Pima Indian Company** became the garrison of the Tubac Presidio. The company, when not fighting Apaches, rebuilt the fort and the church. The eighty-man Indian Company remained at Tubac into the Mexican era of the 1830s, allowing the town to grow and prosper.

The Conquistador and Spanish Colonial Period was 1528-1848. The winter of 1848 and Apache raids forced the abandonment of the fort and mission.

The **Treaty of Guadalupe Hidalgo**, cost the United States $15,000,000 and they received more than 525,000 square miles, bringing an official end to the **Mexican-American War (1846-1848),** Mexico ceded 55 percent of its territory, northern Arizona, California, New Mexico, Texas, Colorado, Nevada, and Utah, to the United States.

The **Mexican era** ends, and the **American period** begins in **1854** with the **Gadsden's Purchase.** Mexico sold the southern half of Arizona, $10 million for a 29,670 square mile portion of Mexico that later became part of Arizona and New Mexico. The Gadsden's Purchase provided the land necessary for a southern transcontinental railroad.

Camp Calabasas (Tumacácori National Historical Park) *(1837 - 1858, 1862)*

Located near the current community of Rio Rico. Access to site only by NPS (**National Park Service)** ranger-led guided tour.

Calabazas was established in 1756 by Francisco Xavier Pauer, who relocated at least 78 Pimas from their village of Toacuquita near the Santa Cruz River to establish the mission. Because of continuing conflicts with the Apaches, Calabazas was abandoned in 1786 when the last of the O'odham left. From 1807 to 1830 it was used as a farm for the Tumacácori mission. In 1844, Calabazas was sold to **Manuel Gándara, governor of Sonora, Mexico**, who converted the church into a ranch house. After the Gadsden Purchase in 1854, Calabazas became part of the United States and the US Treasury Department set up a port of entry and used the old church as the **first customs house** in the area.

During the **American Civil War**, support for the **Confederacy** was strong in the southern part of the New Mexico and Arizona Territories. The Apache were defending their territory against encroaching white settlement, fighting off ranchers and miners, leading to open warfare. With no protection from Army Troops fighting in the East, Arizona settlers were also disturbed by the **closing of the** Butterfield Overland Mail **route and their stations in March 1861**, which had connected the Arizona settlers to the East and California. Some residents felt neglected by the United States government and with good cause they worried about the lack of sufficient troops to fight the Apache. Seeing all Army Troops leave the area, the Apaches thinking that they had finally chased away the intruders set out to finish the job. Some settlers left their communities and fled to Tucson for safety.

Fort Mason was established at Calabazas in 1864, but after 300 of the 400 men got sick with malaria, the fort was also abandoned. Squatters and homesteaders also occupied the site at various times and the various occupants changed frequently. By 1878, Calabazas was totally abandoned, and the buildings soon turned into ruins. Briefly, the fort was occupied by the **Confederate States Army in 1862**. The Arizona Historical Society took over site management and ownership in October of 1974. Like Guevavi, Calabazas was added to Tumacácori National Historical Park in 1990.

Fort Buchanan *(1856 - 1865), near Patagonia*

Originally called **Camp near Calabasas**, and then renamed **Camp Moore** before given its final name in 1857. Fort Buchanan, the first American military post built in the Gadsden Purchase 1854, was abandoned, and burned in July 1861 prior to the **Confederates States Army** arrival. The CSA left in May 1862 when a **Union unit of California Volunteers** arrived. The Californians decided not to keep the post, as it was considered unhealthful and poorly sited.

Camp near Nogales *(1887 - 1888), Nogales*

A temporary Army camp established after Mexican troops had crossed the border and attacked local authorities.

Camp El Reventon *(1862, 1864), near Tubac*

The El Reventon Ranch was occupied by the **California Volunteers** in July - August 1862 and April 1864. Located seven miles northeast of town. Also known as **Camp Reventon**. (See biographies: Brevoort, Elias: Reventon Ranch)

Camp Tubac (1862-1865)

The **California Volunteers** established **Camp Tubac** nearby in 1862. Abandoned in 1865 for Camp (Fort) Mason but reoccupied in 1866 by Army Regulars. Abandoned again in 1868 for Camp Crittenden.

Camp Mason *(1865 - 1866), Calabasas*

Located on the high ground south of the confluence of the Potrero and Santa Cruz Rivers, opposite Camp Calabasas, it replaced Camp Tubac. Originally called **Post at Calabasas**, renamed **Camp McKee** briefly in 1866. Also known as **Fort Mason**. It was manned by the California Volunteers from August 1865 until May 1866, when they were replaced by U.S. Army Regulars. The garrison was transferred back to Camp Tubac in September 1866 due to a high rate of illness, and the post itself was then replaced by Camp Cameron. No structures remain and the site has been subdivided into building lots by developers and their bulldozers. Progress over history. *(thanks to Stephen Siemsen for providing corrected info)*

The name, **Camp Moore**, was changed on November 17 to **Fort Buchanan** to honor **James Buchanan, then President of the United States**. It is significant that the postmaster for this location was **Elias Brevoort**. At that time Tucson was a small and unimportant location, and it would seem that the post office established as "Tucson" on December 4, 1856, moved with the troops in November to the new location, particularly since Brevoort came from New Mexico specifically to be a sutler* for the troops. The name "Tucson" for the post office was changed to Fort Buchanan on June 5, 1857, with **Elias Brevoort** remaining as postmaster. The delay is not surprising, considering slowness of communication, the dragging tendency of red tape and the vast distance between Washington and Arizona.

*a civilian provisioner to an army post often with a shop on the post.

FORT MASON CAMPAIGN

On August 21, **1865**, a garrison of California Volunteer Infantry and Cavalry established the site of **Fort Mason** under command of **Colonel Charles W. Lewis**. The fort was established below the Spanish Colonial Mission site of **Calabazas** close to the present-day International Wastewater Treatment Plant in Rio Rico, on the Upper Santa Cruz River 8 miles from the Mexican border. **Fort Mason** was established to conduct operations against **Apaches**, monitor the **French** secessionists, protect mail and transportation routes, and patrol the border area against **Mexican** imperialists and the **Confederate Army**. The old mission church ruins of Calabazas, which are now part of Tumacacori National Historical Park, were reused as the officer's quarters for Fort Mason.

Fort Mason was never finished and the fort was moved to Fort Buchanan at the headwaters of Sonoita Creek in 1866. The cavalry at Fort Mason included the California Native Cavalry lancers, the last of their kind who came to AZ looking to serve their country and to prospect for land and new beginnings. The Fort consisted of a tent camp, barracks buildings, hospital, some adobe quarters, corrals that were never finished. Almost forty soldiers died from "malarious fever," most of who are now buried at the **San Francisco National Cemetery.**

The old mission church ruins of Calabazas, are now part of **Tumacacori National Historical Park**, were reused as the officers' quarters for Fort Mason. Although the history of Fort Mason is mentioned in a few local histories and by scholars of California military history the full story of this short lived military outpost remains untold.

The archaeological site of **Fort Mason** and the earlier **Camp Moore** (1856-57) are located on private property owned by Rio Rico Properties. The site was excavated by faculty and students at Defiance College, Ohio, from the early 1970s through mid-1980s. The collections were never analyzed and there is not a final report on the results of the investigations. **Rio Rico Properties** has deeded the artifacts and archives to the **Arizona State Museum**, but the **collection remains in Ohio,** where it has languished for 30 years. With help from the Arizona State Museum AAHS arranged for the transport of these materials back to the Arizona State Museum. Volunteers, under the leadership of Homer Thiel, are currently preparing the 88 boxes of materials for analysis and curation. The goal to is to finally tell the full story of Fort Mason, and of those who were there during a particularly turbulent time in southern Arizona's history.

This acquisition is significant, both because of its obvious historical relevance to southern Arizona and its research value as a "snapshot in time" of military life in the Arizona Territory. We anticipate that the outcome will include proper curation of the collection (to which the Arizona State Museum has already committed), collection research, a final report and publication on the Defiance College excavations, and a temporary exhibit at the Arizona State Museum. Donations are accepted to help support the acquisition and study of this important collection

Source: Fort Mason » Arizona Archaeological and Historical Society (az-arch-and-hist.org)

Camp Cameron *(1866 - 1867), Madera Canyon*

The U.S. Army Regulars abandoned Fort Mason due to persistent malaria. A temporary camp at the northwestern base of Santa Rita Mountain, about 16 miles northeast of Tubac, established in October 1866 and abandoned in March 1867 for Camp Tubac.

Camp Arivaca Junction *(1910's), Arivaca Junction*

Built by the U.S. Army for border patrols. Also known as **Camp Reventon**. Camp Arivaca (1916 - 1920), Arivaca, a U.S. Army post for border patrols, located in the block between 4th and 5th Streets, and 4th and 5th Avenues. (names have been changed) Initially a tent encampment in 1916, frame buildings were erected in 1917. All buildings were dismantled after the Army left.

Camp Stephen D. Little *(1910 - 1933), Nogales*

Arizona's Statehood was in 1912. The post was renamed on December 14, 1915, for Private Little killed in action during the border troubles which climaxed with the taking of Nogales, Sonora, during the Mexican Revolution. The post was abandoned May 5, 1933.

Pvt Stephen Littles (findagrave.com)

BIRTH   Jan 1894 Dillon, Dillon County, South Carolina
DEATH   26 Nov 1915 (aged 21) Nogales, Santa Cruz County, Arizona
BURIAL   Body lost or destroyed.

Born in Dillon, SC, Soldier, Pvt. in Company L, 12th US Infantry. He was killed by a gunshot wound of head received in cross-border action against Mexican soldiers at Nogales, AZ 11/26/1915. US Army Camp Stephen Littles was named after him to honor and memorialize him. Shipped on 11/29/1915 for burial in Lumberton, NC. R.I.P.

Source: Copyright by Silas Griffin, G.R.a.V.E., 1999-2012

Camp Christianson Ranch *(1910's), near Nogales*

Built by the U.S. Army for border patrols. Located east of town.

Source in part: www.northamericanforts.com

U.S. Army Heliograph Stations
(1886, 1889 - 1890), various locations

The U.S. Army employed heliograph signaling devices to flash coded messages (Morse or Myer) with mirrors across southern Arizona and New Mexico during the 1886 campaign (May-September) by **General Nelson Miles** to capture **Apache Chief Geronimo** and his band of followers.

(In **1880**, Miles was promoted to brigadier general and given command of the Department of the Columbia. Remaining in this position for five years, he briefly led the Department of the Missouri until being directed to take over the hunt for Geronimo in **1886**. Abandoning the use of Apache scouts, Miles' command tracked Geronimo through the Sierra Madre Mountains and ultimately marched over 3,000 miles before Lieutenant Charles Gatewood negotiated his surrender. Eager to claim credit, Miles failed to mention Gatewood's efforts and transferred him to the Dakota Territory.)

Source: Lieutenant General Nelson Miles in the Indian Wars (thoughtco.com)

Heliograph stations were located in those areas where the telegraph had not yet been wired and were usually situated on treed summits to enhance the contrast of the flashing mirror against the dark forest backdrop and the natural light of the sky. The camps consisted of a ramada-type brush structure which sheltered usually five to eight men and held a 30-day supply of food in case of an attack.

The 13 heliograph stations within Arizona (from a September 1886 summary) were located at the following sites: (the heliograph stations useful in this writing are in bold print.)

(Elevations listed were the reported station elevations, not the summit elevations.)

Fort Bowie (elevation 5150 feet)

Bowie Station

Bowie Peak (elevation 6225 feet)

Cochise Stronghold (also Fourr's Ranch), on west side of Dragoon Mountains.

White's Ranch (Sulphur Springs Valley) (elevation 4450 feet), northeast of Swisshelm Mountain, northwest of Camp Rucker.

Rucker Canyon (Camp Rucker) (elevation 6125 feet)

Swisshelm Mountain (also Emma Monk) (elevation 4950 feet), at extreme northern point.

Henry Forrest's Ranch (also Bisbee Canyon) (elevation 4950 feet), near Bisbee.

Antelope Springs (elevation 4750 feet), south end of Dragoon Mountains.

Fort Huachuca (elevation 4912 feet)

Little Baldy Peak (elevation 7000 feet), about 1.5 miles south of Old Baldy, **Santa Rita Mountains**. The wooden base for the instrument supposedly still existed in situ in the 1980's, but not the actual device.

Crittenden (Fort Crittenden)

Tubac (elevation 3110 feet)

The system's only qualified success in locating Indian warriors came in June 1886 when the station at Antelope Springs observed a renegade group and flashed a message to Forts Huachuca and Bowie, enabling troops to surprise and capture the Indians.

Francis Beaugureau, the artist had an ambitious plan to paint the entire history of Arizona's Army Indian Wars. He found a sponsor in Walter R. Bimson, the board chairman of the Valley National Bank of Arizona.

Geronimo has been mentioned often, who is he?

GERONIMO, Goyahkla, or "one who yawns".

Born: June 16, 1829 upper Gila River country.
Died: Feb 17, 1909 Fort Sill, OK.
Buried: Beef Creek Apache Cemetery, Fort Sill, OK.
COD: Pneumonia.
1851 Mother, Wife and 3 children murdered by Mexicans.
P.O.W. Sept 4, 1886, 23 years of his life.

General George Crook was able track **Geronimo**. Crook wanted to enter negotiations, but things were too tense at first. After a short skirmish, Geronimo and his band sat on a cliff above Crook's company exchanging taunts with Crook's Apache scouts. They entered into negotiations in a way no one could have predicted. Crook was a compulsive hunter, and the next day he wandered off on his own tracking an animal. Before long, he found himself alone face-to-face with Geronimo and some of his best warriors.

Geronimo didn't kill Crook. He had found the same truths about life on the run as Cochise before him. The U.S. was too well-supplied and had what appeared to be an endless number of troops. Constant vigilance and hiding was no way to live. The Chiricahua were of a low morale and wanted to enter negotiations. The **Chiricahua respected Crook**, and after some deliberating, they struck a bargain that the Chiricahua would move to a new reservation called **Turkey Creek**. (east of Fort Apache) Lieutenant Britton Davis became the agent.

Geronimo eventually heard a rumor that he was going to be arrested. He decided to instigate another breakout. Davis wired Crook, but it was too late. Carnage followed in the wake of the **Apache escape from Turkey Creek.**

Most of the Chiricahua remained on reservations this time. The remaining free Chiricahua took up hiding once again in the Sierra Madre Mountains. **Crook** pursued **Geronimo** into **Mexico** one last time. When he found him, Crook was upset with Geronimo for breaking all of their deals. Geronimo pleaded that he wouldn't have broken the deals if he hadn't heard that he was going to be arrested. Crook was not able to offer the terms of surrender that he was able to before. Geronimo knew his cause to be hopeless and surrendered once again.

After this last failed surrender, **General Crook** contacted President Grover Cleveland. Crook told him he still wanted to offer the Chiricahua terms for their surrender. Cleveland rejected this, stating that the surrender needed to be unconditional. Crook disagreed with this method and felt that his way would bring about better results. Crook resigned and was not looked upon favorably afterwards.

A $25,000 bounty was placed on Geronimo's head and a new general took over: Nelson Miles. General Miles would earn little respect from the Chiricahua Apache. Unlike Crook, **Miles lead from faraway forts**. Miles also came up with a shrewd and cruel idea that would bring about a final Chiricahua surrender.)

Source: The Apache Wars Part II: Geronimo - Chiricahua National Monument (U.S. National Park Service) (nps.gov)

General Crook and Geronimo deliberate over the Chiricahua Apache's terms of surrender. Geronimo is third from the left wearing a bandana, and Crook is second from the right. They are among US soldiers, Chiricahua warriors, and Apache scouts.

Public Domain/ Library of Congress, C.S. Fly 1886

Below the photo are names left to right. Capt. Roberts, Geronimo, Nana, Lieut. Maus, Three Interpreters, Capt. Bourke, Gen. Crook.

RAILS MAKE NOGALES ©

Rails through ambos (both) **Nogales** have been a fact of life for Nogalians since the dual nationality community of Nogales existed. Before the arrival of rails in 1882, **Pete Kitchen** settled his **El Potrero Ranch** eight kilometers north of the border in 1862 at an ideal place by the Potrero Creek. As the Apache threat subsided in the 1870s, some of the first local pioneers settled in the Rio Rico (then known as Calabasas) area including **Colonel Charles P. Sykes** and **Joseph Wise**. Russian immigrant, **Jacob Isaacson** traded from a tent across the border, called "Line City."

By **1880**, Isaacson persuaded the U.S. government to provide mail service and make him postmaster and call the town Isaacson. The border area was straddled by a ranch, "Rancho Nogales de los Elias," established by a grant to the Elias family who first arrived in this northern most region of the Spanish empire in the 1700s. The name "Nogales" came from their ranch abundant with walnut trees, but it took a Kansas entrepreneur to unknowingly "baptize" the ambos communities with that name. Born in Pennsylvania in 1826, **Cyrus K. Holliday** helped create the new capital city of Topeka, Kansas. Following that, Holliday planned a railroad from Atchison to Topeka then to continue over the old Santa Fe Trail, a cattle drive route to the capitol of New Mexico.

The **Atchison, Topeka and Santa Fe railroad** expanded further south to Deming, New Mexico from where Holliday hoped to proceed westward to the Pacific coast. In so doing, he could realize his ultimate dream to connect Chicago to the west coast and an anticipated lucrative Pacific Ocean trade with the Far East. The **Southern Pacific**, however, held the rail rights from the U.S. government for the southern route from the Pacific coast eastward to New Orleans, including Deming, which stopped Holliday's expansion, literally, in his tracks. The president of the Santa Fe, T. Jefferson Coolidge, conducted protracted negotiations with the SP's Charles Crocker, who feared competition from the **Santa Fe**. Collis P. Huntington, one of the **Central Pacific**'s and **Southern Pacific**'s "big four" founders (Huntington, Hopkins, Crocker and Stanford), and Crocker contemplated a rail line into Mexico, but the Santa Fe chose to not to joint venture with the Southern Pacific and the SP decided not to compete. Holliday decided he would reach the coast at the port of Guaymas, Sonora.

In November of **1878**, the **AT and SF** sent a locator engineer, William Raymond "Raime" Morley, to plan a route. The first and more difficult plan called for the line to extend southward from Deming to Janos over a well-known wagon trail down to the area near the Yaqui River then west to Guaymas. The second plan and the one adopted called for a line south from Benson to the border, and north from Guaymas through Hermosillo to the border, meeting at the future site of Nogales. The downside of the second plan necessitated using the Southern Pacific between Benson and Deming. Advertisements at the time revealed the inconvenience for freight and travelers of having to change from Santa Fe to Southern Pacific trains at Deming, disembark again in Benson, and wait for the Santa Fe's New Mexico and Arizona Railway train to the border. Two subsidiary companies of the **AT and SF** were organized; The **Sonoran Railway, Ltd.**, operating between Guaymas and Nogales, and the **New Mexico and Arizona Railway** operating over 88 miles of track between Benson through Fairbank, Sonoita and Patagonia to the border crossing point in a valley that would become Nogales.

The low wages offered the construction crew necessitated importing **Chinese labor** to southern Arizona, which resembled the Old West of films, with robberies, riots, shootouts and murders to which was added racial tension. The difficult terrain and heavy rains of summer which made solid ground go loose and deaths from malaria added to the problems. Finally, the rails reached the present day **Rio Rico golf course** at the confluence of the **Sonoita Creek** and **Santa Cruz River** where Colonel Sykes constructed his Santa Rita Hotel. The town of **Calabasas** consisted of 150 people who supported 16 saloons, some offering gambling and some segregated for the Chinese who also supported an opium den.

On October 5, **1882**, **Colonel Sykes** held a grand opening gala for his new and well-appointed hotel and important guests and a brass band from Tucson who traveled the rails to **Calabasas** for the historic event. At the border, the Santa Fe constructed a wooden depot straddling the boundary with the south end in Mexico and the north end in the United States. The international line and its later attendant fences, wires, walls, buildings, turnstiles and uniformed authorities did not exist to impede the Santa Fe railway construction crew who among themselves referred to the site as Nogales, from the maps showing the Elias grant.

They built a single, practical, "international" building over and on both sides of the boundary and painted a simple sign, "Nogales," not to name a town, just a depot. **Nogales**, Sonorans contemplated other names for their little cluster of buildings, but like "Line City" and "Isaacson", none stuck. (Isaacson was too difficult for the Mexican speaking people to pronounce) That first depot straddling the international boundary with one name, Nogales, most probably determined that an international community would grow as one and with one name, irrespective of a man-made boundary line, at least until the security era of the 21st century.

On October 25, **1882**, the rails met at the border. A large crowd of ladies in long dresses and bonnets and men in top hats gathered for the event. Two flag bearing, diamond stacked locomotives faced each other and touched cow catchers at the border just after Mrs. William Morley, representing her husband away on assignment, drove a silver spike into the tie amid cheers and toasts that forever linked the west coast of Mexico and beyond to the entire United States. The crowd retired to **Calabasas** and **Sykes' Santa Rita Hotel** for a very "liquid" celebratory dinner. While the anticipated Pacific Ocean traffic through Guaymas never materialized, the rail lines through Nogales made feasible international trade and attracted the early Nogales pioneers and entrepreneurs. But as early as 1883, the **Santa Fe** obtained rights from the SP to three ports in California and quickly lost interest in the money losing line from **Benson to Guaymas**.

Nonetheless, rail service between Benson to Guaymas continued which further stimulated the mining industry. The names of **Titcomb, Bowman, Mix, Karns, Chenoweth**, and **Escalada** are a few among many who traveled those rails to Nogales seeking opportunity. Acquire the line from Santa Fe. The Santa Fe's line again became of interest to the Southern Pacific in 1897. **CP Huntington's nephew, Henry Huntington**, at the urging of the SP's superintendent in Arizona, **Colonel Epes Randolph**, considered a plan for the SP to serve the west coast of Mexico. Huntington arrived from California and with Randolph, inspected the line and a deal was made to acquire the line from the Santa Fe in **1898**. Later that year, the U.S. government ordered a 60 foot neutral zone along the border. All buildings within that zone were removed, including the original depot. Parts of the old depot were used to construct two depots on either side of the border, and the Benson depot may have been moved to Nogales.

As of **1900**, the SP launched a passenger train, the "burro", between Tucson and Nogales via Benson, not always peacefully as some "wild west" lawlessness continued. The train was held up at Fairbank by 5 masked bandits. **Jeff Milton**, a Wells Fargo Express messenger, when ordered to surrender, grabbed his rifle, shot one bandit and they fired back shattering Milton's arm causing it to heal shorter by some three inches. Milton had been a **U.S. Marshall** and **patrolled the U.S. border**, making him the first federal border patrol officer in Arizona – one man to control the entire Arizona southern border.

The newly reconstructed depot in Nogales remained until June **1904**, when several box cars caught fire, thought to be arson, setting the depot on fire. An attempt to remove the box cars spread the fire and threatened the Morley Avenue business district in what was Nogales most severe fire. As a result of the disaster, a new stone depot was constructed which remained until 1963 when the federal government expanded U.S. Customs facilities. Meanwhile, the Union Pacific's **Edward Harriman** maneuvered for control of the Southern Pacific made possible with the power vacuum created by **Collis Huntington's** death in 1900. E. H. Harriman took control of the Southern Pacific and became its president. Harriman consolidated many of the smaller lines in Sonora into a new company, the Southern Pacific of Mexico. Harriman had established other lines into Mexico from Texas and recognized Mexico's potential.

In February **1909**, the great New York railroad baron himself arrived in his luxurious private car in Nogales to travel the newly completed SP track to Culiacan, Sinaloa. Impressed by what he saw, **Edward Harriman** commented that no country in the world offered the investment opportunity for American capital as did the west coast of Mexico. Those fateful words forebode the future of U.S. – Mexican commerce. Harriman's 1906 other venture consisted of building 6,000 rail cars with ice bunker cooling capacity to facilitate the shipment of fresh produce from California to the east, and after his 1909 trip to Culiacan, he saw the same possibility for the west coast of Mexico. His **Pacific Fruit Express company**, jointly owned by his two railroads, established Mexican icing facilities and a massive rail service yard in Empalme. Harriman's trip in 1909 facilitated the transportation of fresh produce which began in earnest but restrained by the Mexican Revolution of **1910**.

By the **1920s**, the produce business became a big operation and by the 1930s the west coast of Mexico shipped over 6,000 reefer (refrigerator) cars of fresh produce each season, none of which traveled over the old **NM and A** (New Mexico and Arizona) route, which was falling into disuse, but direct from Nogales to Tucson over a line constructed in 1910. While the old "burro" passenger train remained until the **1950s**, there was one first class passenger train with deluxe Pullman cars. This was "El Costeno" which first operated between Tucson and Guadalajara in 1927.

To further promote passenger service, the **Southern Pacific** constructed a luxury destination resort in **Guaymas, the Hotel Playa de Cortes**. In future years, the Mexican government nationalized the **Southern Pacific of Mexico** and later again, sold it to private interests. Meanwhile, the produce industry beginning in the 1950s, turned to more efficient truck transportation and the number of trains through Nogales diminished in the **1970s and 80s**, but was re-energized by a new **Ford Motor Company plant in Hermosillo**, and now trains, once again, are a regular part of Nogales life. The beginnings came from **Holliday**, who wanted rails to the sea, **Huntington**, who wanted to control the southern Arizona and Sonoran rails, and **Harriman** who could see vast trade and commerce far into the future. And the rails made Nogales our home.

Source: Axel Holm, lifelong Nogales resident and champion of local history and culture.

Morgan Ringland Wise was born in Waynesburg, Pennsylvania in 1867, the son of a Pennsylvania congressman. Wise first came to Arizona in 1879 and **Joseph** joined him in 1883. The Wise family built up large cattle holdings around Calabasas, their land was part of the 100,000 acres disputed by the **Baca Spanish land grant**. The Wise family fought the case for 25 years in courts but were finally dispossessed of the land in 1918. Joseph Wise married Lucia Sykes (daughter of Charles P. Sykes) in 1899 and lived at the Santa Rita Hotel in Calabasas which was built by her father from 1899-1910. In 1910, Wise had a spacious home built in Calabasas, also acquired many business properties in Nogales and moved his family there in 1916. After the court decision, he acquired the **El Rancho Arizona in Sonora, Mexico**. Wise served as **Mayor of Nogales** from 1933-1935 and was a **director for the Sonora Bank and Trust Company**. Lucia died in 1946 and Joseph died in 1952.

Source: www.arizonahistoricalsociety.org/wp-content/upLoads/library_Wise-Joseph.pdf

Not all commerce was on a grand scale. Some, like **Harry Karns**, local historian, entrepreneur (Mayor of Nogales 1927-1933), began in 1907 with two vehicles providing a taxi service from Santa Ana, Sonora to nearby mines. A half century apart, two German barbers, **George Januel** and **Albert Gute** traveled west from Europe eventually finding a comfortable place at Nogales to practice their trade. Unable to find work for women in New York, widow **Lucretia Roberts** kept moving west to find someone willing to hire a woman, eventually finding work as a ranch hand in Sonoita. Not long after, Mrs. Roberts, in what began a joke to humiliate her, was elected the **first female deputy sheriff in the United States**. A prosperous mercantile trade was established in Nogales with names like Bracker, Berk, Beatus, Savitt, Levy, Marcus, Chernin and Capin who found opportunity in the burgeoning international business at the pass through of Nogales. But these **Jewish merchants** were only but a few, with others from the middle east, like Karam and Kory and **Greece**, like Kyriakis, Karam and Panasoupolis and others from just about anywhere else who in time found Nogales.

Source: Tumacacori.; Calabasas.; Charles P Sykes; John Currey

1899 at Nogales International Border

Tucson Sentinel 2010

NOGALES (Spanish for walnuts)

EXITS 3-8 Nogales, Arizona is a US-Mexico border community established in **1880** by **Jacob and Isaac Isaacson**, who built a trading post along the border. The name "Nogales" is derived from the Spanish word for "walnut" or "walnut tree." It refers to the large stands of walnut trees that once stood in the mountain pass where Nogales is located.

Thousands of years ago, before European explorers sailed across the Atlantic, Nogales was part of a migratory path and trade route. Eventually, regiments of **Conquistadors** came in search of metals and gems. Missions built by the Spanish still can be seen. In **1914, Pancho Villa's army** occupied Nogales, Mexico during the Mexican Revolution. The military buildup and growth attracted many businesses to Nogales, some of which still remain today. Nogales became a city in 1922, and the first passenger rail service from Tucson through Nogales to Mexico City was established in 1927.

Nogales, part of Santa Cruz County, has **200 historic properties** included in the **National Register of Historic Places**. The 1904 Santa Cruz County Courthouse has gone through extensive renovations, thanks to a combination of private, state, local, and federal resources. It is a great example of a community-based partnership working together to bring an important historic property back to life. The courthouse reopened to the public in 2005 and now houses the **Cowbells and Rangers Museum**, which provides information on local heritage and offers public tours of the building. In addition, **Cochise College** moved into the courthouse and now offers college classes. These adaptive reuses of the historic building contribute to the economic vitality of the city and share the community's heritage with visitors.

Two other major historic preservation projects are currently underway: the Old Nogales City Hall and Fire Station and the former Anza and Bowman hotels. Built in 1914, the Old Nogales City Hall will be restored by the **Pimeria Alta Historical Society**, in conjunction with the city of Nogales. The Anza and Bowman hotels will be acquired by **Nogales Community Development** and will be redeveloped for use as retail space and affordable housing.

The nonprofit Pimeria Alta Historic Society is actively engaged in Nogales preservation efforts. Their museum offers tours, a library, artifacts, and a vast archive. In addition, the society hosts open houses during community holidays, an annual remembrance of the community's **Buffalo Soldiers**, and sponsors an annual **Jazz Festival** to celebrate the heritage of Nogales-born musician Charlie Mingus. The society also offers summer school programs to teach children about their community heritage. Nogales received a **2008 Preserve America Grant** of $157,000 for its Rediscover Nogales campaign. With the grant, Nogales will create materials about individuals and events that have shaped the region's heritage.

Source: Nogales, Arizona | Advisory Council on Historic Preservation (achp.gov)

Nogales was established by Jacob and Isaac Isaacson who built a trading post at the border in **1880**. Two years later, in **1882**, brought the arrival of the Southern Pacific Railroad and the first rail connection between the United States and Mexico. Nogales was also known as Isaacson for a short time. The U.S. Postal Service opened the Isaacson Post Office but renamed it to Nogales in **1883**. Nogales was incorporated in **1893**.

In **1917** Nogales was the site of the last engagement in the Indian Wars.

The beautiful San Rafael Valley near Nogales was the filming location for the movie version of the musical Oklahoma! in **1955**. Nogales was chosen because it looked more like the turn-of-the-century Oklahoma. In 1955, the state of Oklahoma was so heavily farmed and developed, few suitable areas could be found that resembled the highly-rural and undeveloped Oklahoma of the turn of the century.

Today, Nogales is the county seat of Santa Cruz County. The area is known for unique shopping, historical artifacts, and cultural opportunities. Over 60% of Nogales' sales tax comes from Mexican shoppers crossing the border on a daily basis. Nogales is home to one of the largest cooperative manufacturing factories in Mexico run by a foreign company and exporting its products to the country of origin, enabling American manufacturing plants located on both sides of the border to take advantage of favorable wages, low operating costs, and excellent transportation and distribution networks.

Source: Nogales, Arizona - Hotels and attractions - DesertUSA

Isaac & Jacob **Isaacson** were born in Gulding, Russia; Isaac in 1851 and his brother Jacob in 1853, built a trading post along the border.

Isaac Isaacson arrived in New York via London, arrived in San Francisco via Chicago in 1879. Along the way . . . Isaac Isaacson partnered with Samuel Graaff in a German pawn brokerage, (who moved to San Francisco.)

Source: Nogales, Arizona: Life and Times on the Frontier, by Jane Eppinga.

BIOGRAPHIES of PEOPLE and PLACES
Contributing to the SANTA CRUZ VALLEY history.

EUSEBIO FRANCISCO KINO
JUAN BAUTISTA de ANZA II
MARTINEZ HILL
SAHUARITO
CYRUS S. RICE
ALBERT C. BENEDICT
JAMES KILROY BROWN
ELIAS BREVOORT
WILLIAM A. HARTT
JAMES B. BULL
WILLIAM B. ROODS /RHOADES
FREDERICK MAISH, THOMAS DRISCOLL and THE CANOA RANCH
ANTONIO FERRER AMADO
SABINO OTERO
CARMEN CELAYA ZEPEDA
TERESA CELAYA, LA DOÑA DE ARIVACA
Col. CHARLES PATTERSON SYKES
HISTORIC YERBA BUENA RANCH
SILVER LAKE and THE SANTA CRUZ RIVER
PETER KITCHEN
JOHN ROSS BROWNE
RAPHAEL PUMPELLY

EUSEBIO FRANCISCO KINO

Statue of Padre Kino a Jesuit priest who founded missions in present-day Arizona and northern Mexico. Three copies of his statue are located around the world:

1. Tucson, Arizona located at the intersection of 15th Street and Kino Avenue in Tucson.

2. Magdalena de Kino, Sonora, México, where Kino died.

3. Segno, Trentino, Italia - Kino's place of birth.

Eusebio Francisco Kino (1645-1711), an Italian-born Jesuit priest and former royal cosmographer in the service of Spain, explored southern Arizona and northern Mexico in the 1680s and 1690s. Being a skilled cartographer, his maps and writings added greatly to the knowledge of the Southwest. Kino founded a total of 27 missions and won many converts among the natives, whose customs he respected.

Kino laid the foundations of the mission of San Xavier del Bac in 1692 on the Santa Cruz River, south of present-day Tucson sometimes called the White Dove of the Desert. The mission is located on the reservation of the Tohono Òdham nation. Kino introduced horses, cattle, and new crops such as wheat to the native peoples of the Pima region.

Kino headed north on horseback traveling with horses and mules; as many as fifty to one hundred. A familiar sight in Pima and Santa Cruz County, he was easily the cattle king of his day and region. Kino did not own this stock; he provided it to furnish a food supply for the converts of the missions he established, to give them economic independence, and to train the native Pimas in the ways of civilized life.

It was customary for Kino on these missionary tours to make an average of thirty or more miles a day for weeks in a stretch, and making long stops to preach, say Mass, baptize the Pimas and instruct them in building and planting.

Kino crisscrossed Arizona during his time here during 1691-1700 from Tumacacori, San Xavier del Bac, to Casa Grande-the first European to visit Tucson and the Casa Grande Ruins, through O'odham Land to Sonoita, among many other locations in Arizona.

Source:
www.nps.gov/tuma/learn/historyculture/eusebio-francisco-kino.htm

JUAN BAUTISTA DE ANZA

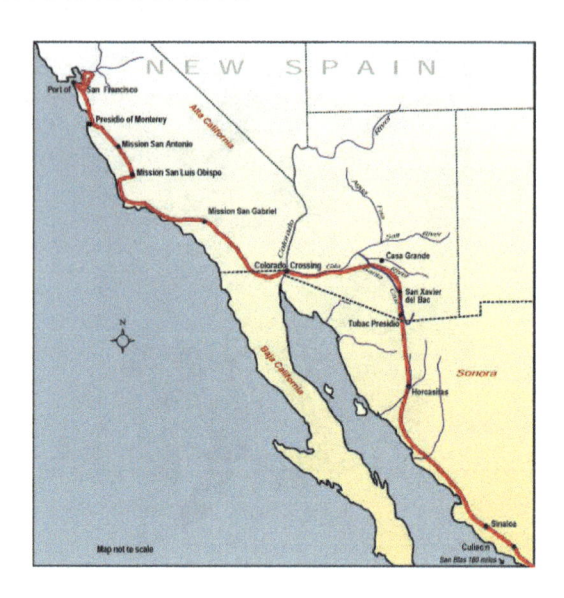

Another historic personage who passed through the area was the Spanish explorer De Anza. In 1759 Juan Bautista de Anza became commander of the presidio of Tubac to protect the presidio (fort) against Apaches.

By 1770 the Spanish feared that California would have to be abandoned to the Russians unless supplies could be delivered to the settlements in California. Routes by sea and over the peninsula of Baja California were not dependable

Based on Kino's maps and notes, de Anza and his Conquistadors with the approval of the King of Spain, volunteered to make the trip through Arizona to find a dependable route to San Francisco in 1774. De Anza's traveling companions were 3 padres, 20 soldiers, 11 servants, 35 mules, 65 cattle, and 140 horses. That must have raised some dust on the trail.

De Anza selected the site for the pueblo of San Francisco and then returned to Mexico and was made governor of New Mexico (Arizona). De Anza fought against the Apaches and Comanches bringing temporary peace to the Southwest.

Colleges and public schools named 'De Anza' are in Arizona and California. It makes one wonder how many there truly are on the De Anza Trail to honor this explorer.

The **Juan Bautista de Anza National Historic Trail** is 1,210-mile (1,950 km) from Nogales, Arizona to San Francisco, California. Parts of the trail are open as walking paths along the Santa Cruz River north of Nogales.

Source:
www.nps.gov/juba/learn/historyculture/places

MARTINEZ HILL south view.

From <u>David Leighton of the Arizona Daily Star,</u> August 25, 2014
"The hill is named in honor of **Jose Maria Martinez**.

From 1836 to 1838, Lt. Col. Jose Maria Martinez served as commandant of the Presidio de San Agustín del Tucson and overall commander of the Mexican troops stationed at Tubac, Altar and Santa Cruz.

On March 5, 1836, prior to becoming commander of the Tucson Presidio, he was one of several people to sign a peace treaty between the Pinal Apaches, represented by war chiefs **Navicaje** and **Quiquiyatle,** and Mexican troops, commanded by Col. **Jose Maria Elias Gonzalez.** The treaty helped reduce hostilities between this band of Apaches and Mexicans in Sonora.

In 1838, Martinez retired from the Mexican military and was granted land in Tubac by the Presidio commander, **Don José M. Villavacencuia**.

Ten years later, in December 1848, an Apache attack left Tubac abandoned, with many residents relocating to Tucson but some, including the Martinez family, taking refuge at San Xavier del Bac.

The laws of Sonora on Feb. 4, 1851, said that each family that was forced to flee Tubac should be given vacant land at San Xavier Mission or Tucson. Martinez petitioned for land under these laws and his petition was approved. The Martinez family built a house on the west side of the plaza in front of San Xavier church, drew water from his fields from an irrigation ditch called 'Ojo de Agua,' or spring, and loaned his oxen to neighboring Indians to cultivate their own land.

In 1856, two years after the United States bought Southern Arizona; Mexican troops left Arizona and handed keys to the San Xavier and Tumacacori churches over to Martinez.

On March 2, 1859, Martinez sold his land holdings in Tubac to **Manuel Otero**, the father of **Sabino Otero**.

In February 1863, while looking after his cattle at the foot of the Black Mountain at San Xavier, he was attacked by Apaches and suffered a rifle shot to the left side and an arrow through the left shoulder. Tohono O'odham Indians rushed to his aid and likely saved his life, but he ultimately died from the wounds he suffered during that fight, on Sept. 22, 1868.

SAHUARITO

The first known person to settle at "el Saguarito," Spanish for the little saguaro, was **Cyrus S. Rice**, who was born in Maine in 1832 and traveled to California, possibly for the gold rush. In December 1861, he enlisted in Company I, 5th Infantry Regiment of the California Volunteers as a corporal, at Marysville, California, and served until he was discharged in 1864, in Las Cruces, New Mexico Territory.

Around 1867, Rice settled at "el Saguarito" along the Santa Cruz River. His new home was called the Sahuarita Ranch, which was likely a corruption of the original Spanish name for the area. On Dec. 23, 1868, he sold the ranch for $600 to **Albert C. Benedict**. The deed of sale describes the boundaries as, "Commencing at the Sahuara in front of and West from the house ... "

Instead of using a normal land deed (aka general warranty deed), **Rice** used a quit claim deed to sell his ranch. This type of deed can indicate the seller is unsure whether he owns the property, so Rice may have settled near the little saguaro or landmark without purchasing the land from a previous owner. Whichever is the case, Rice likely was the first to live here and is therefore the founder of what is now known as the town of Sahuarita.

Benedict… married **Gregoria Alvares** just prior to his purchase of the Sahuarita Ranch. His Spanish-speaking wife might have pointed out the misspelling of the ranch name, because it was changed to the Sahuarito Ranch.

John Spring, who was stationed at Camp Lowell, would write years later about a stop on his trip from Tucson to Santa Cruz, Sonora. "At nightfall we stopped at a place called **Sahuarito** (little giant cactus), for an isolated plant of that kind growing near the place, which was an eating and watering station kept by one **Benedict**, about twenty-five miles south of Tucson and one mile west of the Santa Cruz River."

In July 1872, Benedict and two ranch hands were in the field about 300 yards from the ranch house, planting beans and pulling up weeds, when Apaches attacked. Benedict took several bullets, including one to his foot that plagued him for life. That November, he was elected treasurer of Pima County, and later served as territorial auditor. In January 1874, Benedict began caring for horses and mules at the Sahuarito Ranch, charging $2.50 per animal per month with an unlimited quantity of grass (grain was available for an extra fee). The following year, he advertised the Sahuarito Ranch for sale in the Arizona Citizen newspaper, but apparently didn't find a buyer.

By 1877, he had abandoned the **Sahuarito Ranch** and moved to the Huababi Ranch, on the Santa Cruz River south of Calabasas.

Sometime between April and November 1877, **James K. "Jim" Brown** and **Tom Roddick** obtained the Sahuarito Ranch from Benedict. In June 1879, Roddick was preparing to go to Texas to obtain cattle for the Sahuarito Ranch when he died suddenly. A couple of years later the ranch legally became the sole property of Brown. (Roddick was the first owner of the Yellow Jacket gold mine July 31, 1874.)

In December 1879, Brown returned to his home state of Ohio and brought back a bride, **Olive S. Brown**. When she arrived at her new home, Olive found an eight-room ranch house with adobe walls and high ceilings. The front two living rooms had floors, while the rest of the house had hard-packed dirt floors. This structure was surrounded by a tall, thick, adobe wall.

On Sept. 4, 1882, the Sahuarito post office was established, with Brown as the postmaster and Olive as the assistant. It was used until June 11, 1889. Brown served as Pima County sheriff from 1891 to 1892.

Early in the new century, when the Twin Buttes Railroad was being built from Tucson to the mining camp called Twin Buttes, Brown granted the railroad right of way through his property with the agreement that the train station be called Sahuarito. A few years later, he sold off his ranch and holdings and moved to Tucson.

According to **Olive S. Brand**, granddaughter of James K. Brown, the family ranch was always known as the Sahuarito Ranch, not the Sahuarita Ranch.

On Oct. 11, 1915, the post office was reestablished as Sahuarita with T.G. Dumont as its postmaster. In time, the train station became known as Sahuarita as well.

As the town grew, it maintained the name Sahuarita, which it still has today.

Source:
tucson.com/news/blogs/streetsmarts/street.

First Owner of Sahuarito

CYRUS STANTON RICE
Birth: June 14, 1832, Anson, Somerset, Maine
Death: Aug 5, 1915. New Portland, Somerset, Maine
Burial: West New Portland Cemetery, Somerset, Maine

Cyrus S. Rice, traveled to California, possibly for the gold rush. In December **1861**, (age 29) he enlisted in Company I, 5th Infantry Regiment of the California Volunteers as a corporal, at Marysville, California, and served until he was discharged in **1864**, in Las Cruces, New Mexico Territory.

1867 Rice settled at "el Saguarito" along the Santa Cruz River.

1867 Age 37, resident in Jaguierrata township, Pima Arizona Territory. Informant was Maria Rice age 22.

(The name Jaguierrata is not found in research, remove a few letters and the name Aguierra appears, that name is found near the Godfrey ranch south of Tucson on the 1922 COUNTY MAP)

Dona Maria Montaria Rice, A K A: Maria Sarafiel

Birthdate: 1848
Death: 1877 (28-29)
Family: Wife of Cyrus Stanton Rice
Mother of William Cyrus Rice

TIMELINE:

1866 During that year Charles Adams located at what was afterwards Adamsville. He took out a ditch there and irrigated his quarter section of land and it soon became a prosperous village. In the winter of 1866-67, the first store was opened, according to James M. Barney, the names of the proprietors I have not been able to ascertain. Thomas Edwin Farish, Arizona Historian says the first modern flour mill in Arizona was erected here 1868.

1868 Dec. 23, Rice sold the Sahuarita Ranch for $600 to **Albert C. Benedict.**

1869 Nick Bichard moved his steam flouring mill from the Pima village, known as Casa Blanca, to Adamsville.

1870 Age 38, Adamsville, Pima, Arizona Territory. Occupation Miner, Real Estate value $250

Adamsville, Pima, Arizona Territory, the village dating from about 1866, on the north side of Gila River, 3 or 4 miles west of Florence on the old Hwy 89. Located 1866 by and named for Charles Adams. One of the first settlements in Pinal County.

1871 the name changed to Sanford for Captain George B. Sanford the district was of sufficient importance for a post office. 1st U.S. Cavalry, then stationed at Fort McDowell. Later the name of Adamsville was restored.

According to McClintock and other writers this was rather a wild and woolly place in the early Seventies. Hinton, 1873, writes: 'At Adamsville there were two stores and a mill. It is 4 miles to the Ruggles Ranch.'

Source: "History of Arizona, Vol. VI" by Thomas Edwin Farish, Arizona Historian. Copyright 1918 by Thomas Edwin Farish. Printed by the Filmer Brothers Electrotype Company, Typographers and Stereotypers, San Francisco.

"After the departure of Mr. Adams, the founder of the place, who moved to the Salt River Valley, Adamsville became the headquarters of the Bichard Brothers, well known businessmen of the Gila Valley, who erected a modern flouring mill at that place. The Bichards were the first traders with the Pima Villages, and about the year 1865, became the owners of a primitive flouring mill at Casa Blanca, which was destroyed in the winter of 1868 by one of the great floods which occasionally occurred in the Gila Valley. Before its destruction, this mill was used to grind corn and grain furnished by the Pima Indians. The Bichards constructed a new mill at Adamsville in 1869, which was provided with the most improved machinery of that day, shipped in at great expense from the Pacific Coast, and it was called 'The Pioneer Flouring Mill.' This mill was the first modern flouring mill erected in the Territory."

Source: "History of Arizona, Vol. VI" by Thomas Edwin Farish, Arizona Historian.

1873 Age 40, Voter Registration in Milford, Lassen, California

Milford, Lassen, California, located on Mill Creek 15 miles (24 km) south of Litchfield and Susanville. The settlement began when Judson Dakin and J.C. Wemple opened a flour mill at the site in 1861. The first post office at Milford opened in 1864 and closed for a period during 1879

1877 Maria Montaria Rice died 18 Feb. 1877 at Honey Lake Judicial Township, Lassen County, California. Cyrus is with his two children in Maine.

1880 Sept. Age 57, Divorced Sarah Rice [Sarah Ingalls] defendant, Home at Chesterville, Franklin, Maine Occupation: Farmer

Children:

Henry D. Rice

    b. 27 Aug. 1871, Woolwich, Sagadahoc County, Maine

    d. 15 Feb. 1920, Woolwich, Sagadahoc County, Maine

William Cyrus Rice

    b. 16 Aug. 1875 Honey Lake, Lassen, California

    d. 04 Jan. 1958. **New Portland Cemetery**, *Somerset County, Maine,*

1884 Cyrus married Sarah Welch

1900 Age 68, Married for 16 years

Cyrus S Rice's Spouses and Children

    Sarah W Rice   Wife F 63 Maine, (Sarah Welch Rice 1836–1898)

    William C Rice   Son M 25 California

1915 Aug 5 death. West New Portland Cemetery, Somerset, Maine

Second Owner of Sahuarito

ALBERT CASE BENEDICT

Birth: 13 Oct 1830, Barton, Tioga County, New York
Death: March of 1880 of typhoid pneumonia, Potrero Ranch AZ.
Buried   Tucson Arizona

TIMELINE:

1858 Residence: Marysville, California, enlisted in Union Army

Joseph R. Walker led a group of explorers and miners on an expedition in **1861** that started in California and went through portions of Northern Arizona, Colorado and New Mexico before ending here two years later. John W. (Jack) Swilling joined the party in New Mexico.

The other twenty-three members of the "Original Prospectors" listed in their organizational document were: Joseph R. Walker, Jr., John Dickson, Jacob Linn, Jacob Miller, James V. Wheelhouse, Frank Finney, Sam Miller, George Blosser, **A. C. Benedict**, S. Shoup, T. J. Johnson, Daniel Ellis Conner, Abner French, Charles Taylor, H. B. Cummings, William Williams, G. Gillalan, Jackson McCrackin, Rodney McKinnon, Felix Cholet, M. Lewis, James Chase, and George Coulter. The company was officially disbanded six months later" Problems with Indians was a reason given and the following article was unearthed.

Source: www.hmdb.org

1863: Hot-Head Miners Murder 20 Yavapai

"The starting of Indian troubles in this section (was) due to mining and the first 'war whoop' occurred at Antelope hill in (1863.)" It started with a group of miners from California who one morning, when they could not find their four burros. Without these beasts of burden, the miners activities came to an immediate halt. There was nothing they could do but begin to look for them. They spiraled around their camp searching for the lost animals.

As they spent the better part of the day searching, the miner's thoughts began to wonder if the burros had been stolen by the Indians. The longer their fruitless search continued, the more they became convinced of their theft. The aggravated miners turned away from searching for the burros, to searching for the Indians they were sure stole them. When they found a group of Yavapai close by, they angrily confronted the Native Americans, demanding the return of the four beasts.

The Yavapai denied taking them, but the miners were sure they were lying. The latter warned the Native Americans that if the burros weren't returned immediately, they all would pay. Again, the Yavapai insisted that they knew nothing about the animals. Frustrated and angry, the miners drew their guns and poured their fury into the rapid fire of their weapons, while the Yavapai attempted to flee in terror. The blood, the screams; the crying, the dying; it was a massacre.

When the smoke cleared, twenty Yavapai Indians lay dead--a ghastly retribution of five human beings for each burro! The miners headed back to camp proud of themselves. They thought that they taught those ignorant savages a lesson they would never forget.

But as they made their way back, they came upon their answer. Before them were their four burros "grazing leisurely within one mile of camp!" The epiphany of utter guilt was crushing. Their "valiant vigilantism" quickly melted into a panicked paranoia. They were sure that they were now marked men. What if one of them followed us? They'll know where we camp! They don't need to follow us, you fool, they can easily track us here come first light... The murderers immediately dropped everything but their gold and absconded the area forever."

Source: #PrescottAZHistory: 1863: Hot-Head Miners Murder 20 Yavapai

A member of the Joseph R. Walker expedition to central Arizona in 1863, "The Walker party" was suspected of Confederate activity, therefore Gen. James H. Carleton arranged for **Benedict** to accompany the expedition and report on their activities. A.C. Benedict was a well-known Arizona pioneer, Tucson Mason, later worked as a miner, expressman, proprietor of Tucson's Buckley House hotel, rancher, U.S. Customs Inspector, Pima County Treasurer, 1873 to 1874, Territorial Auditor, 1873 to 1875, and postmaster of the Monument post office, 1876 to 1880.

Source: prescottazhistory.blogspot.com/2018/03/a-union-spy-in-joseph-walker-camp.

A Territorial Auditor account book are present mostly concerning the Walker prospecting party, Benedict's ranches near Sahuarita and Calabasas, Arizona, postal business, family news, and letters from business associates about mining, Apache Indians, and business transactions. The account book contains expenditures of Arizona Territory for the period 1873 to 1876. Highlights include letters from **Benedict** to his cousin, Judge Kirby Benedict of Santa Fe, N.M. regarding the gold discoveries of the Walker Party. There is a document giving **Benedict** power of attorney to register mining claims in Arizona for James H. Carleton, 1865. A few letters to James Benedict relate to the estate of Pete Kitchen (f.12, 41, 43).

Source: Benedict, Albert Collection (arizonahistoricalsociety.org)

In **1865** Benedict married Gregoria Alvarez, born in Santa Ana, Mexico. Together they had 4 children, 3 boys and a daughter, Mary.

1880 March 27, **A.C. Benedict** died, age 49 of typhoid pneumonia at the residence of Peter Kitchen, friend and neighbor. Benedict is buried in the Court Street Cemetery in Tucson, AZ.

1882 March, Gregoria Alvarez Benedict remarried to E.A. Chamberlain and had 2 more boys in. E.A. Chamberlain died in California in 1884.

1884 February, Gregoria died of tuberculosis, leaving behind 6 children under the age of 15. Gregoria is buried at the leading edge of the Guevavi Mission ruins.

Frank L. Proctor, acquaintances with A.C Benedict, knew of the Benedict tragedies and raised Mary after the age of 11. Frank L. Proctor and Mary E. Dowdle adopted Mary Benedict, in 1885.

Mary B. Proctor became a typesetter for the Tucson Daily Citizen in 1890s and was a popular young Tucsonan. She married the "Copper King", Colonel William C. Greene in February of 1901.

Source: Notables & Pioneers | Amber M. Douglas (wordpress.com)

James Benedict (**son of A.C. Benedict**) was adopted by Pete and Rosa Kitchen following Albert Benedict's death.

The **Hacienda Corona de Guevavi (Bed & Breakfast)** – built in 1935 and located at 348 South River Road was the former Guevavi Ranch headquarters was originally homesteaded by the Benedict family in the early 1900s.

Third Owner of Sahuarito

ELIAS BREVOORT

Born: 22 Sep 1822, Detroit, Wayne, Michigan.
Death: 12 Mar 1904, Silao, Guanajuato, Mexico.
Buried: Silao, Guanajuato, Mexico

s/o Major Henry Bregaw Brevoort, naval officer during the War of 1812 and wealthy landowner. Husband of Marie-Catherine Navarre.

SIBLINGS:

Mary Ann	(b. 1812)
John	(b. 1816) Brevoort Farm manager
Henry	(b. 1819) Dry goods merchant and banker
Robert N	(b. 1821) Surveyor. 5 Apr 1851, Panama, Acapulco, San Francisco.
Elias	(b. 1822) Frontiersman, trader, author. Not in family 1850 CENSUS

TIMELINE:

1860 CENSUS. Age 37.
Residence: (Tubac) Lower Santa Cruz, Arizona, New Mexico Territory.
Occupation: Merchant, Real Estate Value $57,500, Personal Value $1,600.

1860 CENSUS Household Members	Age
Elias Brevoort	37
Jesusa Aldecoa, from Mexico, could be Brevoort surname. (*probably housekeeper*)	26
Monte Christo, Native, birth 1852	8
Paul Christo, Native, same	8
A L Jackson, druggist from S. Carolina	46

1870 CENSUS, Age 47
Residence: Polvadero, Socorro, New Mexico Territory.
Occupation: General Merchant, Personal Real Estate Value, $1,200.

Household Members	Age
Thomas Jefferson Jeffords (see pg 86)	34
Born: 1832	
Died: 1914	
Buried: Evergreen Cemetery, Tucson, Pima, Arizona	
Epitaph Erected in 1964 by Daughters of the American Colonists, Friend and Blood-Brother of Cochise Peacemaker with hostile Apaches 1872	
Elias Brevoort	47

1874, Brevoort authored, New Mexico: Her Natural Resources and Attractions

1880 CENSUS, Age 57. Residence: Santa Fe, Santa Fe, New Mexico.

Occupation: Real Estate, Household Members: 1

1900 CENSUS, Santa Fe Real Estate and Loan Agent.

Santa Fe City Ward 1, 4, Santa Fe, New Mexico Territory

Brevoort was an author and a longtime, important pioneer citizen of the New Mexico Territory. As early as 1874, Brevoort had written an important book, "New Mexico: Her Natural Resources and Attractions." He was a citizen of the New Mexico Territory as far back as the Civil War when it appears he was a Southern / Confederate sympathizer... Be that as it may, he seemed like a very interesting guy and an important figure in Santa Fe by the time he was much older in 1899.

1904 Death at Hotel Victoria in Silao, Guanajuato, Mexico. COD: Kidney disease.

THOMAS JEFFERSON JEFFORDS

Born: January 1, 1832, in Chautauqua County, New York

s/o Eben Rockwood and Elmira Jeffords

Never married.

Died: February 19, 1914 at Owls Head, Pinal County, Arizona. Age 82.

(His funeral was under the auspices of the Arizona Historical Society.)

Jeffords as a young man became a riverman on the Ohio; steamboats on the Mississippi and Missouri Rivers; helped to lay out the road from Leavenworth, Kansas, to Denver, Colorado; prospector in the San Juan Mountains, Taos, New Mexico; a military messenger in New Mexico; a guide to the advance companies of the California Column; trader with the Apaches in New Mexico; a stage driver; Superintendent of the mail line between Fort Bowie and Tucson.

Jeffords was wounded by Apaches arrows shot from an ambush, he determined to have a talk with Cochise, Chief of the Chiricahuas. Jeffords went alone to the camp of Cochise who, in admiration of his courage and after a visit of some days agreed that the Apaches would never again disturb him. A Charter Member of the Society of Arizona Pioneers, Tucson. Jeffords Point on the west wall of the Wand Canyon is named for him.

Source: yokb353.tmp (asu.edu)

Elias Brevoort: REVENTON RANCH

When **Brevoort**, owner of the Reventon decided to sell, Lt. Col. Pitcairn Morrison, 7 Infantry, commanding at Fort Buchanan, after examination of the ranch in Oct. 1860 wrote to his superior, Col. James Loring, commanding the Dept. of New Mexico, recommending the purchase of the ranch in the event it was desired to establish a new post in the area. In his letter of April 2, 1861, dated at Tucson he made the recommendation and he enclosed two letters by **Elias Brevoor**t which dealt with the matter.

The first of these letters was dated at Tucson, March 29, 1861. It was addressed to Col. James Loring, R[egiment] M[ounted] R[ifles], U.S.A., Dept. of New Mexico. Brevoort stated that he recently visited Santa Fe the colonel, but finding him absent, handed Col. Fauntleroy a petition signed by over 200 citizens of the region praying that a military post be established at Reventon. Lt. Col. Pitcairn Morrison recommended the purchase after examining the ranch in Oct. 1860. Sylvester Mowry (mine owner) objected to the sale on the grounds that Reventon Ranch was a part of a large tract bought by him in Sonora. Mowry has since withdrawn his protest.

In a letter written to Fauntleroy about the 18th of Feb. 1861 while **Brevoort** was at Santa Fe, he handed the colonel a lithographed map of the country showing the position of Reventon "as being central to the mining, as well as the farming and stock raising community." The map given to the colonel at the time the petition was delivered.

Brevoort proceeds to describe the improvements on the ranch and its military and practical advantages. He went to on to say: "For some reason or other Col. Fauntleroy has failed to act, probably it is from the fact that he told me Capt. R.S. Ewell and Indian Agent Jno. Walker had expressed the opinion that Fort Buchanan was the best site, I will here remark that both these gentlemen are opposed to me from personal difficulties, all others condemn Fort Buchanan as a miserable sickly place. So situated that it is of no benefit or protection to anyone except eight or ten settlers on the Sonoita River [Creek]. The entire community you may say reside west of the Santa Rita mountains and along down the Santa Cruz Valley to Tucson."

Brevoort requests an early decision. "In the meantime you are at liberty to place troops on the premises free of charge agreeable to the letter addressed to Colonel Fauntleroy about the 18th."

The second letter is a brief one, addressed to Morrison and dated at Tucson, April 2, 1861. Here **Brevoort** again recommends the Reventon Ranch as a suitable place for a military post. Since Morrison examined the place in Oct. 1860. [Sylvester] Mowry withdrew his protest of the proposed sale. Brevoort now offers it free of charge to the Department provided the buildings are kept in repair in accordance with a letter to Fauntleroy about March 18, 1861.

Brevoort closes by saying: My object is to close it out to the Government for the sum of $6,500 (less than cost) with the officer commanding. The Department may see proper to purchase." Morrison is here addressed as commanding the Regiment of the Infantry. The lieutenant colonel was then in Tucson.

Morrison's covering letter to Col. Loring was dated at Tucson April 2, 1861, and the two letters of **Brevoort** are enclosures.

Source: (RG393, LR, Department of New Mexico, 36M-1891)

ARIZONA PLACE NAMES by Byrd H. Granger 1960

On May 20th, **1862**, Captain Emil Fritz with his Company B, 1st California Volunteer Cavalry entered Tucson, Arizona Territory, not approaching from the west as expected, but from the north and east via the Canada Del Oro Road.

Lieutenant James Tevis, with a small detachment from Captain Sherod Hunter's Company A, having been ordered to remain, so as to keep a watchful eye on the advancing Union troops. Lieutenant Tevis, who had been watching the western approach, the Main Road from Yuma, was completely surprised by Lieutenant Guiardo's sudden appearance from the north on the Canada Del Oro Road, almost capturing his detachment.

Tevis and his men narrowly evaded capture by the Union forces. Tevis beat a hasty retreat to the south and east along the Overland Mail Route to Mesilla. Fortunately for Tevis and unfortunately for Guiardo, Tevis escaped. Without a single shot being fired the Union forces again occupied Tucson, after an absence of 10 months.

On May 21st, the garrison of Tucson now established their headquarters to await the advancement of the remainder of the Union troops who were now rapidly advancing towards Tucson.

The next detachment of the column, Battery A, 3rd U.S. Artillery, under command of Lieutenant John B. Shinn arrived June 2d, 1862. Colonel Carleton with his escort entered Tucson, June 6th. with a salute by the guns of Battery A, 3rd U.S. Artillery in the Main Plaza of Tucson. Colonel Carleton now entered upon the business of establishing some order in Tucson and ordered the confiscation of property of known or suspected Southern Sympathizers. Also the property of Mr. Alfred Fryer, Granville Oury, Frederick Neville, Charles Lauer and **Elias Brevoort.**

Sources:
legendsofamerica.com/we-explorerindex2.html.
latinamericanstudies.org/19-century/Arizona-places.

militaryhistoryonline.com/civilwar/southwest

Elias **Brevoort** penned an influential work of 176 pages, entitled:

New Mexico, Her Natural Resources and Attractions: Being a Collection of Facts, Mainly Concerning Her Geography, Climate, Population, Schools, Mines and Minerals, Agricultural and Pastoral Capacities, Prospective Railroads, Public Lands, and Spanish and Mexican Land Grants (Santa Fe: E. Brevoort, 1874).

Brevoort was a speculator who in the era wrote one of the earliest locally printed histories and the definitive work of its period, based on information furnished by early settlers and the author's own residence of 24 years. He already had substantial interest in land grants he had purchased so he was the best known of the promoters of the state. His friend William F.N. Amy had written a smaller book in 1873 but allowed his name as a reference. He writes while many disparage the land for farming, the Navajo, Zuni, Paiute and even the Apache cultivate the soil.

Source: newmexicohistory.org/people/bowler-thomas-f#_ednref20

HISTORY OF ARIZONA, Volume II

The discovery of the Patagonia mine dates only from the Fall of **1858**, during the year 1858–9 to **Mr. Brevoort**, who thereupon became superintendent of the mine and principal owner.

The administration of **Mr. Brevoort** was not a happy one. The mine, which as I have before stated, had been badly opened and badly worked, being turned into inexperienced hands, fared much worse. A certain quantity of ore was extracted, but, whether the proceeds were expended in useless operations or for any other purposes, they were not sufficient to cover the costs incurred.

These failures gave rise to disagreements between the owners, which could not be settled except by the sale of their whole interest, which **Capt. Ewell** and his partners made to **Mr. Brevoort**, this last-named gentleman turning the interest immediately over to **Mr. H. T. Titus**. But these negotiations did not put a stop to the difficulties, which were renewed on account of the payment of the purchase-money. Consequently, the sale of the whole was resolved upon, and the conveyance took place in the Spring of **1890**, in favor of **Lieutenant Mowry**, all the interested parties joining in the deed.

Fourth Owner of Sahuarito

JAMES KILROY BROWN

BIRTH 9 Dec 1849, Ohio
DEATH 25 Feb 1922 (aged 72)
BURIAL Evergreen Memorial Park,
Tucson, Pima County, Arizona

James Kilroy Brown, pioneer rancher and Pima County Sheriff, was born in Ohio in 1849 and moved to Arizona as a young man. He married Olive Letitia Stephenson (1858-1953) in 1879 and they moved together to Sahuarita where they homesteaded and ran the Sahuarita Ranch as a stagecoach station and post office until 1890. They moved to Tucson in 1890 when J. K. Brown was elected Sheriff for Pima County. At the turn of the century, the family permanently moved to Tucson where they eventually bought a house at 422 S. 5th Avenue.

OLIVE LETITIA STEPHENSON BROWN
BIRTH: Jul. 24, 1858, Ohio, USA
DEATH: May 4, 1953. Tucson, Pima County, Arizona
Daughter of John A. Stephenson and Clarissa Birge
Olive was a schoolteacher. COD: heart disease

CHILDREN:

Clarissa B. Brown Winsor	b. Sept. 3, 1880, AZ	d. March 1974, Yuma AZ
James Kilroy Brown, Jr.	b. Mar 7, 1882 Ohio	d. May 14, 1942, Sahuarita, AZ
Harriet E. Brown Carpenter	b. July 16, 1884, AZ	d. Nov. 18, 1918, Tucson AZ
John S. Brown	b. Dec. 20, 1889, AZ	d. June 27, 1962, Tucson AZ
Marguerite Brown Strong	b. Aug. 14, 1888, AZ	d. Feb. 1966 Tucson AZ

In 1879, **James Kilroy Brown** and **Olive Leticia Brown** established **Sahuarito Ranch** in Pima County with 4,000 head of cattle. The name meant "little saguaro," reflecting the many saguaro cacti in the area. By **1884**, the ranch served as a post office and station on a stagecoach line that ran from Tucson south to the border at Nogales.

Numerous small mines around the Sierrita Mountains to the west had been worked sporadically for decades, with varying success. In **1906**, a boom prompted the construction of a railroad connecting Tucson and the Twin Buttes mines with a station at Sahuarita. Here, the trains were loaded with hay from ranches in the surrounding area.

In **1910**, the Tucson Chamber of Commerce, looking to boost trade with Mexico, convinced the Southern Pacific Railroad to extend the line from Sahuarita south to Nogales.

The **1960s** brought new housing developments such as Santo Tomås. In the **1970s**, the development of Green Valley on part of the old Canoa Land Grant and the construction of Interstate 19 brought more residents.

Recognizing the needs of their growing community, Sahuarita residents voted to incorporate as a town in 1994. Planned residential communities, led by Rancho Sahuarita and Quail Creek, boosted the town's population to 25,659 in the 2010 Census, up from 1,900 in 1994.

James B. Bull   1887- 1975
Southern Arizona Farming Pioneer
Written by Gladys (Bull) Klingenberg and Rena (Allen) Klingenberg

"Jim (**Bull**) moved to Continental ahead of his wife and daughters, and until his family joined him in Arizona he lived in a two-story boarding house. When his family arrived, they moved into a house originally built by the Intercontinental Rubber Company, directly south of Continental School. This house has since burned down.

Other residents in the houses behind the school were Mr. Phillips, who was the farm manager for Ivy, Dale and Owens; a man for the Continental cotton gin; the train master; and Mr. Owens, who lived in the house on the corner. The Continental School teachers lived in two nearby duplexes.

Jim and Lee's daughters, Gladys and Margaret, attended the Continental grade school. Gladys was one of three students, all girls, in the school's 1926 graduating class. The Bull family enjoyed the rural life at their new home, only a short distance from the pleasant town of Tucson, which then had a population of about 25,000.

Lee ran the Continental Post Office, which was connected with the **Continental** Store, across the railroad tracks from the **Continental** School. The mail was picked up and delivered by train. Jim's bookkeeping office was in the building that housed the company store, where the employees shopped and charged against their pay.

The town of **Continental** was sparsely populated by about 200 people when the **Bulls** arrived in **1926**. The town had no modern utility services for many years. Residents used appliances such as wood cook stoves, flat irons and kerosene lamps, and heated their homes with woodstoves and fireplaces. Only the farm office had a crank telephone, and the town had just one party line. The cotton gin generated its own electricity with oil. Later, in the late 1950's and early 1960's, the Continental area acquired improved utilities. Bull Farms was one of the first in the area to use natural gas for pumping water, because it was less expensive than electricity and Tucson Gas and Electric Company encouraged the use of gas. Later, use of electric power was resumed.

The **Bull** family's life in **Continental** was interrupted abruptly late in the summer of 1927, the year after they arrived. Summer rains brought profuse growth of weeds, to which Jim was highly sensitive. Because he was not in good health due to his previous illness, his allergic condition was the deciding factor in resigning from his job and returning with his family to El Paso."

In 1928 the **Bulls** opened a grocery store in a part of a newly constructed building on the northeast corner of **Tucson** Boulevard and Sixth Street. The building was a concept for various small businesses, and the area around the intersection was undertaken as a housing development. Unfortunately, with the economic crash in 1929, development slowed drastically.

As Mr. **Bull** continued in accounting jobs in Tucson, he kept his eyes on the farmland near Continental. He acquired his first 160-acre parcel of land two miles north of the Intercontinental Rubber Company of Continental (which is now part of the FICO pecan orchards) in the 1930's by paying the back taxes accumulated during the Great Depression, and over the next 36 years he established a large-scale farming operation in the Continental area.

Mr. **Bull** began farming in earnest in **1937** on his first 160 acres of land. He purchased a second parcel of land bordering both sides of the Nogales Highway (then State route 89).

In **1939** The Westerner, an Academy Award-winning film starring **Gary Cooper** and other well-known actors, was filmed in southern Arizona. The film production company was headquartered at Canoa Ranch, south of Continental, and the scenes and action were shot in other locations. The spectacular scene of the burning cornfields was made on the Bulls' farmland. The movie was released in theaters in October 1940.

In September **1940**, Jim and Lee moved from Tucson to their small farming operation two miles north of Continental.

With the onset of World War II, Mr. **Bull** kept pace with the demands of suitable crops on his land. A camp for about 50 **German prisoners of war** was located on the Bulls' land, on the west side of the Continental Madera Canyon Road, three miles north of the Continental School. The camp consisted of barracks to house the prisoners and four 20-foot tall guard towers, one at each corner, surrounded by a 10- foot high barbed wire fence. It was run by Army personnel and served as a labor cooperative, with the prisoners of war repairing roads, weeding, and picking cotton on the surrounding farms in the Sahuarita/Continental area. The cotton produced with their labor was used in the United States war efforts.

During the mid-**1940's**, before Farmers Investment Company acquired the Continental Rubber Company's holdings, Mr. **Bull** leased the entire holdings for one year. He cultivated the land suitable for crops, and sub-leased the remaining land for cattle grazing to a rancher from the Magee Ranch, west of Continental. In **1947** the Bulls built a permanent home on the **older Nogales Highway**, which followed along the west side of the foothills.

Although cotton had been a major crop for **Bull Farms** during World War II, years of producing it had depleted the soil. Also, a 1940's government allotment program limited farm production of some crops, so Mr. Bull considered alternative crops to produce on his land. Vegetables, alfalfa, and grains were diversified crops grown on Bull Farms in the late 1940's. Mr. Bull's farming operation introduced peanut production to Arizona, and today Jackrabbit Hill, where the peanut crops were grown, can still be seen from Interstate 19, several miles east on the mesa.

During the **1950's**, the old POW camp buildings were used to house a new group of farm laborers. Jim employed a number of Papago Indians on his farm, and 8 their families lived in the old barracks, cooking their meals over wood fires outside the buildings. The Papago children attended Continental School. Eventually, in the late **1950's**, buildings in the camp caught fire and burned down.

Occasionally **Bull Farms** suffered crop losses due to severe weather. Hailstorms damaged crops periodically, and runoffs were heavy at times after rains.

Jim suffered seasonal allergies in the fall of each year, and he frequently drove to nearby Madera Canyon for relief. In mid-1950 he finally acquired a cabin there, enabling him to remain longer and derive greater relief from his allergies.

From 1950 until the retirement of **Bull Farms'** operation in January 1970, additional land was acquired which justified increased crop production. The crops included long and short staple cotton, milo maize (red), barley, corn, love grasses, peanuts, and sorghum.

In addition to operating his farming enterprise, Mr. **Bull** was also an active and influential member of community and agricultural groups. He served on the Continental School Board for 15 years. Over the years he became a supporter and friend of the College of Agriculture at the University of Arizona in Tucson.

Mr. Bull's achievements caused him to be recognized as a progressive and successful farmer in Arizona's Santa Cruz River Valley. He received two specific awards for his contributions to Arizona agriculture: **Outstanding Farmer in Arizona**, awarded by the Arizona Bank Association in 1955; and **Farmer of the Year**, awarded by the Tucson Kiwanis Club in 1962.

In January **1968** Lee died and Jim remained actively engaged in the Bull Farms operation until he sold his entire holdings two miles north of Continental to the Anaconda Mining Company (Anamax) in **1969**. At that time **Bull Farm** became known as **Bull Ranch**, and local ranchers ran cattle on the land.

After the sale of his land, Jim moved to nearby Green Valley in January 1970. After several subsequent ownerships of the Bulls' holdings, a retirement community called **Quail Creek** was established on part of it in **1989**."

Source: www.digplanet.com/wiki/Continental,_Arizona

WILLIAM B. ROODS / RHOADES

Birth	1824 Fleming, Kentucky
Death	29 Apr 1870, Arizona City
COD:	Accident (Drowned)

s/o - Samuel Rhoads and Susannah Wishard
Husband of Felicitas Gonzalez
1860, Arizona territory
Occupation: Brickmaker
Real Estate Value: 9,100

Reproduced from the original in the Huntington Library and Art Gallery

WILLIAM B. ROOD

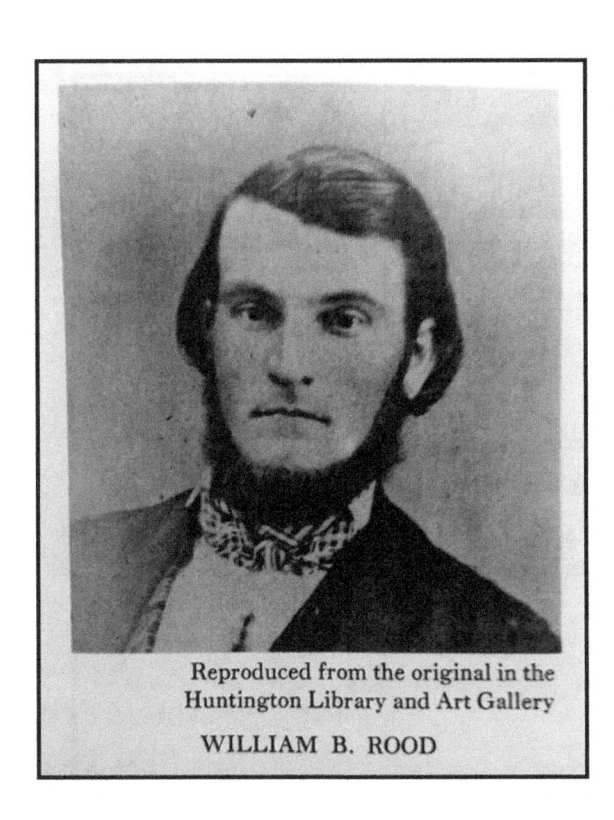

CHILDREN:

ADELAIDE C ROODS GODFREY

BIRTH	17 Mar 1860, Tucson, Pima AZ
DEATH	6 Jun 1920 (aged 60), Yuma AZ
BURIAL	Yuma Pioneer Cemetery
1879	married Joseph H Godfrey, Yuma Arizona

CIVIL WAR RECORDS

Name:	William B. Rhoads
Side:	Union
Regiment State/Origin:	Kentucky
Regiment:	11th Regiment, Kentucky Infantry
Company:	B
Rank In:	Private
Rank Out:	Private
Film Number:	M386 roll 22

ROOD PROBATE AFTER DROWNING

IN THE PROBATE COURT OF YUMA COUNTY, DOCKET NO. 19
NAME OF DECEASED ROODS, WILLIAM B.
ADDRESS OF DECEASED ROODS RANCH, YUMA COUNTY, ARIZONA
DATE AND PLACE OF DEATH IN THE COLORADO RIVER   APRIL 29, 1870.
BURIED AT (TOWN) _____ (CEMETERY) _____
WHEN AND WHERE BORN KENTUCKY   ABOUT 1835.
NAME OF ADMINISTRATOR Isaac Polhamus, Jr.
NAMES AND ADDRESSES OF ATTORNEYS C. W. C. Rowell, Yuma, Arizona

HEIRS AND RELATIVES CLAIMING AN INTEREST IN THE ESTATE
(NAME)   (ADDRESS)

Adelaide Gonzales Roods, (a minor child) Los Angeles, California

Mary A. Landers, (sister)   Yuma, Arizona

Thomas G. Rude or Roods (brother)   Unknown
Thompson Rude
John S. Rude   (relationship not given) Unknown

LIST OF PROPERTY AND APPRAISED VALUE OF EACH ITEM

Real Estate, Roods Ranch, estimated value $3,500.00

Cattle and horses, estimated value   2,500.00

No will left by the deceased. No itemized inventory and appraisement of the estate could be found. The above estimate was that of the administrator in his petition for letters of administration.

TOTAL VALUE OF THE ESTATE . . . . $ 6,000.00
DATE WHEN THE ADMINISTRATOR WAS DISCHARGED January 6, 1874.

Please return to Carl Hayden, 131 Senate Office Bldg. Washington, D. C.
(Attach extra sheets of paper if necessary)

WILLIAM B. ROODS/RHOADES RANCH

As the story goes from **The Conquest of Apacheria**

By Dan L. Thrapp:

"Roods went west from Illinois in 1849 with the Jayhawker Party and in Death Valley carved his name and date on rocks in the desert in case they did not survive. Leaving California in 1855 for Arizona he became cattleman south of Tucson. Apache raids encouraged Roods to move to the Colorado River north of Yuma with the La Paz gold rush of Civil War times. William B. Rood owned a ranch on the E side of the Colorado River, about halfway between Yuma and La Paz. Roods was drowned in the Colorado River under mysterious circumstances April 29, 1870.

One day in 1861 with the company of a Mexican boy, Roods set out for his ranch to gather some loose horses, eighteen miles north of Tubac on the road to Tucson.

The pair stopped at **Canoa**, a stockade inn about four miles from Rood's ranch, finding two men there cooking supper, and went on, gathered their stock, and drove it back to Canoa. A scene of utter wreckage met their gaze.

In the hour or more since they had left, the Apaches had visited the place, killed the two occupants,* and withdrawn into the surrounding brush. Rood discovered them a few hundred yards off the path, and he and the Mexican clapping spurs to their mounts, fled toward **Tubac**. They were hotly pursued by a hundred mounted Apaches and many more afoot. About a mile from **Reventon**, an inn along the way, Rood's horse seemed to be playing out, so he, with an arrow through his left arm, separated from his companion, veered toward the mountains, drawing after him the Indian riders, sure now of their triumph.

Scarcely two hundred yards ahead of pursuit, he threw himself from his horse and crawled into a thicket, lying close to the warm, soft earth in a small charco, or mudhole, near its center. The thicket was dense. Rood spread his revolver loads and caps before him. He snapped off and drew out the arrow. Feeling the loss of blood, he buried his wounded elbow in the earth to clot the wound. All this was the work of a minute.

The Indians formed a cordon around his hiding place. Rood brought down the first who charged toward him. Each succeeding brave met the same fate until six shots had been fired. The Apaches, believing his weapon empty, then charged with a loud yell, but the cool frontiersman had reloaded after every shot, and a seventh ball brought down the foremost of the attackers, and the eighth another one.

The Indians fired volley after volley into the thicket. Bullets and arrows coursed within inches of his head, snipping off twigs that showered down upon him, and sent up little puffs of dirt as they chunked into the ground.

Miraculously all missed him. Rood at length had but two bullets left. With one of these he killed another Indian; the rest whirled off and stood within shouting distance. One of them, who knew him well by name, called out: "Don Guillermo! Don Guillermo! (Guillermo [Gee-air-mo] is William) Come and join us, you're a brave man, and we'll make you a chief."

The ranchman was not to be fooled. "You devils!" he called. "I know what you'll do with me if you get me!" He added, "I'll kill the last one of you before you shall take me!" The Indians consulted, apparently concluded Rood was unbeatable that day, and galloped wildly off. The frontiersman waited until he was sure they were gone, then staggered into **Reventon**."

walden* The 1860 Census shows Edwin Tarbox of Maine was 23 and occupation was 'artist'. Edwin Tarbox managed the hotel on the Canoa Ranch and a whipsaw operation to supply the mines with lumber. He lost his life at the Canoa Massacre by Apaches in 1861.

William B. Rhodes's Ranch as sketched by J. Ross Browne
(Notice Mt. Wrightson and elephant Head in the background

William B. Rood owned a ranch on the East side of the Colorado River, about halfway between Yuma and La Paz as the crow flies and between the area of Walker and Draper Lakes, except on the East side of the river. Rood drowned while crossing the river in 1870 and it was widely known that he had various amounts of gold coins hidden on the ranch, called Rancho de los Yumas. He was a very wealthy man, but only a few hundred dollars was found after his death. Various relatives, and others, searched for his caches at different times, but there were no reports of any recoveries.

In 1897, Alfredo Pina dug up a baking powder tin containing $960 in gold coins. Another small cache is believed to have been found by Leonardo Romo. The recovered caches are but a small portion of what is still awaiting recovery. The remains of the old ranch buildings can still be located.

Source: dailyoddsandends.wordpress.com/2017/10/05/7654/

1866 CENSUS of the Eureka District in the Arizona Territory, lists:

William B. Roods, and daughter Adelaide under 10 years old, who later went to a convent in Los Angelos, California. Unknown when her mother died.

1867 CENSUS of the Arizona Territory, lists:

William B. Roods at the Roods Ranch and two families:

Reno: Manuel
        Felicita and Hijo, (Baby boy)
Salazar:
        Nofacis (sic) head of family
        Juan, Andrea, Francisco: all single and over 21 years old.

THE REAL TREASURE IS THE MAN HIMSELF AS WRITTEN BY:

"Rancho de los Yumas", "Apache Fighter" by Rafael Pumpelly,

"When Rhodes Returned to Death Valley" by George Miller,

"Rhodes Told Me of the Lost Gunsight" by J.A. Guthrie,

"The Gold of Don Guillermo" by Mike Mendivil,

"The Secret of Ruined 'Los Yumas'" by E. B. Hart,

"Death of Wm. Roods" by Peter Doll, April 30, 1870

"Letters From Frontier Arizona" by Wm B. Rood

(All out of print.)

Frederick Maish and Thomas Driscoll and Canoa Ranch

Lynn R. Bailey
And you think the "Cowboys" were bad . . .
Sun Sep 8, 2013

Frederick Maish and **Thomas Driscoll** were typical early-day entrepreneurs. Maish was born in York County, Pennsylvania, on October 12, 1834, but spent his youth at Frankfort, Indiana. It was from Frankfort that Frederick struck out for the west.

Born in New York state about 1837, Thomas Driscoll migrated to Colorado in 1866 where he farmed for a short while. Moving on to **Montana** he engaged in the lumber business which took him into the Black Hills. It was in South Dakota that Driscoll hooked up with Maish. In 1869 the two men came to Arizona.

The following year Maish and Driscoll opened a **butcher shop** in **Tucson**. They prospered from the very start, for Maish had a net worth of $5,700 in **1870**. It was to furnish beef for that business that the men each took up 640 acres in the Santa Cruz Valley. They added to that acreage on November 18, 1876, by purchasing a portion of the **Canoa Ranch** from **Tomas Ortiz** for $1,000. This 17,000 acre tract straddled the Santa Cruz River, thirty-five miles south of Tucson in the heart of what is today **Green Valley**.

Despite Apache depredations and inroads of Sonoran rustlers, Maish and Driscoll did well. Besides their Tucson business, Maish and Driscoll supplied beef to other outlets, mainly mining camp butchers. Through the government contracting firm of William B. Hooper and Company, with which Henry C. Hooker was affiliated, the **Canoa ranch** furnished beef on the hoof to Arizona military posts and Indian reservations.

Although Maish and Driscoll had 5,000 head of cattle by **1877**, they could not keep up with demand. This forced them to set their sights on hundreds of square miles of grassland lying between the Santa Cruz and Altar Valleys. Acquiring a portion of the **Buena Vista grant**, they pushed into range lying between Fresnal and Gunsight.

At the foot of **Baboquivari Peak** the stockmen drilled to a depth of 500 feet and brought in several wells, one of which flowed at a rate of 2,000 gallons a day. In **1889** the range was stocked with 2,000 head of cattle brought in from the Canoa Ranch. Maish and Driscoll spent more than $30,000 setting up their range cattle operation in what is today **Avra Valley.**

In moving west of the Santa Cruz Valley, Maish and Driscoll, as well as other stockmen, collided with an enormous obstacle. They took up land contiguous to the **Tohono O'odham reservation**, a meager tract of 69,200 acres allotted the Indians in 1874. Although these Indians had some livestock, they mainly cultivated corn, beans, and squash. They also hunted and gathered wild plants over an immense expanse of territory extending to the Gulf of California. Their existence was, at best, a marginal one.

The Papagos, as Arizonans called these Indians, had always been friends of the whites. Anglo-Americans considered them an "inoffensive Christianized people" who traded baskets, pottery and field products in southern Arizona towns. At times they joined the whites in wars against the Apaches.

In **1872** Tucsonans enlisted their aid in wiping out troublesome **Arivaipi Apaches** near old Camp Grant. Environmental circumstances and governmental fickleness, however, threw a monkey wrench into the relationship which this people had with white stockmen.

In the late 1870s and early '80s the **Tohono O'odham** suffered hardships. A series of droughts wiped out their crops, forcing them to consume their grain and cattle. They sought aid from the government but nothing was done to relieve their plight. Meanwhile, their mortal enemies, the **Apaches**, received corn, flour, sugar, and tobacco at San Carlos and the White Mountain reservations. Millions of pounds of beef were delivered to a people the Papagos detested.

To the starving Indians living in the shadow of **Baboquivari Peak** this was an insult that could not be overlooked. In mid-1883 the Papago began striking back.

Their resistance was subtle at first. A few horses disappeared in the Arivaca region; some cattle were slaughtered on the **Sonoita**. At first the butchery was attributed to starving Mexicans. Then on September 15th at Antelope Springs near the southern end of the Dragoon Mountains, a roving band of Papagos killed George Ward. Shortly thereafter a number of Indians from the **Altar Valley** appeared in Tombstone with fourteen horses for sale. Tombstoners bought them all.

A day or so later, a rancher appeared claiming the animals were stolen from his ranch in Sonora. As he presented proof of ownership, the sheriff compelled townsfolk to give up the animals. Then it got worse, especially in the Altar Valley.

Of the 2,000 head of cattle that Maish and Driscoll stocked their **Buena Vista Ranch** with, when it came time to round them up, 400 head were "all that could be gotten together." Eighty percent of the herd had been slaughtered by "thieving Papagos." Other ranchers had similar losses.

Frank Procter drove 673 head of brood cattle to the Fresnal about the time **Maish** and **Driscoll** established their **Buena Vista Ranch**. When he made his roundup only 400 head were left. Four missing steers were trailed to the village of Topowa where the animals had been slaughtered. The hides were gone but the meat remained. When stockmen questioned villagers as to who killed the steers, they were told the men had gone to Tucson.

If the Indians had not molested the cattle, **Procter's** herd would have increased to at least a thousand head. **Sabino Otero**, who range bordered Papago country, lost nearly his entire herd of 1,500 head of cattle. At roundup time he found ninety-two head remaining.

Livestock losses mounted steadily with each passing year. By spring of **1896** Papago Indians had slaughtered cattle worth $100,000. The **Arizona Daily Star** called it "wholesale butchery." Indeed it was. A gentleman traveling to Tucson from the Papago country reported passing three carcasses of which only choice parts had been removed. It was obvious to all-

-the herds were the sole support of the Indians.

With their wealth and livelihood being eaten away, cattlemen sought relief first from the Interior Department and then from local authorities. The government refused to move in the matter and the Pima County Sheriff said he was powerless to stem the depredations. Whenever an Indian was arrested, local courts discharged him for "alleged want of jurisdiction." That was enough for cattlemen. Beginning in August **1896** stockmen huddled in a series of meetings to curb Indian butchery.

At a conference in the **Palace Hotel**, owned by **Maish** and **Driscoll**, cattlemen talked of summary punishment; a fine idea if a few thieves were involved. The Indians, however, were formidable in numbers, and well-armed. At another meeting in the district courtroom stockmen formulated a plan to employ six men to patrol the Indian country to discover cattle theft and arrest thieves.

Charles Procter, however, pointed out the plan's weakness. No system of patrols could prevent the slaughter of cattle, the country being extensive and the Indians too shrewd. The only remedy, Procter believed, lay in the government and if the government turned a deaf ear, "attention might be awakened by hanging or shooting some of its wards." A bad idea, proclaimed Ramon Soto. Such an extreme measure would "make life insecure for miners in that country and other persons not interested in the cattle trouble."

The **Pima County Cattlemen's Association** finally adopted a plan. A detective was hired at a salary of $100 a month to patrol the country adjacent to the Papago reservation and arrest Indians slaughtering cattle. The detective's expense was paid by cattlemen, "in proportion to the valuation of their herds as shown by the county assessment roll." The detective had the authority to call in assistance from **Indian Agent J. Roe Young,** based at Sacaton.

Despite the detective's efforts the slaughter continued. In desperation, cattlemen exerted enough influence to convince the War Department to station soldiers at Arivaca.

In the mid-**1890s** the famed **Seventh Cavalry** was positioned along the border, contingents being posted at **Fresnal, Arivaca, and Calabasas**. That did the trick; livestock slaughter subsided after 1897. A decade later the Arizona Daily Star reported the Papagos "in very good circumstances owning cattle, horses and farming land." That wasn't the case with Maish and Driscoll.

From **1890** to **1894** the **Tohono O'odham** inflicted more than $300,000 worth of damages on Pima County stockmen, forcing stockmen from the Fresnal and Avra Valley region.

Maish and **Driscoll** pulled what remained of their herds back to the Santa Cruz Valley. They abandoned $40,000 worth of range improvements: wells, stock tanks, buildings and corrals. But their actions were too slow and they went bankrupt. Disposing of their remaining cattle to an Idaho buyer, the lives of **Maish** and **Driscoll** spiraled downward. They lost the Canoa and Buena Vista ranches, the butcher business, and the Palace Hotel.

Frederick Maish spent his remaining years in a (hovel ?) on Meyer Street. He died in Tucson in May 1913. His body was returned to Frankfort, Indiana, for burial.

Thomas Driscoll fared a little better. Hanging on to some land in the Santa Cruz Valley, he lived into the 1920s.

-- From "The Cowboys," by Lynn R. Bailey, 2012.

Antonio Ferrer Amado's recollections of his ranching life

"Contributed by Antonio Ferrer Amado, owner of several ranchos in Pima and Santa Cruz counties."

"In these days we raised horses by the hundred as the range was all open and we had a good opportunity to sell horses to freighters and to the government for cavalry horses and we broke horses from fifty head to one hundred at a time and took all of this hard work as a good pastime as we thought it was lots of fun to ride these wild outlaw horses raised out in the wild on the range. With some of them it took a week to get them in to the herd of horses that were tamer that we drove in a herd to run the wilder ones in to this herd so as we could drive them in to a corral to pick out the ones we wanted to break as we called it in those days.

Now-days they say taming a horse; we rode our bronc right out on the open range. One man saddled a gentle horse to herd through bronc busters on wild horses. I and my brother John and two other men done the riding act and had lots of fun. The two herders helped to turn out broncs and herd us back to the corral where we would unsaddle and resaddle a fresh one. Thus was done every day for a month until we got where the six of us could ride twelve head in the forenoon, and twelve head in the afternoon until they were all gentle and then we would turn them out and herd them and get them picked out to a certain height for the inspection for the government sales and the culls were held for cow ponies and used on range for our own stock work and farm work and stage horses which carried the mail seventy-five miles a day by making two changes 150 miles a "round trip" from Willcox to Aravaipa mines. This mail was delivered twice a week.

These old pictures bring a great remembering of those later days and none of these roads are traveled today and no horse breaking is like in those days."

Hardy Cowman Recalls Days Of Apache Raids
The Arizona Daily Star 1-31-1965

90-Yr.-Old Rancher Recently Quit Riding

By BOB THOMAS

AMADO - In a house he built beside the old stagecoach road to Nogales, **Antonio Amado** looks back over a life that began in Arizona's Indian wars and extends into the space age.

At the age of 90, Amado probably is the oldest working rancher in the state. Born in Tucson in a house on the corner of Meter Ave. and Jackson St. in 1874, **Amado** started work on his father's ranch as a six-year-old cowboy. Until two years ago he rode a horse every day.

He still was able to mount a horse last year but has foresworn long rides that carried him in to the foothills of the Santa Rita Mountains nine miles from his home when he was 88. "That's nine air miles; it's a lot longer on the ground," says Randy R. Riley, forest ranger for the Santa Ritas. "I've seen him ride up those ridges several times and that's a rough haul."

Amado, who customarily speaks in a slow, thoughtful manner with frequent pauses, can remember when Geronimo passed nearby in a raid. A cousin of his was killed by the Apaches while chopping wood in nearby White House Canyon.

He has known such Tucson pioneers as Sheriff Bob Leatherwood, the Hughes brothers - Tom, Sam and L. C. Hughes, founder of the Arizona Daily Star. Amado knew Ed Echols when he was a young cattle inspector.

Still slim and straight, Amado looks much younger than he is. He has most of his own teeth, has good hearing and doesn't wear glasses except for reading. He smokes but doesn't drink.

Asked what he credits his long life to, **Amado** shook his head wonderingly and said: "I don't know. I've never taken care of myself." Amado said he has no desire to reach 100. "I feel all right. I haven't seen a doctor in many years. But I may die any day," he said.

His father, who came to Arizona from Hermosillo, Sonora, Mexico, in 1850, started the ranch in 1852 between two old Spanish land grants, the Canoa and Otero land grants. A year later he started another ranch two miles from the **San Xavier Mission**. It ran dairy cattle and supplied Tucson with milk and butter.

Amado's father started other ranches at Patagonia and in Sonora. He died at the age of 73 after fathering three sons and four daughters.

Amado, the middle son, is the only one alive today. He has two sons, Pablo and Gustavo, and a daughter, Amalia, all of Tucson. Another son, Antonio Jr., died recently.

Amado remembers how the U. S. government evicted his parents from their **San Xavier Ranch** in 1880 because it was located within the boundary of the newly created **San Xavier Indian Reservation.** The ranch, like others lying within the reservation, was burned by the government agents.

The family moved to Tucson where **Amado** attended the old Congress St. school and then transferred to Safford School. He received the equivalent of a college education when his family send him to the San Ignacio Loyola Jesuit school in San Francisco.

At the age of 23 he was married in the newly completed San Agustin Cathedral in Tucson and in 1909 he bought his ranch - 160 acres of patented land for $300. Today it is worth $900 an acre. In addition to the patented land he holds state and Forest Service grazing leases for 6,000 acres.

In the days before the barbed wire fence **Amado's** cattle ranged all the way from the Mexican border to Cortaro, north of Tucson. His ranch branded as many as 1,500 calves a year. "The land was different." said **Amado**. "There was more grass and less mesquite trees."

In a lifetime of hazardous work as a rancher, **Amado** never broke a bone. He did, like many other cowboys, lose the tip of the index finger on his right hand when he caught it between the saddle horn and his leather riata, which he had used to lasso a big steer.

Amado built his home and all the buildings on his ranch. The ruins of the old stage station are still visible. The **Amado ranch** was a stopping place for the Nogales stage for many years. In 1910 the **town of Amado** came into being when the railroad track from Tucson to Nogales was laid. When the Nogales Highway was built the town was moved to its present location.

Amado never succumbed to the prospecting urge, despite the heaving mining activity, especially at nearby **Helvetia**, in the early part of the century.

Although he carried a Colt .45 revolver until his middle forties, Amado said he was never threatened or had to resort to violence to protect himself.

"And I never had to call the sheriff. Things were quiet. But I did lose a few calves (to rustlers)," said **Amado**. "I carried a gun to shoot coyotes. I killed two deer with it. I was a pretty good shot," he said in a matter of fact manner. Dressed in frayed work clothes and wearing the old fashioned wide brim cowboy hat, Amado showed his ranch to visitors. He pointed to towering slat cedar trees he had planted when he first built his home.

In the front yard was a giant mesquite tree that had shown no appreciable growth in the time **Amado** has lived there. The adobe home with galvanized iron roof is an outdated type still seen here and there in the Southwest: high, narrow windows, thick walls to keep out the heat and high ceilings.

A fireplace heats the living room, its façade decorated with tile featuring scenes from Don Quixote. Every morning **Amado** cuts wood for the day's fire. He does his own cooking. The pioneer rancher took his first airplane ride in 1950 when he flew to Mexico City. He has flown several times since. Until advancing age forced him to stop a few years ago, **Amado** drove his own car.

SABINO OTERO

BIRTH   30 Dec 1842, Tubac, AZ
DEATH   22 Jan 1914 (aged 71), Tucson, AZ
BURIAL Holy Hope Cemetery and Mausoleum
            Tucson, Pima County, Arizona
            s/o Manuel Otero and
            María Clara Martinez

Sabino never married as his father passed away when he was 19 years old and left a family of 7 children. Eventually the family settled in Tucson as some of Tucson's first settlers. Sabino was prosperous enough to travel to Paris in 1878 but returned several months later stating he was content with his home in Southern Arizona.

Sabino Canyon, a popular recreation site in the Santa Catalina mountains north of Tucson is named after Sabino Otero.

Sabino was, **Great-grandson of Torrivio OTERO** who was awarded a home property and a nearby ranch in Tubac, Pimaria Alta, Sonora, Mexico from the King of Spain on 10 January 1789. That property became a part of the United States through the **Gadsden Purchase** in 1853.

Source: www.findagrave.com/memorial/90157394/sabino-otero

As for the small Otero Grant, Toribio Otero had received title in **1789** to a house-lot and four suertes (suerte: an area of 276 x 552 varas, or about 26.4 acres) of farming land. The grant had been made by the commander of Tubac under a 1772 Spanish regulation that allowed him to grant up to four leagues (17,354 acres) of land near the presidio to attract settlers. Under the terms of the grant, Otero had to keep arms and horses for defensive purposes, but by **1838** had abandoned his land because of the hostilities of the Apaches.

Manuel Otero and **María Clara Martinez** were the parents of seven children:

1. Francisca Otero, born circa 1839/1840 in Arizona. Married to Ramón Comaduran.
2. **Sabino Otero**, born 30 Dec 1842 in Tubac. Never married.
3. María Manuela Otero, born on 6 June 1844. Married to Louis Quesse.
4. María Helena de Jesús Otero, born on 17 August 1846. 1864 Married Mauricio Castro.
5. Gabriela Otero, born circa 1849 in Arizona. She was still alive in 1879.
6. Fernando Otero, born circa May 1860 in Arizona. died on 5 February 1878.
7. José Teofilo Otero was baptized on 13 April 1863 in Tucson.

'A big rancher in the area was **Sabino Otero**, who employed about twenty vaqueros. It was recalled "lots of little Indian scares" in those early days, times when the townspeople would take refuge in Otero's store. "It had a dirt roof. We huddled in there and told Indian stories—they were enough to scare anyone to death." "They wanted these men to go to Tucson, then they wanted to take the women in but they wouldn't go, they were not built that way, so we all stayed here," the pioneer teacher said. "No, I never worried much about the Indians." '

Source: www.nps.gov/parkhistory/online_books/tuma/hrs/chap7.htm

'James H. McClintock the Arizona historian, states that for a number of years he (Sabino) engaged in hauling freight-to Arizona army posts but Apache attacks caused him such losses that he disposed of his freighting outfit and used the proceeds to buy a herd of cattle from Texas; subsequent Indian depredations against his cattle led him to make an arrangement to graze them in Sonora which he did for five years; became a member of the Society of Arizona Pioneers, February 5, 1888, at the time of his death the Tucson Citizen gave an account of his life and activities from which the following is quoted: 'Sabino Otero, one of the oldest native sons of Southern Arizona, passed away at 6 o'clock this morning at his home at 21g South Main Street in Tucson, where he had lived for nearly fifty years.

Sabino outlived all of these save one brother, Teofilo Otero. Sabino Otero was the father of the whole flock. He said that he never married because he had too many responsibilities. after raising the large family which his father left him, he raised his nephews and nieces and when they had grown up raised grand-nephews and grand-nieces and at the time of his death their children, comprising the fourth generation, were living at his home.

Sabino Otero devoted his attention to farming the grant which he inherited and lands to the south below the Tumacacori mission. He farmed lands at Buzani across the line. He used to travel at night to escape the renegade Apaches. They made serious inroad on his stock at times.

In **1881** he began to give his entire attention to the cattle business and at the time of his death had large herds grazing near Tubac, on the east and west side of the Baboquivari mountains and in the Santa Rosa valley. **Sabino Otero** has always been a very charitable man. He was a patron of the Sisters of St. Joseph, not only here in Tucson but in Phoenix, Prescott and Los Angeles. He practically 'build the Catholic Church at Tubac and was a heavy contributor to churches built in this diocese.'

Source: www.asu.edu/lib/archives/azbio/bios/OTEROS.PDF

Carmen *Celaya* Zepeda

Birth: Nov. 21, 1879, Mexico
Death: Sep. 3, 1968, Nogales, Arizona
Burial: Arivaca Cemetery
d/o Teresa Celaya-Bustamonte. 1918, opened a trading store and homesteaded 300 acres.

CARMEN ZEPEDA, TUCSON DAILY CITIZEN, SEPTEMBER 5, 1968

A Rosary will be recited tomorrow for Mrs. Carmen Zepeda, founder of the town of Carmen, who died yesterday at the Casa Solana Rest Home. She was 93. A Mass will be said at San Agustin Cathedral at 9 a.m. Saturday. Burial will be in Arivaca.

Mrs. Zepeda, most recently a resident of Nogales, had operated a general store at Carmen, about 19 miles North of Nogales, for 41 years before retiring in 1958. A native of Saric, Sonora, Mrs. Zepeda came to Arizona when she was 12 and first resided in Arivaca. In 1914, she built the Carmen Hotel in Tubac, selling it three years later.
Survivors include a brother, Bert T. Arce, and a sister, Mrs. Dolores Landero, both of Tucson.

Created by: Lanette Estill Cooper

Now-closed store remains core of Carmen's identity
By Kendal Blust, Nogales International, Sep 5, 2017

Carmen Zepeda, the town's namesake and a local legend, had a reputation as a tough, independent woman who always kept a shotgun on her hip at the **Carmen Store**, which for years was the only business for miles around, Renee Shultz said. Divorced from her husband Charles Wilbur and in possession of her own head of cattle, Zepeda was known for maintaining order in the little town that grew around her store, refusing to sell cigarettes or Levi's to girls, and putting rowdy drunks in their place, according to a book called "Arizona Twilight Tales," by Jane Eppinga.

Herminia "Minnie" Trujillo, whose family moved to Tumacacori in 1941 when she was 14, remembers walking to the one-room store, where Zepeda would be sitting behind the counter next to the cash register, surveying everyone who came in. "She was a very quiet lady, very respectable," said Trujillo, now 90. "You went in and she'd look around at what you were doing and what you were touching. She was very, very strict. Very nice, but don't try to get away with anything."

With her hair combed back into a bun at the top of her head, **Zepeda** rarely smiled or talked to customers, Trujillo said. But she always had everything you needed at her store, which served not only the small population of Carmen, Tumacacori and Tubac, but also travelers on the old U.S. Highway 89 that passed right by the store's front door.

"It was very, very quiet then. It was only a few people," Trujillo said of the Tumacacori-Carmen area. "Everybody knew each other. Everybody was very friendly and always one helping another one."

Angie Montenegro, 59, grew up in a small three-room house just behind the Carmen Store. Though she didn't know Zepeda personally, her five older brothers and sisters told her stories about evenings spent watching TV at **Zepeda's** house, which was attached to her little white store.

"She had the only TV in town," Montenegro said. **Zepeda** would always tell the children not to take any candy, she added, but when she would fall asleep they would slip into the store and sneak a few pieces. "My oldest brother (Edmundo Valdez) said she had a soft spot for Frank, the younger brother. He could get away with anything."

After running the store and her ranch for 41 years, **Zepeda** retired to Nogales in 1958, where she died 10 years later at the age of 93. She was buried next to her mother Teresa Celaya, in the Arivaca Cemetery.

TERESA CELAYA, LA DOÑA DE ARIVACA

Posted on May 3, 2020, by southernarizonaconnection

by Mary Kasulaitis

'What does it take to move to a new land, settle down, and make a success of your life? Especially when you are a middle-aged, sometime single mother from Mexico, the new land is Arizona Territory, and the year is 1886? Teresa Celaya had what it took.

'**Doña Teresa Celaya** (later Bustamante) was from Saric, Sonora, just sixty miles below the border on the Tres Bellotas Road. She came to live in Arivaca in the 1880s because it was an up-and-coming mining camp with ranches just getting started. Things looked promising and perhaps back in Saric they weren't. As they said, "Teresa was a businesswoman." It is rumored that she was a "dance hall lady" back in the old days and that she had part of her ear cut off to mark her as a lady of the night. She is always pictured wearing a rebozo (shawl), but then, that was common in those days.

'By **1890** Teresa owned the building just west of what is now **La Gitana Saloon** (17240 W 5th St.). Now it is a ruin, but at that time it had four rooms that faced the Arivaca Plaza or Main Street and rooms running along the west side also, with a walled area in the middle. Who built this building is not known it may have been Teresa, but it may have been old already. Teresa had a saloon in the easternmost room, lived in some of the rooms, and rented out other rooms. Over the years, a barbershop run by José Membrila, a shoe repair business owned by George Clark, and a store run by the Gallegos family were two of the businesses. Even into the 1950s that building was roofed and plastered. Then in the early **1900s** she built a dance hall next door, which now houses the La Gitana saloon. By the time she died, she also owned the building across the street, which became Double L Feeds, and more recently owned by the late Laurence Smets.

'Teresa was the mainstay of Arivaca for at least forty years, when the town was like a little Mexican village and everyone, Hispanic or not, spoke Spanish. Frank Krupp, Sr. of Nogales, remembered her as: "the Lady Bountiful and the friend in need of rich and poor alike throughout the area. She was the first visiting nurse service, helped to attend the sick and bury the dead, and acted as friend and midwife to many a woman far from real medical aid…She ran the cantina and in that capacity was her own bouncer, and an effective one."

'Gipsy Harper Clarke remembered staying at Teresa's place when she first arrived to teach at the Arivaca School. Armando Membrila remembered a strong personality, a funny lady, who kept stray children in line with a cane, while she smoked cigarettes. She would get the little girls to dance while she sang. Her little dog, Pipo, was very protective. Doña Teresa lived in Arivaca until her death in **1937** at the age of 102. In 2004, her descendants returned to Arivaca with good memories of their tenacious great-grandmother.

'It is possible that the old Catholic chapel, El Sagrado Corazon de Jesus, was built at Teresa's behest, when priests from Nogales came to promote the building of churches in the early 1900s. The best picture that exists, taken in 1916 by the cavalry photographer, was donated to the Arizona Historical Society by her family.

'One daughter, **Carmen Zepeda**, went on to become well known in her own right. Carmen Zepeda was a beautiful, accomplished and very independent woman. Born in Saric in 1874, Carmen came to Arivaca with her mother and helped her with the rentals. Fred Noon remembered her as one of the first women to drive a Model T Ford, all alone, a big accomplishment given the frequency of tire repairs. Carmen was briefly married to Charlie Wilbur (uncle of Eva Antonia Wilbur-Cruce).

'About the time of World War I, Carmen opened a one-room store near the Tumacacori Mission on the Nogales road. At that time "practically in the middle of nowhere," the store sold everything from toothbrushes to salt licks, pinto beans and everything else. As time went on, she added more rooms, cabins and a filling station. Soon the area was being known as Carmen, as it is to this day. She retired at the age of 83 and passed away at the age of 93 in 1968. Both Carmen and Teresa are buried in Arivaca cemetery.'

References: Fred Noon notes; remembrances of Armando Membrila, Nogales and Tucson newspaper articles, Pima County records, and information donated to the Arizona Historical Society. (A reprinted article.)

TERESA CELAYA-BUSTAMONTE

BIRTH	Oct 1835, Sonora, Mexico
DEATH	15 Aug 1937 (aged 101) Tucson, Pima County, Arizona
BURIAL	Arivaca Cemetery, Arivaca, Pima County, Arizona

d/o: Jesus Celaya and Ramona Montano
Wife of Angel Bustamonte

Col. CHARLES PATTERSON SYKES, "DREAM SPINNER"

TIMELINE:

1824 Sept 16,	Birth :Madison County, New York
1850s	Wisconsin, founding the *La Cross Democrat*
1861 Mar 4,	Married, Mary E Knight. La Crosse, Wisconsin
1876	Residence 2202 Pine, San Francisco, California. Age 51,
1881 Dec 20,	Passport Issue Date
1882	San Francisco, California
1882 Dec 19,	Postmaster Appointment Date, Calabasas, Pima, Arizona
1892 May 4,	Registration Date, Age 67, Precinct, Pima, Arizona
1895 Jul 1,	Residence Pima, Arizona
1901 Mar 6,	Death : New York, New York
Burial:	East Homer Cemetery, Homer, Cortland County, New York

The primary "dream spinner" in Santa Cruz Valley was **Colonel C.P. Sykes**, a New Yorker who hoped to become a Universalist minister in his youth. After his stepfather persuaded him to quit school and run the family farm, however, the 'consuming entrepreneurial spirit of the time' enflamed his soul and drove him across the North American continent.

He rode the land boom of the **1850s** to **Wisconsin**, founding the La Cross Democrat newspaper in 1858 just after the boom collapsed. Two years later, "being a bold and adventurous business man," he sold his newspaper and "started for the wilds of Colorado," according to a biographical sketch in the Pacific Coast Annual Mining Review." He soon accumulated an ample fortune, owning large interests in some of the best gold mining property in Colorado," the sketch continued. "He was the first to perceive the necessity for placing the mining interests of Colorado before Eastern capitalists, going to New York himself, where he organized a number of first-class mining companies."

Sykes lost most of his Colorado fortune after the Civil War. Returning to New York, he formed a partnership to publish another newspaper, but mining soon drew him west again. By **1875**, he was in **San Francisco**, the center of Western capital. There he cast about for investments as the U. S. economy struggled to pull itself out of the first major depression of the industrial age triggered by the failure of Jay Cooke's financial empire and the ensuing Panic of 1873. (Martin 1980)

After hearing about the fabled mineral wealth of southern Arizona, he organized the San Xavier Mining and Smelting Company, securing title to the San Xavier Lode south of Mission San Xavier del Bac. In **1878**, he also purchased the **Tumacácori grant** from Gándara, who died shortly after the sale (Mattison 1967).

Sykes, wasted little time in developing the grant. He quickly sold a three-sixteenths interest to John Curry, an ex-judge of the California Supreme Court, for $9,000. The new partners then convinced other prominent San Francisco businessmen including Senator John P. Jones, Eugene L. Sullivan, and George C. Perkins, a partner in the shipping firm of Goodall, Perkins & Company, to form the **Calabasas Land & Mining Company**. Curry was elected president. Sykes became managing director. The Tumacácori grant's transition from a landscape of community to a landscape of speculation was complete.

……. New technological innovations in electricity and coal-powered steam engines stoked this growth, while new industries like steel built its industrial infrastructure. But every enterprise depended upon the revolutionary expansion of the railroads, which turned the United States from what historian Allan Nevins called an "invertebrate" to a vertebrate nation after the Civil War. In **1860**, there were only **30,000 miles of railroad** in the nation. By **1890**, that number had soared to **170,000 miles**, with an average 8,000 miles added each year during the boom decade of the 1880s. …..

During this heady era, the **Calabasas Land & Mining Company** did everything it could to live up to its name. The company took over five of the six mining locations of **Sykes' San Xavier Mining and Smelting Company**. The new enterprise also laid out a townsite on "old Don Gándara ranch" of Calabasas. Sykes clearly wanted **Calabasas** to eclipse Tucson as the gateway to northern Mexico, and he used his contacts in the press to advance his vision. "Tucson does a trade with Sonora of at least $6,000,000 per annum. It is seventy-five miles from the northern line of Mexico," wrote "Explorer," a columnist for the New York Daily Graphic. "Calabasas is but ten miles therefrom. ……."

Setting a precedent for future promotions, Sykes' company used the Santa Cruz Valley's mission (history) to sell itself. The same issue of the New York Daily Graphic featured six lithographs entitled

> "Views on the Property of the Calabasas Land and Mining Company, Pima County, Arizona".
>
> A portrait of Sykes, bearded and judicious, is flanked by a brooding "Mount Wrightson, From Calabasas, Santa Cruz Valley"
>
> on the left and the "Ruins of Mission Tumacácori, Destroyed by Apache Indians" on the right.
>
> Below Sykes is an "Ear of Corn Grown on Calabasas Rancho in 1876 without Irrigation."
>
> To the left of the corn is the "Plan Of The Hotel And Plaza At Calabasas As It Will Appear When Completed."
>
> To the right is "San Xavier del Bac."
>
> At the bottom is a "Map of the San Xavier Mines, 1878" divided into the six "locations" owned by Sykes.

Sykes, the Yankee entrepreneur, presides over and unites the romantic past with the industrious future—a future of agricultural abundance, luxurious amenities, and mineral wealth apportioned into the precise rectangles of mining claims. "Views on the Property of the Calabasas Land and Mining Company" was a representation of space bursting with speculative exuberance.

Key to Sykes' schemes was the construction of a railroad through the Santa Cruz Valley linking Mexico and the United States. His first venture was the **Arizona Southern Railroad Company**, which was incorporated on August 16, **1880**, five months after the Southern Pacific Railroad reached Tucson. The incorporators included Arizona entrepreneurs like Sykes, ex-territorial governor Anson P.K. Safford, and Tucson businessmen C.H. Lord as well as investors from Boston with ties to **Southern Pacific**'s rival, the **Atchison, Topeka, and Santa Fe**. The Santa Fe itself bought 1000 shares of stock in the Arizona Southern for $10,000.

Sykes emphasized the importance of a rail line by portraying Calabasas as the center of a transportation network linking southern Arizona and northern Mexico. He also geared his promotions to various audiences, with Calabasas growing ever more grandiose the further away from Arizona prospective investors were. According to a sardonic article in the Tombstone Epitaph, three prospectuses were circulating by **1882**—one in Arizona, another in the United States, a third in Europe. "This **European prospectus** was a grand affair," the Epitaph jeered. "It was filled with magnificent drawings representing the raging Santa Cruz at high tide, with steamboats and heavy vessels at the docks unloading while yonder in the distance could be seen the smoke of a dozen furnaces with lively locomotives hauling [?] to the numerous mills."

Where **Sykes** conjured up the image of a navigable Santa Cruz remains to be determined. According to journalist Sybil Ellinwood, the illustrations were adapted from those circulated in Boston and New York newspapers by Sylvester Mowry nearly three decades earlier. "With them the ambitious **Sylvester Mowry** had tried to promote Eastern capital for mining ventures by picturing a line of steamers puffing up the Colorado River to Yuma, thence up the Gila to Maricopa, and finally up the Santa Cruz, invisible for much of its course, to within twenty miles of the Mowry mine," Ellinwood (1964:35) wrote. But Mowry himself made no mention of steamboats on the Santa Cruz in his major published work, Arizona and Sonora:

The Geography History, and Resources of the Silver Region of North America (1866). On the contrary, he correctly stated, "Like most streams, the Santa Cruz is intermittent, sinking and rising at irregular intervals" (Mowry 1966:25). Whatever the origins of Calabasas as bustling river port, Arizonans scoffed. Stung by the sarcasm, **Sykes** offered a reward for any poster portraying steamers on the river (Ellinwood 1964). No one replied. Nonetheless, Sykes continued to use the mythical waters of the Santa Cruz to woo investors across the ocean.

But even a Danube River in the desert could not make the Arizona Southern a reality. **Sykes** managed to convince Congress to grant his railroad a right of way through the Papago Indian Reservation around San Xavier, but the city of Tucson turned down his request for financial support. More damaging was the construction of the **Santa Fe's New Mexico & Arizona Railroad**, which built eighty-eight miles of line between Benson and Nogales in 1881-1882.

The road ran south along the San Pedro River, servicing the booming mining district of Tombstone. Then, at Fairbanks, it veered west and followed Babocomari Creek until it crossed a divide into the Sonoita Valley. Cattlemen moving onto the finest grasslands in Arizona suddenly had rail access to markets across the United States, and cattle proliferated like flies.

To reach the Mexican border, the **New Mexico & Arizona** snaked down Sonoita Creek to **Calabasas**. Sykes lobbied hard for the railroad to build its international depot there, but the New Mexico & Arizona chose the infant border community of Nogales instead. On October 25, **1882**, a crowd cheered and poured champagne on the engineers as a locomotive of the **New Mexico & Arizona**, draped in red, white, and blue, steamed south to face a locomotive of the **Santa Fe's Sonora Railway**, sporting Mexico's national colors of red, white, and green. The silver spike driven into a mahogany crosstie to commemorate the occasion drove a stake through the heart of **Sykes'** visionary community as well (Myrick 1975).

But **Sykes** was more than a decade away from giving up. That evening, he hosted a banquet for the seventy-five guests who attended the Nogales ceremony at his new **Santa Rita Hotel**. By then, Calabasas had grown into a community of about 150 people with five stores, two dancehalls, two Chinese gambling dens, an opium den, and sixteen saloons. The Santa Rita was easily the most elegant structure in town. With its two stories of solid brick surrounded by a white picket fence, the Santa Rita looked like a Yankee vision of prosperity and decorum. Sykes made sure the interior was elegant as well, furnishing it with three carloads of furniture from Boston and staffing it with proper Bostonian women (Myrick 1975).

During its brief heyday (1882-1893), famous visitors like General Nelson Miles and prominent settlers like Sabino Otero slept under its roof and ate in its famous dining room. One guest pronounced the hotel "the best between San Francisco and Denver" (Ellinwood 1964:37).

Source: www.nps.gov/parkhistory/online_books/tuma/hrs/chap6.htm

The Calabasas, Tucson and North Western Railroad Company and the Arizona Cattle and Improvement Company

Even though the **New Mexico & Arizona** brought patrons to his hotel, however, Sykes still wanted a railroad of his own. In 1885, backed by New York capital, he therefore organized the **Calabasas, Tucson and North Western Railroad Company**. John Rice, a former member of Congress from Maine, was president. Sykes was vice-president. The treasurer was Thomas James, former Postmaster-General of the United States and president of Lincoln Bank in New York. General C.C. Dodge, "Late of Phelps, Dodge & Co.," served on its board. With such distinguished names on its masthead, the **Calabasas, Tucson, and Northwestern** planned to extend a rail line down the Santa Cruz to Tucson, Florence, and Phoenix. It also projected two feeder lines: one to Arivaca and the mining boom town of Quijotoa to the west, another to the coal fields of Deer Creek along the San Pedro River and the mining district of Globe to the northeast.

Sykes was initially more successful in capitalizing his second railroad venture. He asked the Pima County Board of Supervisors to issue $200,000 worth of bonds to construct the line to Tucson and the northern border of the county. The supervisors liked the proposal and scheduled a special election on May 23, 1885. The bond issue passed by an overwhelming majority of 939 to 87. (Myrick 1975)

The **Calabasas, Tucson and North Western** also proposed to pay for itself by issuing first-mortgage, six-percent thirty-year bonds guaranteed by a second corporation, the **Arizona Cattle and Improvement Company**. The directorships were largely interlocking, with Sykes serving as vice-president and general manager and James as treasurer for both companies. The president of the Arizona Cattle and Improvement Company was the Honorable William Windom, ex-Secretary of the U.S. Treasury, with Rice serving on its board. In return for forty-nine percent of the capital stock of the railroad, Sykes received 99,940 of the cattle company's 100,000 shares of capital stock. According to the **"Prospectus of the Calabasas, Tucson and North Western Railroad Company and the Arizona Cattle and Improvement Company**," cattle were the currency that would bankroll the rails.

The first order of business was to sink deep wells along the route and then pump the water through a pipeline "sunk in the road-bed, for the use of stock in desert places." In italics, the prospectus proclaimed, *"The right of way of the railroad, with a pipe line to carry water for cattle, will practically control the grazing land along* the line of the road, for many miles upon each side for many years to come, as the lands are not yet surveyed." During the late nineteenth century, controlling water meant control over the open ranges of the West.

What followed was an elaborate bovine house of cards. In order to construct the line, the **Calabasas, Tucson and North Western** signed a contract with an unspecified "English Syndicate." For the first fifty-five miles of construction between Calabasas and Tucson, the English Syndicate would supply 370 head of cattle for each mile of construction. In return, it would be paid "all the railroad first mortgage bonds on that division, which will be issued at the rate of $30,000 per mile." Upon completion of this first stage, the **Arizona Cattle and Improvement Company** would have a herd of 20,350 head.

The prospectus then marched through a series of Alice-in-Wonderland-like calculations to show how rapidly the herd would increase, how quickly the railroad would be paid for, and how handsomely the investors would be rewarded. During the first year, 4,400 three-year old steers would be sold at $30 per head, generating $132,000 in revenue. Second-year revenues would be the same, but by the third year, 4,400 cows would be sold as well, raising revenue to $220,000. When the entire 350-mile line was built, the cattle company's herd would have swelled to a staggering 129,500 head, "with annual sales of 56,000 head, equal to $1,400,000." Interest on the entire line's bonded debt, in contrast, would only be $530,000. Deducting another $100,000 for estimated ranching expenses, the company would have $770,000 to distribute as a thirty-percent annual dividend to stockholders in the cattle company.

And that was a conservative estimate that did not take into account revenues from cargo hauled by the railroad itself *"There are at least one thousand mining claims within ten miles on each side of the proposed railroad,"* the prospectus trumpeted. There were also the Deer Creek coalfields, which would produce 51,333,000 tons of coal. And finally there was southern Arizona's great agricultural fertility, where "*it is not an uncommon occurrence that sixty bushels of wheat per acres is harvested.*" Judicious and understated after such astonishing numbers, the prospectus concluded, "*With this safe financial outlook the companies have no hesitancy in declaring that the public has never had a better prospect presented for a safe and profitable investment.*"

The public was less than impressed. On October 16, **1885**, the Pima County Board of Supervisors approved of Sykes' plans and stipulated that the first county bonds would be issued if work on the railroad began within three months and was finished within a year. But Sykes was unable to raise much capital in New York because of a **national depression that began in 1882** and culminated in the **so-called Panic of 1884**, when one major New York brokerage firm and two New York banks failed. (Myers 1970)

During this period, business failures rose from 6,738 in 1883 to nearly 10,000 in both 1884 and 1885 as production declined by one-fourth. Unemployment climbed to fifteen percent and labor unrest intensified, especially in 1886, when a series of strikes and their brutal repression swept the country. (Rezneck 1956) As a result, the **Calabasas, Tucson, and North Western** did not lay a single rail. A year later, after the venture failed to meet any of its deadlines, 109 individuals petitioned the board to grant a six-month extension. The supervisors refused, "the company not even having made a good showing at commencement". (Myrick 1975:258)

Sykes tried to revive his railroad one last time. In January **1891**, he circulated petitions to convince the Pima County board of supervisors to once again issue $200,000 in bonds. He also promised to build a $100,000 hotel and sanatorium if the Tucson City Council gave him the old Military Plaza. In an article in the *Tucson Citizen* on February 5, 1891, prominent citizens generally supported Sykes' schemes but recommended that no county funds be expended until the railroad was completed. "If the parties mean business and will do as they say in a specified time I am heartily in favor of the propositions," merchant Samuel Drachman commented. But then he bluntly added, "I want to see the contract drawn up in such a shape that not a dollar of money or fit land will be given till the work is satisfactory [sic] performed."

Once again, it was the same sad story. The supervisors approved the bonds as long as the first stretch of rail was constructed by March 1, **1892**. March 1 came and went, Sykes requested another extension, and New York investors continued to ignore the Tucson, Calabasas and North Western. Then the **Panic of 1893** plunged the nation into a much deeper depression than the one a decade before. The 1880s witnessed the construction of more railroads than any other decade in U.S. history. The 1890s saw many of those lines end up in receivership. By 1895, companies controlling forty thousand miles and representing $2.5 billion in fixed capital that could not be transferred to other industries had failed.

Railroads were already consolidating before the **Panic of 1893**, with main lines buying up feeder lines to become self-sustaining systems. In 1892, thirty-three railroads capitalized at more than $100 million apiece controlled 70 percent of the tracks and even more of the traffic in the United States. After the Panic of 1893, investment bankers like J.P. Morgan swallowed up the weaker roads and established the shape of the railroad industry for the next fifty years. The proliferation of railroads encouraged overbuilding and ruinous competition. Morgan and his fellow bankers reorganized the U.S. system into six or seven "communities of interest" in which big companies bought one another's stock. (Chandler 1980; Martin 1980; Moore 1980) Those big companies-were the largest business enterprises on the globe.

A speculator like Sykes was hopelessly out of his league in such an environment. In **1903**, two years after he died on another fruitless search for capital in New York, the **Calabasas, Tucson and North Western** bonds were destroyed in the presence of the Pima County board of supervisors and the county clerk. Two other companies—the **Twin Buttes Railroad** and the **Tucson and Nogales Railroad Company**, a Southern Pacific subsidiary—connected Tucson with Calabasas, Nogales, and Mexico in 1910. (Myrick 1975) That was the year that Sykes' widow, who had remained in the Santa Rita Hotel, died. By then, Calabasas was little more than a ghost town slowly being reclaimed by mesquite.

Source: Tumacacori NHP:Historic Resource Study (Chapter 6) (nps.gov)

(NOTE: Sykes' wife and daughter's grave information do not connect with Charles.)

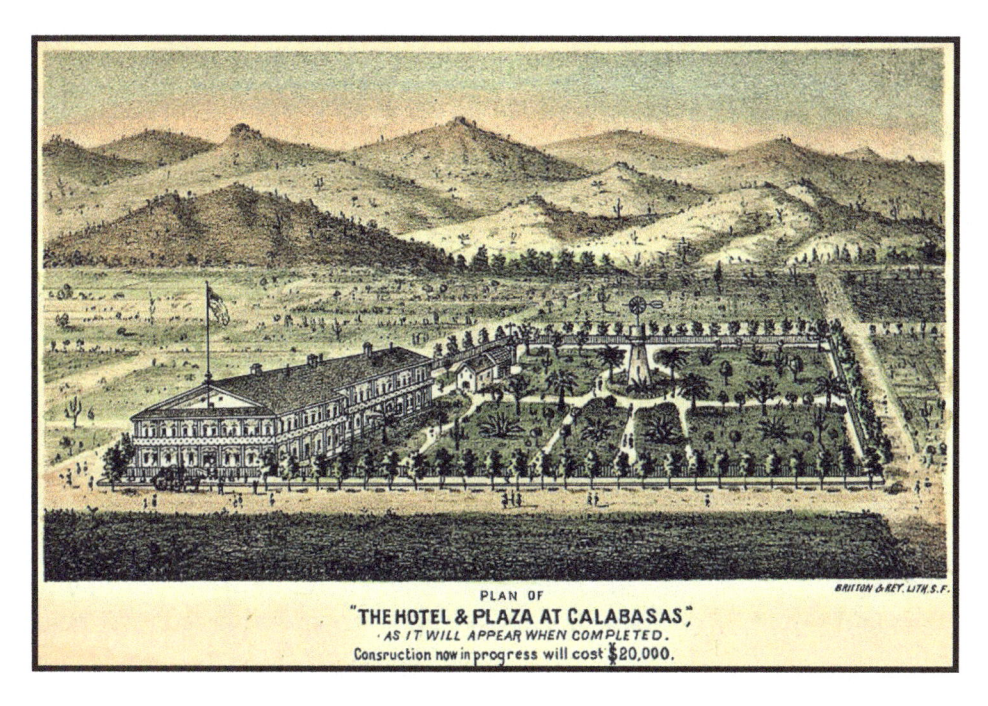

PLAN OF
"THE HOTEL & PLAZA AT CALABASAS"
AS IT WILL APPEAR WHEN COMPLETED.
Construction now in progress will cost $20,000.

Ruins of the old Hacienda del Santa Rita, where Wrightson, Grosvenor, Hopkins and Slack, lost their lives, and part of the defense of which in 1891, is so graphically described by Professor Raphael Pumpelly, now of Harvard University, in his book "*Across America and Asia*."

Calabasas' post office was established October 8, **1866**, and discontinued August 15, **1913**. Calabasas was once a Papago Indian village, a Mexican garrison, a U.S. Military base, a mining camp, and a farming community before becoming a railroad stop that was determined to become the gateway to Mexico. The Hotel Santa Rita was supposedly the finest hotel between San Francisco and Denver. Unfortunately, Nogales took over as the gateway to Mexico and Calabasas declined into non-existence.

The Arizona Historical Society took over site management and ownership in October **1974**; the Mission was incorporated into Tumacácori National Historical Park in 1990.

It was declared a National Historic Landmark in **1990**.

'A well-defined road evidently long used, and now made quite easy and accessible, is the route from the valley. To the north, Salero Hill looms up boldly, and the explorer in search of the old Tumacacori mine will follow a rough but still good road for a couple of miles to the Salero House, used by the Tyndall Company since 1875. From this point for another mile or so, the explorer will follow a rude bridle path to the Jefferson mine, one of the most valuable of those now worked by the Aztec Syndicate. To the north and east of the Jefferson for less than half a mile, an old mule track, evidently once heavily used, may be traced.'

www.ghosttowns.com/states/az/calabasas.html   8 miles north of Nogales on the Rio Rico Ranch.

www.kinospringsgc.com

HISTORIC YERBA BUENA RANCH near Nogales, Arizona.

Hollywood actor **Stewart Granger** and actress-wife **Jean Simmons** purchased Yerba Buena, a 10,000-acre ranch on the American side of the border. Granger's guests included his favorite drinking buddy John Wayne along with Clark Gable, Bob Hope, Richard Burton and Elizabeth Taylor, just to name a few. Film personalities could relax without being photographed by the *paparazzi* or swarmed by enthusiastic admirers. From Yerba Buena, it was a 10-minute drive to the Mexican side of Nogales where stars and their entourages unwound at La Caverna, a nightclub located in the entertainment district along Calles Elias. White-jacketed waiters served cocktails and champagne in a unique environment illuminated by sparkling chandeliers and elegant sconces. A portion of the Cavern exists today as La Roca and is still a popular destination for dining or hosting an event.

As Western films passed out of popular favor, fewer movies were made at Old Tucson, a large movie set located near Tucson's Sonoran Desert Museum. As a result, studio executives and the Hollywood crowd found other places to vacation.

The historic Yerba Buena Ranch dates back to the **1700's**. Beginning with a Spanish Land Grant to the Oritz Family, the ranch was then purchased in **1881** by the cattle barons Fredrick Maish and Thomas Driscoll. The 30,000 acre ranch was acquired in **1930** by Thomas F. Griffin, a Chicago industrialist (Griffin Wheel Company, 1887).

The Griffin's raised Santa Gertrudis cattle and leased grazing rights to other ranchers. In the **1950'**s, actor Stewart Granger purchased 5,280 acres of the Yerba Buena (now Kino Springs Golf Resort) to raise Charolais cattle. When the Griffin family sold the balance of the land, they retained the prime 1,000 acres for the family Trust.

By **1969**, the aging Granger had completed the sale of his Yerba Buena ranch to a group of investors who transformed it into the Kino Springs golf resort. Granger's luxurious home was incorporated into the facility's clubhouse.

Source: onmilwaukee.com/articles/nogales

HISTORY AND FACTS CONCERNING WARNER AND SILVER LAKE AND THE SANTA CRUZ RIVER

By C. C. Wheeler

At different times, the papers have mentioned items of these lakes, and several have asked me to describe them. And as this is to be a story concerning water, I will begin with the Santa Cruz River. Early writers tell that many years ago that the river was an ever flowing stream of clear water, not a large stream with a wide channel and deep as the present time, but enough so that fur animals were trapped on both it and the Gila River.

Many lagoons or sloughs were located along the Santa Cruz. Two very large ones at Calabasas formed by the overflow of the Sonoita Creek and Santa Cruz, with others along the stream. The condition at Calabasas on account of this swampy land malaria was very bad and settlers suffered greatly with Chills and Fever and many were obliged to move from that section.

There was also much swampy land south of Tubac, also another south of the San Xavier Mission, another about Nine miles Northwest of Tucson. The Santa Cruz valley then was a dense forest of trees and many ranchers were located along the river, several very large; Geo. Atkinson, Geo. Allison, Jos. and Morgan Wise, J. Piskorski, Casanega, and others near Calabasas, further north T. Lilly Mercer, Sabino Otero, and many others, Maish and Driscoll at the Canoa station, and others up to the Papago Indian reservation.

The settlers cleared the land of the timber and irrigated lands from the river. Much of the land had been farmed by the Mexican people long before Arizona became a part of the United States. All varieties of grain, produce and considerable fruit was grown.

There were several acres of fruits close by the old Tumacacori Mission, some also at Amado such as Grapes, Peaches, Pears, Quinces, Pomegranates.

Copyright Information: October1889 - Arizona Historical Society. Photo ID: 2922
Description: Falls on the Santa Cruz River. "A" Mt in the background.

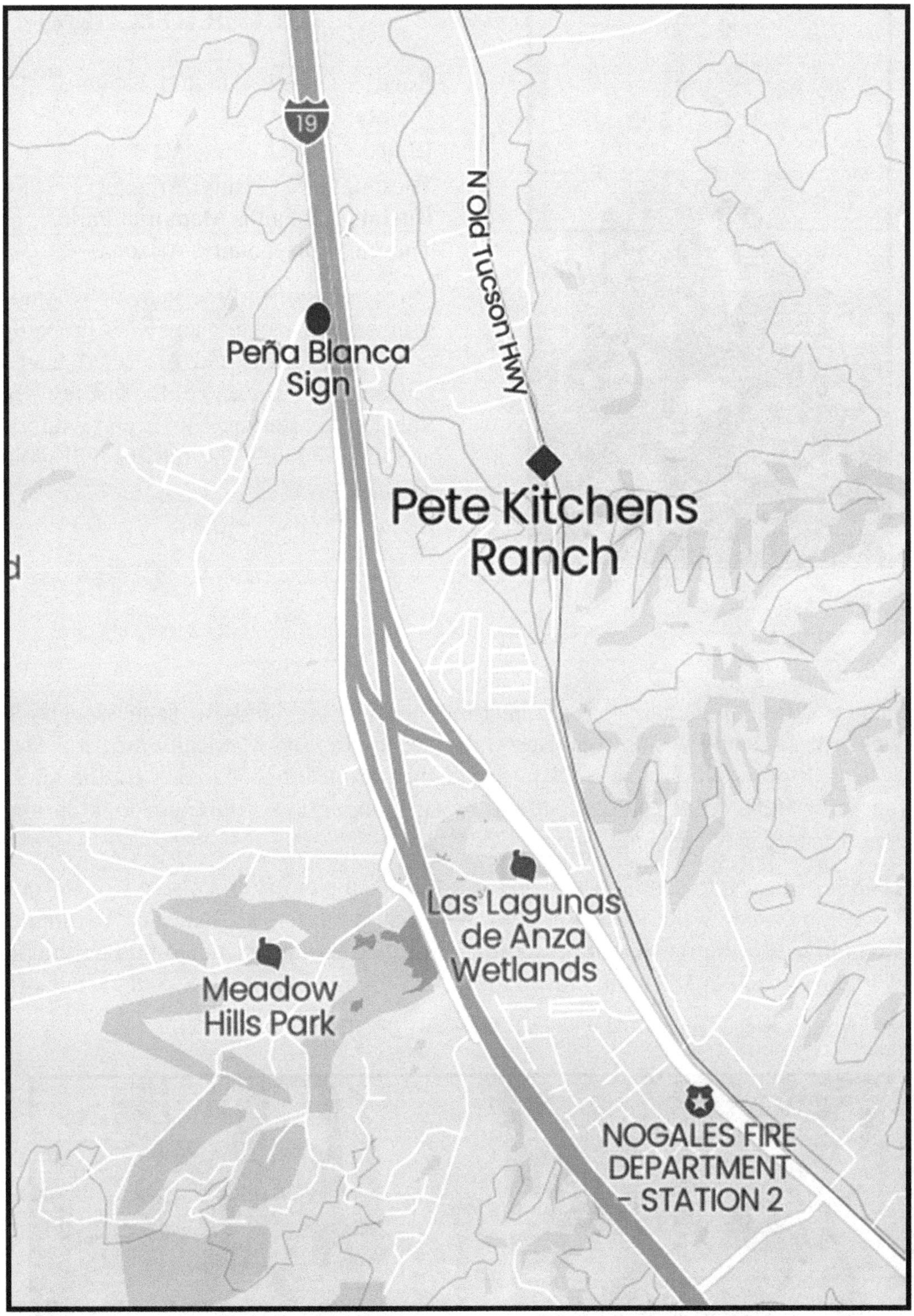
19
N Old Tucson Hwy
Peña Blanca
Sign
Pete Kitchens
Ranch
Las Lagunas
de Anza
Wetlands
Meadow
Hills Park
NOGALES FIRE
DEPARTMENT
- STATION 2

PETER KITCHEN

Born: 1819 Covington, Kenton County, Kentucky

Died: 1895 Aug (aged 75–76) Tucson, Pima County, Arizona

Burial: All Faiths Memorial Park Tucson, Pima County, Arizona

"In the days of early settlement by Anglos in southeast Arizona, there was probably no one more feared and respected than Pete Kitchen. He was one of the last few settlers to hang on after the 1861 troop withdrawal, and consequently, he felt the full wrath of Cochise's war."

C. Fahey, 11 Jun 2007

Kitchen was born in Kentucky 1819, later moving with his family to Tennessee. By **1846** he was in Texas employed as a teamster with Zachary Taylor's Mexican War army. He was then in California working at odd jobs and then attracted to Arizona by the Gadsden Purchase of **1854**. After being wiped out by an Indian raid in **1861** at Canoa Springs he operated a store in Magdalena, Sonora, Mexico.

In **1868** he returned to southern Arizona & established a ranch on Potrero Creek. He took as his common-law wife, Rosa Verdugo, who was the sister of Francisco Verdugo who was employed on the ranch. Pete's stepson was killed during an Indian raid on the ranch. Pete sold the ranch in **1883** and moved to Tucson where he died in **1895** at the age of 73.

Source: Historic Ranches of the Old West by Bill O'Neal - EAKIN PRESS - Austin, Texas.

Tucson, Tubac, Tumacacori, To Hell by Gil Procter – 1956

This book has several pictures, including Pete Kitchen, Dona Rosa Verdugo Kitchen, the original one room adobe house and the "stronghold".

1. Pete Kitchen was born **1822** in Covington Kentucky.

2. He joined the U.S. Army at the age of 24 and after serving as a wagon master with the mounted rifles along the Rio Grande in **1846**, he went across country with his outfit to Oregon, where he received his discharge. After receiving his discharge he started moving south spending some time in the California gold fields.

3. Pete arrived in Tucson in **1853**.

4. At the age of 31, he settled in the Santa Cruz Valley, 1st stopping at La Canoa on the Santa Cruz River north of Tubac but soon afterward moved his outfit to Potrero Creek five miles north of which would later become the International Boundary Line between Mexico and the United States.

5. First he built a small one-room adobe house.

6. From Sonora, he brought in 30 Opata Indians to help establish the ranch, do the farming and act as guards.

7. He brought in Manuel Ronquillo, a fine young Mexican, like himself an expert rifle & pistol shot, an excellent horseman & vaquero, and also brave & intelligent, to assist him in running the ranch.

8. He acquired the services of Francisco Verdugo, an outstanding frontiersman to take charge of the Opata Indians.

9. Francisco "Pancho" arrived with his sister Rosa Verdugo who took on the supervision of running the household.

10. Pete soon fell in love with Dona Rosa and it wasn't long until she became Dona Rosa of the Hacienda.

11. Pete built a new "stronghold" and as soon as it was finished he and his new wife, Dona Rosa, moved in and the one room adobe was turned over to Manuel Ronquillo and his wife Jesus Verdugo who was the sister of Dona Rosa. (Pete, Manuel & Francisco "Pancho" was brothers-in-law).

12. In 1859, Dona Rosa bore a son, Santiago (James in English) and on June 8, **1871**, Santiago, who was 12 yrs. old, was murdered and scalped during an Apache attack.

13. As time progressed, although Pete had no more children, the ranch prospered and the household grew. Five of Dona Rosa's little nieces came to live with her.

14. After the Potrero was sold, Pete & Rosa moved to Tucson where Pete died at the age of seventy-seven on August 5th **1895**.

Source: Arizona Territory, Pioneer Marriages - Pima Co.
KITCHEN, Peter m. VERDUGO, Rosa – 4 Aug 1883 - Pima Co., AZ Terr. Volume:1A, Page:161

One of the earliest pioneers of Arizona was Peter Kitchen, who came to the Territory in **1854**. Little is known of his early life beyond the fact that he served in some capacity during the Mexican War. He was a man, as I remember him, about five feet ten inches in height, rather spare, always wearing a wide brimmed sombrero; very quiet in his manner; low and soft spoken. There was nothing about the man to indicate the daredevil of dime novels, which is associated in the Eastern mind with the pioneers of the West.

After coming to the Territory, he lived at the Canoa for several years, and then moved to a ranch near Nogales, called the Potrero, where he (farmed) a little, and raised cattle and hogs. He fortified his residences, both at the Canoa and the Potrero by building the adobe walls of the houses higher than the roofs and having loopholes to shoot through. On many occasions he and his employees stood off Apache attacks. He lived in the heart of the Apache country, and, although subjected to severe losses, he refused to leave the country, but defied the red devils to the end.

The following description of his ranch is taken from Bourke's **"On the Border with Crook."**

"Approaching Pete Kitchen's Ranch, one finds himself in a fertile valley, with a small hillock near one extremity. Upon the summit of this has been built the house from which no effort of the Apaches has ever succeeded in driving our friend. There is a sentinel posted on the roof, there is another out in the 'cienega' (spring, marsh) with the stock, and the men ploughing in the bottoms are obliged to carry rifles, cocked and loaded, swung to the plough handle. Every man and boy are armed with one or two revolvers on hip. There are revolvers and rifles and shot-guns along the walls, and in every corner. Everything speaks of a land of warfare and bloodshed.

"The title of 'Dark and Bloody Ground' never fairly belonged to Kentucky. Kentucky was never anything but a Sunday-School convention in comparison with Arizona, every mile of whose surface could tell its tale of horror, were the stones and gravel, the sage-brush and mescal, the mesquite and the yucca, only endowed with speech for one brief hour.

"Within the hospitable walls of the Kitchen home the traveler was made to feel perfectly at ease. If food were not already on the fire, some of the women set about the preparation of the savory and spicy stews for which the Mexicans are deservedly famous, and others kneaded the dough and patted into shape the paper-like tortillas with which to eat the juicy frijoles or dip up the tempting chili Colorado. There were women carding, spinning, sewing—doing the thousand and one duties of domestic life on a great ranch, which had its own blacksmith, saddler, and wagon-maker, and all other officials needed to keep the machinery running smoothly.

"Between Pete Kitchen and the Apaches a ceaseless war was waged, with the advantage not all on the side of Kitchen. His employees were killed and wounded, his stock driven away, his pigs filled with arrows, making the suffering quadrupeds look like perambulating pin-cushions—everything that could be thought of to drive him away; but there he stayed, unconquered and unconquerable." Many settlers abandoned their **property** and sought sanctuary in Tucson, but **Kitchen** held out until **his** ranch was burned by Apaches in **1861**. "Pete **Kitchen** hams" were a major portion of the business. In **1883**, **Kitchen sold** the ranch for a substantial amount of money ($60,000) after the arrival of the railroad cut into **his** market. He continued to maintain mining, cattle interests and retired to Tucson, losing **his** money to gambling and loans to friends.

The following clipping from the Tucson Citizen of June 15, 1872, shows that under adverse circumstances, Pete Kitchen was prosperous:

"Personal:

'Our friend, Peter Kitchen, was in town this week from the Potrero. He reports that his crops are excellent. He has about twenty acres of potatoes planted and has made this year about 14,000 pounds of No. 1 bacon and hams, which he has sold at an average of thirty-five cents per pound; also 5,000 pounds of lard, sold at the same price. Mr. Kitchen's ranch is located near the Sonora line and at one of the most exposed points for Apache depredations in Arizona.

'The Apaches have endeavored to take his place many times—one partner, and all his neighbors, have been murdered, and last summer his boy was killed within gunshot of his door. Instead of being frightened or discouraged by those bold and numerous attacks, he seems only the more determined to stand his ground and take his chances. The Indians have learned to their sorrow that in him they have no insignificant foe. He never travels the same route twice in succession, and he always sleeps with one eye open; therefore, ambushes and surprises do not win on him worth a cent. He has been on the picket line now for fourteen years and has buried nearly all his old acquaintances and should his luck continue, he may truly be called the first and last of Arizona's pioneers." '

Source: genealogytrails.com/ariz/bios-pioneers.html

Another source discovered:

Kitchen was born in Kentucky 1819, later moving with his family to Tennessee. By 1846 he was in Texas employed as a teamster with Zachary Taylor's Mexican War army. He was then in California working at odd jobs and then attracted to Arizona by the Gadsden Purchase of 1854. After being wiped out by a Indian raid in 1861 at Canoa Springs he operated a store in Magdalena (this would be Magdalena, Sonora, Mexico). In 1868 he returned to southern Arizona & established a ranch on Potrero Creek.

Source: Re: Pete Kitchen (1822KY-1895A - Genealogy.com   Tess Gamez

JOHN ROSS BROWNE

BIRTH	11 Feb 1821, County Dublin, Ireland
DEATH	8 Dec 1875 (aged 54), Oakland, California
BURIAL	Mountain View Cemetery, Oakland, **California**
	COD: Sudden death at home.
WIFE:	Lucy Anna Mitchell Browne
CHILDREN:	1826-1898
	Spencer Cochrane Browne 1845–1896
	Nina Florence Browne Craven 1852–1928

Author, Journalist, U.S. Revenue Service Agent, official reporter of the Constitutional Convention of California at Monterey, Surveyor of custom houses and mints and investigator of Indian and Land Office affairs, prolific writer of many subjects, appointed Minister to China in 1868, but recalled in 1870.

His writings incidental to service with the United States Government in various capacities, Special Agent of the U.S. Treasury of California, mining and real estate investor, passionate champion for the rights of Chinese Americans and American Indians in California. He traveled widely both in government service and his own pleasure.

His father edited a nationalist paper in **Ireland**, inspiring British authorities to put him in prison. They exiled the family to America in **1833**, where they settled in Louisville, Kentucky, and his father became a schoolteacher, editor and proprietor of the Louisville Daily Reporter.

In **1842**, John Browne signed on to a whaling ship, traveling much of the Atlantic and Indian Oceans. The New York firm, Harpers and Brothers, published his writings and etchings of a whaling cruise in 1846. It was said his book may have influenced Herman Melville to write Moby Dick and earned Browne international fame as an author and artist. **1849** found him in California during the Gold Rush and working at a number of government positions.

Further travels to **Europe** and the **Middle East** yielded more Harpers publications in 1853, and in 1860, while in Virginia City, Nevada, after a few days visit, he complained of stomach pain caused by bad water.

By **1855**, he was friends with Mark Twain, who visited him at his Oakland, California, home. In his early days of writing, John heard from Edgar Allen Poe, who published John's articles in his publication, Graham's Lady's and Gentlemen's Magazine. His style of writing influenced a number of author's, not only Mark Twain, but Bret Harte and Dan De Quille.

John Ross Browne married Lucy Anna Mitchell in **1843** and they had ten children. By 1907, only five of their children were alive. He died suddenly at his home in Oakland, California.

Source: John Ross Browne (1821-1875) Find A Grave Memorial

The Hacienda as sketched by J. Ross Browne early in 1864

The Santa Rita Mining Company

RAPHAEL PUMPELLY

BIRTH	8 Sep 1837 Owego, Tioga County, New York
DEATH	10 Aug 1923 (aged 85) Newport County, Rhode Island
BURIAL	Berkeley Memorial Cemetery Newport County, Rhode Island Husband of Eliza Frances Shepard, married on October 20, 1869 at Dorchester, Massachusetts

Five Children:
Mary Margaretta Pumpelly,
Caroline Eliza Pumpelly,
Anna Pauline Pumpelly,
Clarence King Pumpelly
Raphael Pumpelly Jr.

Geologist. An **1859** graduate of the Royal School of Mines in Freiburg, **Germany**, he began his career directing the development of **Arizona** silver mines and working as a consulting geologist to the government of **Japan**.

During **1864 and 1865** he was the first person to conduct a thorough survey of the **Gobi Desert**. Other scientific explorations he undertook during his career were done in **China**, **Russia**, **Siberia**, **Mongolia** and countless other locations around the world.

From **1866 to 1875** he served as the **first Professor of Mining at Harvard**. He later worked for the U.S. Geological Survey, heading up the New England office from 1884 to 1889.

His many contributions to the field of geological knowledge include a number of books and articles, the discovery and excavation of the village of Anau in **Turkmenistan** which he dated to around 4500 B.C., his secular rock disintegration theory and his studies of iron ore.

He was honored by having a mineral named after him, Pumpellyite, which can only be found in Keweenaw County, Michigan.

Bio by: Jen Snoots
(My personal gratitude to Jen Snoots for condensing the biography of this man's busy life.)

History was also made by the humble and lowly who did not have their name in the news, nor could they read or write their memories down. Sometimes we find remnants of headstone documenting the lives of these people. Perhaps the missions had a written record of birth, marriage and death. Often, bones are found in the desert or abandoned property with no identification. Lives that were lived and forgotten.

Arizona has laws regarding burial sites:

Human Burials, Sacred Objects, and You

Human remains and associated funerary objects in unmarked graves and abandoned cemeteries that exceed 50 years in age are protected on state, county, city and municipal lands in Arizona under A.R.S. § 41-844. This statute also protects sacred ceremonial objects and objects of national or tribal patrimony* on State lands that have special importance to American Indians. On private lands, A.R.S. §41-865 provides similar protection to human remains and funerary objects that also exceed 50 years in age. These laws were adopted in 1990 and are similar to federal laws protecting human remains on federal lands.

The intent of these state laws is to ensure that human remains and funerary objects are treated with respect and dignity. Sacred ceremonial objects and objects of national or tribal patrimony (objects of cultural heritage) are given equal consideration.

First and foremost, dignity and respect mean protecting graves and objects of cultural heritage from disturbance.

There will be times when human remains and objects are accidentally disturbed, and times when the locations of known graves, or places with a potential for containing graves, or objects of cultural heritage are threatened. In these situations, the director of the Arizona State Museum (ASM) is required to consult with individuals that can show direct kinship. In the absence of direct kin, the ASM director may consult with groups that can show a relationship to human remains through cultural affinity. For example, when human remains of American Indian ancestry are involved, the director will consult with the appropriate American Indian tribes. The director will also consult with American Indian tribes that can show their ancestors made and used certain special objects of cultural heritage.

In consultation with the director, descendants may decide to leave human remains and associated funerary objects or objects of cultural heritage in place or to rebury elsewhere if disturbance is unavoidable. Some circumstances may require cultural remains, including human remains, be excavated and cared for in a museum.

What This Means to You

In most cases, a landowner will not be certain if bones encountered are human or if they might be more than 50 years old. Individuals should make every effort to maintain the safety and security of the remains and then notify the local police immediately. If the human remains are older, and even if there is some question about whether they are human, ASM should be notified and will assist law enforcement and the landowner in determining if the laws cited in this brochure apply to the situation.

Individuals who think they have come across cultural remains should first stop any activity that might further disturb the remains. They should then call or email ASM to inform the museum of the circumstances and to receive guidance on what to do.

Intentional disturbance of human remains and funerary objects 50 years old or older, or of protected classes of cultural objects, without first gaining written permission from the ASM director is a violation of state law. Accidental disturbance of graves and human remains or objects of cultural heritage is not a crime, but not reporting the accident is a violation of state law.

ARIZONA STATE MUSEUM

The University of Arizona
1013 E University Blvd
PO Box 210026
Tucson, Arizona 85721-0026
520-621-6302

CEMETERIES IN THE SANTA CRUZ VALLEY

A tour of graveyards may seem out of the ordinary or just weird to some folks. However, it is quite an education in stonework artistry, family plots, but easier to take in black and white on paper for many. My personal experience after this research, was to reunite my great grandparents and their five children into the same cemetery in Colorado. My g-g-grandfather, his daughter in law and a young child are buried in a large, lovely plot. My g-g-grandmother and four children are in another town in a dry fenced-in site big enough for just them. Big cost to me but took a chance with a phone call. No can do! Digging in g-g-grandfather's plot turns up unrecorded old bones. The plot will remain as is. It still makes me feel lonely for the family there.

Starting with Los Reales, which is <u>not</u> on the Old Nogales Highway, but included to show how the history of a mining camp turns into a town, then discarded by progress and how the property is recycled. Twin Buttes Mine is seen from Old Nogales Highway SR89 from the Duval Mine Road Exit.

Los Reales Tucson, Arizona
By David Leighton For the Arizona Daily Star (in part)

'A miner named Domingo or S.R. (abbreviation for Senor) Domingo, built his home and a small foundry on the west bank of the Santa Cruz River and would bring his ores down from his mine in the hills for processing.......His home was old and weathered by the time more settlers moved to the rich valley land, then supported by an ever-flowing Santa Cruz River.

The first known settlers were Rafael Herreras, Mercedes Frederico, Joaquin Burruel and Gabino Altamirano, as well as Tomas, Francisco, Ysmael, Juan and Jesus M. Elias. They built adobe homes, planted crops and established the first Los Reales community. Domingo's mine flourished and he employed many miners. Neighbors and laborers believed he kept his wealth buried, since no banks existed there at the time........

One day, residents of the village were shocked to see Domingo's workers carrying a box that was nailed shut, with blood dripping out, to the graveyard.... With no law in Los Reales, nobody was ever brought to justice and it remains unknown what happened to Domingo's money. This is believed to have occurred in the late 1860s.

'The creation of the Tohono O'odam reservation started a second Los Reales on the east bank of the Santa Cruz River, as many Mexican-American families left their former homes.........the new town had two stores, one of which was run by Antonio Bustamante, and a blacksmith shop close to town, run by Samuel Shortridge.

'Residents expanded their crops to include wheat, watermelon, corn, barley, hay and garden vegetables. All of the grain was sold to the government for the cavalry horses and the soldiers. They also sold mesquite wood to supplement their incomes.

'Throughout its existence, Los Reales, like many communities in southern Arizona, faced Apache attacks, with the theft of horses and livestock a common occurrence. …..the town was abandoned in 1912 as a result of Midvale Farms taking most of the water from the Santa Cruz River. The land is now the Midvale Park subdivsion.

'Little remains today of the old Los Reales community except for remnants of the Los Reales Cemetery, located just northeast of Los Reales Road and I-19.'

- The Pima County Board of Supervisors established Los Reales Road or Road No. 64, on Dec. 30, 1922. It is the main east-west street south of Valencia Road.

- Note: Because Los Reales was never incorporated as a town, the exact boundaries of it are unknown. But it is known that, in 1874, much of what is now Midvale Park and directly south of it was part of the first Los Reales.'

- According to Marina Ruiz Olivas, in "Images and Conversations: Mexican Americans Recall a Southwestern Past," (claim of it being in Green Valley is unfounded)

"The area is called Los Reales, and it is part of an old Mexican settlement from the time that Arizona was a part of Mexico. I know that there is an old cemetery over there where there are headstones that date into the 1800s. Only one or two headstones are from the 1900s. That old cemetery doesn't exist anymore. When the developers bought the land, they didn't let people know what their plans were. People didn't have time to protest or to even remove the remains of their ancestors. The cemetery was bulldozed and they built the houses right over it. It should have been saved, because it was a very historical place."

The Nequilla Mine was located on December 11, 1865 and is just southeast of the Saguaro National Park boundary. The claim was recorded by Jesus and Ramon Bustamente and Domingo Gallego on February 17, 1866. Primary: Lead, Secondary: Silver

Bustamente and Gallego's interests in the mine were sold to James Lee and William Scott in 1867 and 1871. The mine was patented on September 28, 1872, making it the first patented mining claim in the Arizona Territory. Lee and Scott recovered silver ore until the early 1880s. The Nequilla Mine changed hands and was reworked a few times but closed for good in 1923 (Clemensen 1987:89- 92).

Source: Amole-Mining-District-Brief-2.pdf (nps.gov)

MORE BITS AND PIECES EXHUMED:

- The now vanished mining settlement of Los Reales accounts for the location of the cemetery: numerous burials at Los Reales are noted in the records of the San Xavier Mission. Of the many more than one hundred burials. only four bear even partially legible markings.

- Little remains today of the old **Los Reales** community except for remnants of the **Los Reales Cemetery**, located just northeast of **Los Reales** Road and I-19.

- **Arizona** Daily Star, June 27, 1937 "Name's Origin Found by Bork: **Los Reales** Was Named as Military Camp of Earlier Days ...

- LOS REALES CEMETERY lies off Los Reales Road. Tucson. Pima County. at the end of the road: it is nearly surrounded by the Los Reales Heights Housing Development. The cemetery is wholly uncared for and has been vandalized.

- The City of Tucson's **Los Reales Landfill**, located at 5300 E. **Los Reales** Road, opened in 1967 and is the only active landfill owned and managed by the City of Tucson.

- KOLD News 13 Staff / Published: Apr. 12, 2021

    TUCSON, Ariz. (KOLD News 13) – As more unaccompanied children and others turn themselves over to authorities at the border, federal officials are looking for options on where to house them.

    According to Tucson Mayor Regina Romero, Border Patrol is constructing a tent facility in the Pima County area. It will be located at 4550 East Los Reales Road, which is east of the airport, and should be completed in late April or early May.

- Brothels were part of the history of any growing town when men out numbered women. Several women and infants are buried with no history, such was life.

LOS REALES CEMETERY

Memorials for:

JUANA ALTAMIRANO
BIRTH 6 May 1891 Phoenix, Maricopa County, Arizona
DEATH 30 Nov 1903 (aged 12) Tucson, Pima County, Arizona
d/o Trinidad and Maria Miranda Escalante.
Wife of Agustine CASTRO. COD: Broncho pneumonia

JOSEFINA ESCALANTE CASTRO
BIRTH 1894 Tucson, Pima County, Arizona
DEATH 7 Nov 1918 (aged 23-24) Tucson, Pima County, Arizona

MARIA OLIVAS CASTRO
BIRTH 23 Feb
DEATH 23 Feb 1910 Tucson, Pima County, Arizona
d/o Manuel and Anita Burruel Olivas.
Cause of Death: Pulmonary tuberculosis (consumption)

PERFECTO CASTRO
BIRTH 1884 Tucson, Pima County, Arizona
DEATH 14 May 1909 (aged 24-25) Tucson, Pima County, Arizona
Cause of Death: Pulmonary tuberculosis

CARMEN QUIROZ CONTRERAS
BIRTH 1843 Sonora, Mexico
DEATH 25 Oct 1913 (aged 69-70) Tucson, Pima County, Arizona

ELOISA FREDIRICO CONTRERAS
BIRTH Unknown Tucson, Pima County, Arizona
DEATH 4 Jan 1903 Tucson, Pima County, Arizona
Age at Death: 27 , COD: Heart

JESUS MARIA FREDERICO
BIRTH 1854 Cobabi, a village on the Tohono O'odham reservation.
DEATH 28 Apr 1919 (aged 64-65) , Pima County, Arizona
Occupation: Teamster
COD: Pulmonary tuberculosis

RAMON FREDERICO
BIRTH 1884 Sonora, Mexico
DEATH 17 Sep 1910 (aged 25-26) , Pima County, Arizona
s/o Jesus Maria and Guadalupe Mindiola Frederico
Occupation: Miner COD: Double pneumonia

JOSE MALDONADO
BIRTH	1857 Sonora, Mexico
DEATH	16 Nov 1917 (aged 59-60) , Pima County, Arizona

s/o Francisco Maldonado and Eulogia Villanueva.
Occupation: Rancher, COD: Apoplexy

ANTONIO RAMIREZ
BIRTH	14 Jun 1882 Arizona
DEATH	4 May 1910 (aged 27) , Pima County, Arizona

s/o Martino and Lupa Romero Ramirez. Occupation: Rancher

ADELA TREJO DE RAMIREZ
BIRTH	March 1876 Arizona
DEATH	16 Oct 1922 (aged 45-46) , Pima County, Arizona

d/o Pedro and Antonia Frederico Trejo.
Wife of Antonio Ramirez.

SALVADOR SANCHEZ
BIRTH	1850 Guaymas, Guaymas Municipality, Sonora, Mexico
DEATH	9 Dec 1926 (aged 75-76) , Pima County, Arizona

s/o Josefa Sepulveda. Husband of Emilia Gastelo

EMILIA GASTELO SANCHEZ
BIRTH	Unknown Hermosillo, Hermosillo Municipality, Sonora, Mexico
DEATH	8 Jun 1923, Pima County, Arizona

d/o Miguel Gastelo and Lauteria ?. Wife of Salvador Sanchez

FLORENCIO TORRES
BIRTH	1873 Mexico
DEATH	29 Dec 1916 (aged 42-43), Pima County, Arizona

Husband of Ygnasa Ramirez de Torres

Occupation: Cattleman. COD: Electrocution

'Florencio and wife lived on a ranch nine miles south of Tucson. Florencio went out to cut the grass. Unbeknownst to him, a live transmission wire had fallen on his barbed wire fence about a half mile away from his home. While cutting the grass he went to go through the fence and as he parted the wires with his hands he was killed instantly. His brother-in-law saw what happened and ran to tell Florencio's wife. She dropped her breakfast dishes and ran to the scene. She attempted to pull him away from the wire and was also killed instantly. She died with her head resting on his breast.'

YGNASA RAMIREZ TORRES
BIRTH	1874 Mexico
DEATH	29 Dec 1916 (aged 41-42) , Pima County, Arizona

d/o Jose Ramirez. Wife of Florencio Torres. COD: Electrocution

PEDRO TREJO
BIRTH	29 Jun 1838 Sonora, Mexico

DEATH   6 Jun 1920 (aged 81) , Pima County, Arizona
               Husband of Antonia Frederico.
               Occupation: Rancher.
               COD: Gastro enteritis

ANTONIA FREDERICO TREJO

BIRTH   1815 - 1875

DEATH   1900 Pima County, Arizona
               Wife of Pedro Trejo

MARIA TREJO GRANILLO

BIRTH   1866 Magdalena de Kino Municipality, Sonora, Mexico

DEATH   10 Jul 1910 (aged 43–44) , Pima County, Arizona

BURIAL   Los Reales Cemetery
               d/o Pedro Trejo. Wife of Jesus Granillo

ANTONIA TREJO

BIRTH   1882 Arizona

DEATH   23 Jun 1909 (aged 26–27) , Pima County, Arizona
               COD: Epilepsy

ROMONA TREJO

BIRTH   Oct 1888 Arizona

DEATH   28 May 1911 (aged 22) , Pima County, Arizona
               d/o Pedro and Antonia Frederico Trejo. COD: Cerebral meningitis

LAMBERTO TREJO

BIRTH   17 Sep 1876 Tucson, Pima County, Arizona

DEATH   28 Apr 1918 (aged 41) , Pima County, Arizona
               s/o: Pedro Trejo
               Occupation: Rancher.
               COD: Pneumonia

FRANCISCA TREJO SANTA CRUZ

BIRTH   1868   Hermosillo, Hermosillo Municipality, Sonora, Mexico

DEATH   22 Nov 1922 (aged 53–54) , Pima County, Arizona
               d/o Pedro and Trinidad Soto. Widow of Lenon Santa Cruz.
               COD: Cerebral hemorrhage

PLACIDA VALENZUELA

BIRTH   1888 Sonora, Mexico

DEATH   30 Nov 1918 (aged 29–30) , Pima County, Arizona
               Cause of Death: Pneumonia

MANUELA FELIX DE VEGA

BIRTH   1859 Tubutama, Tubutama Municipality, Sonora, Mexico

DEATH   20 Sep 1919 (aged 59–60) , Pima County, Arizona
               d/o Pio and Rosalinda Maldonado Felix. Wife of Isidro Vega.

MARTINA VILLEGAS
BIRTH   1 Jan 1886 San Xavier, Pima County, Arizona
DEATH   30 Oct 1904 (aged 18), Pima County, Arizona
               COD: Pulmonary tuberculosis

AGUILAR RANCH CEMETERY
Tucson, Pima County, Arizona

Memorials for:

FELIX JOSEPH DIAZ LOPEZ III
BIRTH   19 Oct 1937 Tucson, Pima County, Arizona
DEATH   19 Oct 1937 Tucson, Pima County, Arizona
               3-hour-old child of Felix Romero Lopez Jr and Delia Aguilar Diaz.

GUILLERMO FELIX DIAZ
BIRTH   *Jun 25, 1876,*
DEATH   *April 03, 1960, Tucson, Pima County, Arizona*
               s/o Francisco Díaz and Delfina Felix Díaz
               Husband of Ramona Díaz, Occupation, Blacksmith

GUILLERMO AGUILAR DIAZ
BIRTH   10 Oct 1920 Tucson, Pima County, Arizona
DEATH   17 Jul 1921 (aged 9 months) Tucson, Pima County, Arizona
               s/o Guillermo Diaz and Antonia Aguilar.

(If a child died young, their name was used again for the next child of the same sex, thereby keeping alive the name of the relative who they were 'named for'. A common practice around the world.)

HELVETIA CEMETERY
Empire Mountains, Pima County Arizona
(see pages 19-20 for description of mining and town)

Celestina Bracamonte
BIRTH   6 Apr 1907, Helvetia,
DEATH   4 Feb 1908 (aged 9M 29D) pneumonia.

d/o Lacaro Bracamonte & Gabriela Valenzuela
Family moved to Yuma, two brothers lived long lives.

Infant Male Carbajal
BIRTH   29 Apr 1907. Helvetia
DEATH   24 Jun 1907 (aged 1M 26D) whooping cough

s/o Carlos Carbajal & Carmen Batia

Matthew Donahue
BIRTH   unknown
DEATH   19 Mar 1906 (68) Prospector.

Maria Escalante
BIRTH   18 Jul 1905   Mexico
DEATH   3 Feb 1908 (aged 2Y 6M 19D)

d/o Francisco Escalante & Carlota "Charlotte" Garcia
Family with 2 other children stayed in Pima Co.

Domingo Felix Jr.
BIRTH   11 Apr 1906
DEATH   27 Jun 1907 (aged 1Y 2M 16D)

s/o Domingo Felix Sr. & Eldafonsa Romero

Pedro Felix
BIRTH   Unknown, Sonora, Mexico
DEATH   27 Sep 1909 (aged 90) Miner

Angelito Figerola/ Figueroa?
BIRTH   11 Dec 1907, Arizona
DEATH   13 Jul 1910 (aged 2Y 7M 2D)

s/o Francisco Figerola & Esabel Olivas

Francisco Figerola Jr.
BIRTH   8 Nov 1908, Arizona
DEATH   20 Jul 1910 (aged 1Y 8M 12D)

s/o Francisco Figerola & Gregoria Lopez

Abelardo Florez
BIRTH   17 Mar 1906
DEATH   9 Oct 1907 (aged 1Y 6M 12D)
s/o Antonio Florez & Florencia ?

Guadalupe Florez
BIRTH   10 Jan 1905, Patagonia, Arizona
DEATH   8 Oct 1907 (aged 2Y 8M 28D)
d/o Antonio Florez & Florencia ?

John Franco
BIRTH   7 Dec 1905, Helvetia,
DEATH   22 Mar 1907 (aged 1Y 3M 15D)
s/o Juan Franco & Marcella Rivera

Maud "Minnie" Gandy
BIRTH   6 Feb 1907, Willcox, Cochise County
DEATH   17 Jul 1909 (aged 2Y, 5M, 11D)   COD: colitis
d/o James Ross "Ross" Gandy & Ida Singleton. Buried by her father

Infant Male Garrison
BIRTH   29 Jul 1906, Helvetia,
DEATH   29 Jul 1906, Helvetia,
s/o S. M. Garrison & Alva Martin

Rogelio Gastelum
BIRTH   27 Jan 1929, Rosemont Camp,
DEATH   4 Feb 1930 (aged 1 COD: Pneumonia)
Son of Ignacio Gastelum & Ramona Martinez. Parents and 3 sibling stayed in Pima County.

Ygnacio Gastelum Jr.
BIRTH   24 Nov 1916, Rosemont Junction,
DEATH   8 Mar 1918 (aged 1), Tucson,
s/o Ygnacio Gastelum of Mexico and Ramona Martinez of Tubac, AZ
Parents and brother stayed in Pima County.

George Gray
BIRTH   11 May 1909, Arizona
DEATH   28 Mar 1910 (aged 10M 17D)
s/o Edward Gray & Ermila Torres

Adela Lopez
BIRTH   29 Dec 1912, Rosemont Camp,
DEATH   22 Jan 1919 (aged 6Y 22D) Tucson,
d/o Francisco Lopez & Francisca Romero. Only child, parents stayed in Pima County.

Cruz Olivas Lopez
BIRTH 1864, Ures, Sonora, Mexico
DEATH 9 Jan 1927 (aged 62–63)
d/o Ruberto O Lopez , g-d/o Ediberto B. Lopez

Rafala Martinez
BIRTH 20 Mar 1895, Mexico
DEATH 3 Sep 1909 (aged 14Y 5M 14D)
d/o Manuel Martinez & Louisa Mallor

Eufracia Cesura Molina
BIRTH 14 Jan 1880, Tucson,
DEATH 29 Mar 1909 (aged 29Y 2M 15D.)
d/o Alonzo Cesina & Maria ?, wife of Frank Molina

Francisco Nevarro
BIRTH Unknown, Mexico
DEATH 22 Oct 1907, aged 20. Laborer, fell into mine shaft.

Miguel Olivas
BIRTH 15 Jun 1830, Mexico
DEATH 12 Sep 1909 (aged 79)

Franco Rivera
BIRTH 18 Oct 1912, Tucson,
DEATH 26 Feb 1916 (aged 3Y 4M 8D)
d/o Norman Wagon & Josefina Rivera

Nicanor Rivera
BIRTH 1878, Mexico
DEATH 24 Mar 1908 (aged 29–30)
s/o Juan Rivera & ?

Frederick George Leslie Rodda
BIRTH 26 Aug 1907, Helvetia,
DEATH 28 Oct 1907 (aged 2M 3D.)
s/o George Henry Morley Rodda & Frances Yeo
Parents and 2 siblings moved to California.

Natalia Ruelas
BIRTH 13 Oct 1920, Tucson,
DEATH 13 Oct 1920 (8 hours old)
d/o Feliz Ruelas Sr. & Cloete Mendoza
Parents and 2 siblings stayed in Pima County.

Antonio Ruiz
BIRTH 21 Dec 1907, Bisbee, Cochise County
DEATH 20 Sep 1908 (aged 8 M) Infantile Diarrhea
s/o Felix Ruiz & Cruz Zamora. Buried by father.

Loretta Ruiz
BIRTH   4 Jul 1903
DEATH   7 Apr 1910 (aged 6Y 9M 3D)
d/o Leopoldo Ruiz & Cruz Mendoza

Maria Sanchez
BIRTH   10 Jun 1910, Helvetia,
DEATH   10 Jun 1910, Stillborn
d/o Lopez Sanchez & Savella Olivas

Tomas Gastelo Sanchez
BIRTH   17 Sep 1882, by Canoa/Canyon Ranch,
DEATH   11 Mar 1909 (aged 26Y 6M)

s/o Salvador Sanchez & Emilia Gastelo
Teamster, died when thrown from a wagon.
Buried by father.
(Cori H. on 8 Oct 2009)

Infant Male Sawyer
BIRTH   30 May 1909, Helvetia,
DEATH   30 May 1909 Stillborn. Buried by parent.
s/o Nelson Sawyer & Florence Nailer.

Manuel Valencia
BIRTH   24 Dec 1879, Tucson,
DEATH   22 Feb 1918 (aged 38) Miner.
            Cancer of stomach.
s/o Jesus Valencia & Delfina Salazar. Parents and brother stayed in Pima County.

TWIN BUTTES CEMETERY

Photo by Daryl and Barbara(Biggs) Mallett

The Twin Buttes Mining and Smelting Company was a mining operation in the Twin Buttes area of Pima County, AZ that was subsequently leased or owned by Bush-Baxter, Glance Mining Company, Midland Copper Company, San Xavier Extension Copper Company. In addition to its mines the company operated a boarding house, store, and railroad.

The cemetery is on private property owned by a mining company and is only accessible to family members of the deceased or by special permission. A fence is erected around the cemetery.

www.airphotona.com

Memorials for:

FRANCISCO ALTAMIRA
BIRTH	unknown
DEATH	Unknown, Arizona
BURIAL	Twin Buttes Cemetery

Possibly the husband of Teresa Mascareno and father of Lydia Altamirano

FRANCISCO REVELLO "CHICO" ARGUELLES
BIRTH	1900, Mexico
DEATH	2 Sep 1982 (aged 81–82), Tucson, Pima County, Arizona
BURIAL	Twin Buttes Cemetery

DOMENICK A. REVELLO
BIRTH	3 May 1875, Cintano, Città Metropolitana di Torino, Piemonte, Italy
DEATH	1 Jan 1953 (aged 77) Tucson, Pima County, Arizona
BURIAL	Twin Buttes Cemetery

s/o Pete Revello & Dionicia Amsabecia. m. Ysabel N. Romo de Revello.
Naturalized citizen. Miner.
Father of Rose Revello Samms, Josephine Nunez Revello and Concha (Revello) Parker.
Grandfather of Jeanie (Parker) Hutchison, Marie Etta Stinnett.
Died of acute peritonitis

YSABEL NUNEZ ROMO REVELLO
BIRTH	2 Sep 1887, Mexico
DEATH	5 Jul 1955 (aged 67), Tucson, Pima County, Arizona
BURIAL	Twin Buttes Cemetery

d/o, Domingo R. Nunez and Josefa Romo Nunez
Wife of Domenick A. Revello
Died at Tucson General Hospital of uremia, due to chronic nephritis and chronic hypertension.

ROSALINA ARMIJO
BIRTH	unknown
DEATH	unknown
BURIAL	Twin Buttes Cemetery

ANGELITA BEJARANO ? (see Rio Rico Cemetery)
BIRTH	unknown
DEATH	unknown
BURIAL	Twin Buttes Cemetery

BERT BIANCHETTI
BIRTH	29 Dec 1879, Issiglio, Città Metropolitana di Torino, Piemonte, Italy
DEATH	23 Mar 1928 (aged 48), Twin Buttes, Pima County, Arizona
BURIAL	Twin Buttes Cemetery

ARTEMISA BONILLAS
BIRTH	5 Oct 1907, San Ignacio, Navojoa Municipality, Sonora, Mexico
DEATH	17 Aug 1921 (aged 13), Tucson, Pima County, Arizona
BURIAL	Twin Buttes Cemetery

d/o Artilano Bonillas & Ramona Coronado. COD diptheria.

IGNACIO BORQUEZ
BIRTH	unknown
DEATH	25 Jan 1927, Tucson, Pima County, Arizona
BURIAL	Twin Buttes Cemetery

Husband of Susana Borquez.

SUSANA BORQUEZ
BIRTH	unknown
DEATH	unknown
BURIAL	Twin Buttes Cemetery

Wife of Ignacio Borquez

NASARIO BURROLA
BIRTH	unknown
DEATH	20 Apr 1918, age 31.
BURIAL	Twin Buttes Cemetery

REYNALDO CABRERA
BIRTH	1906, Tucson, Pima County, Arizona
DEATH	7 Jul 1983 (aged 76–77)
BURIAL	Twin Buttes Cemetery

Possibly the husband of Adelina Martinez and father of Oralia Cabrera

GUADALUPE CARDENAS
BIRTH	3 Sep 1923
DEATH	11 Jun 1954 (aged 30)
BURIAL	Twin Buttes Cemetery

Cardenas was killed when she was run over by Mr. Sanders' truck.

FRANCISCO SERVANTES CASTILLO
BIRTH	unknown
DEATH	unknown
BURIAL	Twin Buttes Cemetery

CARLOS CASTRO
BIRTH	20 Feb 1927, Tucson, Pima County, Arizona
DEATH	21 Dec 1927 (aged 10 months), Tucson, Pima County, Arizona
BURIAL	Twin Buttes Cemetery

Child of Guillermo Castro and Juanita Aguilar.

ENRIQUE CASTRO
BIRTH	unknown
DEATH	Unknown, Baby boy.
BURIAL	Twin Buttes Cemetery

TRINIDAD MARTINEZ CHACON
BIRTH	Unknown, Mexico
DEATH	13 Dec 1925, Tucson, Pima County, Arizona
BURIAL	Twin Buttes Cemetery

Age at Death: 88 COD: Apoplexy

LITO CHAVEZ
BIRTH	unknown
DEATH	1925 Killed in Glance Mine
BURIAL	Twin Buttes Cemetery

BESSIE MAE FARRIS COX
BIRTH	15 May 1890, Oklahoma
DEATH	Dec 15, 1929
BURIAL	Twin Buttes Cemetery / Merged with Tempe, Maricopa, Arizona

RAFAEL ESTRADA
BIRTH	1839, Altar Municipality, Sonora, Mexico
DEATH	1918 (aged 78-79), Pima County, Arizona
BURIAL	Nov. 25, 1918, Twin Buttes Cemetery

JULIAN FIGUEROA
BIRTH	unknown
DEATH	Died, about age 75, of asthma.
BURIAL	Twin Buttes Cemetery

ANTONIO GARCIA
BIRTH	1889, Sonora, Mexico
DEATH	22 Jan 1917 (aged 27-28), Tucson, Pima County, Arizona
BURIAL	Twin Buttes Cemetery

s/o Espiritu Garcia and Angela Soto.
Miner. COD internal injuries as a result of an accident, on the road from San Xavier Mine to St. Mary's Hospital.

CRUZ GARCIA
BIRTH	1905, Ures, Ures Municipality, Sonora, Mexico
DEATH	14 Jul 1935 (aged 29-30), Tucson, Pima County, Arizona
BURIAL	Twin Buttes Cemetery

Occupation: Miner. COD: Heart.

LAURA ROMO GARCIA
BIRTH	14 Aug 1901, Mexico
DEATH	16 Mar 1953 (aged 51), Tucson, Pima County, Arizona
BURIAL	Twin Buttes Cemetery

d/o Antonio Romo and Maria Laura Carpena
Died at Pima County Hospital of uremia.

JESUS GARCIA
BIRTH	unknown
DEATH	unknown
BURIAL	Twin Buttes Cemetery

Brother of Isabel Vidal.
Laura Romo de Garcia

MANUEL GARCIA
BIRTH	unknown

DEATH unknown
BURIAL [Twin Buttes Cemetery](#)

JOSE RAMON GRIJALVA
BIRTH unknown
DEATH unknown
BURIAL [Twin Buttes Cemetery](#)

EUGENE VICTOR JOHNSON
BIRTH 15 Aug 1924
DEATH 11 Oct 1990 (aged 66)
BURIAL [Twin Buttes Cemetery](#)
s/o: Gust H Johnson of Norway and Amalia C Maule Johnson of Italy

JUAN LAUTERIO
BIRTH 1874, Mexico
DEATH 24 Mar 1917 (aged 42–43), Tucson, Pima County, Arizona
BURIAL [Twin Buttes Cemetery](#)
Husband of Manuela Duarte Fuentes

MANELA DUARTE FUENTES
BIRTH Mexico
DEATH 16 Dec 1961, Twin Buttes, Pima County, Arizona
BURIAL [Holy Hope Cemetery and Mausoleum](#)
Tucson, Pima County, Arizona
Wife of Juan Lanterio.

FRANCISCO "Chico Pancho" LOPEZ
BIRTH 15 Mar 1932
DEATH 1 Mar 1999 (aged 66)
BURIAL [Twin Buttes Cemetery](#)

FRANK LOPEZ
BIRTH 18 Jul 1903
DEATH 17 Nov 1964 (aged 61)
BURIAL [Twin Buttes Cemetery](#)

LORETA ROMERO MENDEZ
BIRTH	1888 Las Plomosas, Álamos Municipality, Sonora, Mexico
DEATH	13 Nov 1933 (aged 44–45), Tucson, Pima County, Arizona
BURIAL	Twin Buttes Cemetery
	d/ o Ignacio Romero. Widow of Lautero Mendez.
	COD; Pulmonary tuberculosis

MARGARITA MENDEZ
BIRTH	unknown
DEATH	Died in 1922 or 1923.
BURIAL	Twin Buttes Cemetery

JESUS "Chu" MENDIBLES
BIRTH	1885, Arizona
DEATH	15 Apr 1915 (aged 29–30), Tucson, Pima County, Arizona
BURIAL	Twin Buttes Cemetery
	Miner. COD, labor pneumonia and pulmonary tuberculosis.

MARIA "Marillita" MENDIBLES
BIRTH	unknown
DEATH	unknown
BURIAL	Twin Buttes Cemetery
	Wife of Rafael Mendibles

RAFAEL MENDIBLES
BIRTH	unknown
DEATH	unknown
BURIAL	Twin Buttes Cemetery

TERESA MENDIBLES
BIRTH	unknown
DEATH	unknown
BURIAL	Twin Buttes Cemetery

JOAQUIN MARTINEZ MENDOZA
BIRTH	unknown
DEATH	unknown
BURIAL	Twin Buttes Cemetery

ALBERTO MONTANO
BIRTH	1915
DEATH	1931 (aged 15–16)
BURIAL	Twin Buttes Cemetery

Inscription, "Sus padres...," *Gravesite Details* The stone is very worn and parts of it at the bottom are cracked and/or buried, making the inscription illegible.

JOSE NORIEGA
BIRTH	unknown
DEATH	1925
BURIAL	Twin Buttes Cemetery

Killed in Glance Mine.

(Infant) NUNEZ
BIRTH	unknown
DEATH	unknown
BURIAL	Twin Buttes Cemetery

ANTONIA B. NUNEZ
BIRTH	13 Jun 1917
DEATH	14 Sep 1918 (aged 1)
BURIAL	Twin Buttes Cemetery

d/o Alberto Nunez & Teodora Bustamante.
COD: acute gastrointestinal dyspepsia.

DEMITRIA NUNEZ
BIRTH	unknown
DEATH	Baby
BURIAL	Twin Buttes Cemetery

DOLORES ACUNA DE NUNEZ
BIRTH	unknown
DEATH	1921
BURIAL	Twin Buttes Cemetery

Gravesite Details, Mostly unreadable stone. Her grave is the ring of stones to the right of the picture, about halfway up.

2 (Infants) VEGA
BIRTH	unknown
DEATH	unknown
BURIAL	Twin Buttes Cemetery

Gravesite Details, At the foot of the grave of Dolores Nunez.

DOMINGO R. NUNEZ
BIRTH	1862, Baviacora, Baviácora Municipality, Sonora, Mexico
DEATH	10 May 1944 (aged 81–82), Tucson, Pima County, Arizona
BURIAL	Twin Buttes Cemetery

s/o Juan Nunez and Josefa Romo.
Farmer. Husband of Josefa Romo Nunez

JOSEFA ROMO NUNEZ
BIRTH	Unknown, Mexico
DEATH	Unknown, Pima County, Arizona
BURIAL	Twin Buttes Cemetery

Wife of Domingo R. Nunez

JUAN NUNEZ
BIRTH	1892, Mexico
DEATH	1 Nov 1960 (aged 67–68), Tucson, Pima County, Arizona
BURIAL	November 5, 1960, Twin Buttes Cemetery

s/o Domingo Nunez, born Mexico and Josefa Romo, born Mexico. Occupation: laborer in building industry. COD: lung cancer.

JUAN NUNEZ
BIRTH	unknown
DEATH	unknown
BURIAL	Twin Buttes Cemetery

TEODORA NUNEZ
BIRTH	unknown
DEATH	unknown Baby
BURIAL	Twin Buttes Cemetery

JUAN OLIVAS
BIRTH	unknown
DEATH	1910, 41 age
BURIAL	Aug 29, 1910, Twin Buttes Cemetery

Husband of Mariana Diaz Olivas

LEON OLIVAS
BIRTH	unknown
DEATH	unknown
BURIAL	Twin Buttes Cemetery

RAMONA NUNEZ PADILLA
BIRTH	18 Jul 1903
DEATH	17 Nov 1964 (aged 61)
BURIAL	Twin Buttes Cemetery

d/o Domingo & Josefa Nunez.
Beloved Mother

ANDREA PADILLA
BIRTH	May 1915
DEATH	2 Oct 1915 (aged 4–5 months)
BURIAL	Twin Buttes Cemetery

CONCHA "Connie" REVELLO STINNETT PARKER
BIRTH	13 Apr 1921, Amado, Santa Cruz County, Arizona
DEATH	5 Nov 2005 (aged 84), Pima County, Arizona
BURIAL	Twin Buttes Cemetery

d/o of Ysabel and Dominick Revello. She lived in Ruby, Ariz., and later her parents homesteaded at Twin Buttes.
Wife of James Monroe Stinnett from Oklahoma

ANA JOAQUINA NUNEZ ACUNA SALCIDO
BIRTH	1 Jan 1886, Mexico
DEATH	16 Jul 1958 (aged 72), Tucson, Pima County, Arizona
BURIAL	Twin Buttes Cemetery

d/o Sisto Nunez & Dolores Acuna.
Housewife. Died at Pima County Hospital of acute peritonitis.

RAMON SALCIDO
BIRTH	1885, Mexico
DEATH	25 Apr 1918 (aged 32-33), Tucson, Pima County, Arizona
BURIAL	Twin Buttes Cemetery

s/o Valencio Salcido & Antonia
Miner. Died at St. Mary's Hospital of emphysema.

FRANK FRANCIS SAMMS
BIRTH	11 Apr 1893
DEATH	9 Sep 1981 (aged 88)
BURIAL	Twin Buttes Cemetery

Husband of Rose Revello Samms.
US Navy * World War I

ALEJANDRO SANCHEZ
BIRTH	1868, Altar, Altar Municipality, Sonora, Mexico
DEATH	28 Nov 1958 (aged 89-90), Sahuarita, Pima County, Arizona
BURIAL	Twin Buttes Cemetery

Husband of Jesus Y. Sanchez.

JESUS YUBETA SANCHEZ
BIRTH	11 Nov 1899, Mexico
DEATH	15 Jun 1975 (aged 75), Tucson, Pima County, Arizona
BURIAL	Twin Buttes Cemetery

Wife of Alejandro Sanchez

LUIS SANCHEZ
BIRTH	15 Jul 1934, Pima County, Arizona
DEATH	10 Feb 1959 (aged 24), Sahuarita, Pima County, Arizona
BURIAL	Twin Buttes Cemetery

Husband of Dolores.

FRANCES S. "Winnie" SANDERS
BIRTH	25 Jul 1961
DEATH	5 Jul 1980 (aged 18)
BURIAL	Twin Buttes Cemetery

Sister of Yolanda Sanders Allegria.

(Infant Female) SILICEO
BIRTH	15 Jan 1937, Tucson, Pima County, Arizona
DEATH	16 Jan 1937 (aged 1 day), Tucson, Pima County, Arizona
BURIAL	Twin Buttes Cemetery

Premature. d /o Henry Duarte Siliceo and Guadalupe Aguilar Castro.

MARIA ETTA STINNET
BIRTH	9 Sep 1958, Tucson, Pima County, Arizona
DEATH	10 Sep 1958 (aged 1 day), Tucson, Pima County, Arizona
BURIAL	Twin Buttes Cemetery

d/o James Monroe Stinnett and Concha Revello Parker.

ANTONIA M. DE SUARES
BIRTH	28 Feb 1938
DEATH	40 years old
BURIAL	Twin Buttes Cemetery

JUAN SUARES
BIRTH	unknown
DEATH	unknown
BURIAL	Twin Buttes Cemetery

Unknown "El Diablito" Unknown
BIRTH	unknown
DEATH	unknown
BURIAL	Twin Buttes Cemetery

Died, about age 22, when he fell into a mine.

Unknown
BIRTH	unknown
DEATH	unknown
BURIAL	Twin Buttes Cemetery

Got drunk at the tavern on the hill and was found frozen to death.

ALEJANDRO VALENZUELA
BIRTH	1866, Hermosillo, Hermosillo Municipality, Sonora, Mexico
DEATH	24 Oct 1940 (aged 73-74), Tucson, Pima County, Arizona
BURIAL	Twin Buttes Cemetery

s/o Jose Valenzuela & Angelita
Husband of Rita R. Mendibiles Valenzuela 1883-1955
COD: coronary thrombosis.

RITA R. MENDIBILIES VALENZUELA
BIRTH	1883, Arizona
DEATH	25 Oct 1955 (aged 71-72), Tucson, Pima County, Arizona
BURIAL	Twin Buttes Cemetery

d/o Rafael Mendibiles and Maria Carrello.
Wife of Alejandro Valenzuela
COD:. Died of cerebral hemorrhage.

MARIA LUISA VALENZUELA
BIRTH	unknown
DEATH	unknown
BURIAL	Twin Buttes Cemetery

IGNACIO VELTRAN / BELTRAN
BIRTH	Unknown, Twin Buttes, Pima County, Arizona
DEATH	20 Mar 1922 (age 5), Tucson, Pima County, Arizona
BURIAL	Twin Buttes Cemetery

s/o Celso and Feliz Morales Veltran. COD: Diptheria

YSABEL GARCIA VIDAL
BIRTH	unknown
DEATH	unknown
BURIAL	Twin Buttes Cemetery

Wife of Jesus Vidal. Sister of Jesus Garcia.

CRUZ RUBIO VINDOLA

BIRTH	1868, Hermosillo, Hermosillo Municipality, Sonora, Mexico
DEATH	28 Jan 1944 (aged 75–76), Tucson, Pima County, Arizona
BURIAL	Twin Buttes Cemetery

Widow of Amado Vindola.
COD: Pneumonia

ROSENDO YANEZ

BIRTH	unknown
DEATH	unknown
BURIAL	Twin Buttes Cemetery

EULALIA

BIRTH	unknown
DEATH	circa 1932, Pima County, Arizona
BURIAL	Twin Buttes Cemetery

Died, drunk in Sahuarita, Arizona.

SOPORI RANCH CEMETERY

'Those who enter the Sopori Ranch Cemetery are greeted by a carved chunk of granite stuck in the ground at the entrance.

"Tread softly here," the inscription says. *"These stoney mounds shelter the bones of Arizona's oldest pioneers."*

The cemetery is the final resting place for an unknown number of people, buried as Arizona transitioned to the U.S. from Mexico. But while the rock could be referring to anyone interred there, it's specifically referencing one family whose experience in Southern Arizona was full of hardship and bitterness.

Sopori Ranch dates back to a land grant given to Juan Bautista de Anza. After becoming part of the new territory of Arizona, it would exchange hands several times, abandoned and acquired as owners died or were driven off by Apaches. In the 20th century, it was owned by Jack Warner, one of the founders of Warner Bros. Studios, before being bought by John Croll in 1993. The Croll family still owns a fair portion of it, including the ranch house and cemetery, though they sold more than 10,000 acres for potential development in 2004.

The Sopori Ranch Cemetery is accessed off Arivaca Road, just a few miles from Amado. A barbed-wire gate, easily overlooked, leads to a short hike through cholla-infested desert to the cemetery.

It sits back on private property, so few have the chance to tread into this cemetery, softly or otherwise. A faded wooden sign with a cross and "Sopori Ranch Cemetery" hangs from the fence, keeping any livestock out.

Inside are a handful of rock mounds, showing where people have been interred, though nothing remains of any grave markers. There is also a raised concrete tomb with a tree growing out of the top. Several old headstones are scattered here or there. One inscription is worn away completely. Another, that of "Diego Valenzuela," is still visible, if nearly illegible. The headstone itself has fallen over.

The oddity here is a clean, modern headstone for John Brissot Croll (Dec. 31, 1940 – June 29, 1999). It sums him up as "Owner of the Sopori Ranch." He is the newest known burial in the cemetery in over a century.

And then there were the Penningtons.

The pioneers

'Three more carved granite chunks match the warning stone at the entrance. One reads "Ann Pennington, died at the Sopori, 1867." Another, "James Pennington, killed by Apaches, August 1868." And finally "In memoriam, Elias G. Pennington, Green Pennington, killed on the Sonoita 1869, Ellen Pennington Barnett Died at Tucson, 1869."

Elias Green Pennington and his wife, Julia Ann Hood, were originally from South and North Carolina, respectively, and had relatives who fought in the Revolutionary War and the War of 1812. The couple moved to Tennessee shortly after marrying in 1831. Ever mobile, the Penningtons relocated to the new state of Texas. Julia died in 1855, leaving behind 12 children. The motherless family would start for California but came to a stop in Arizona along Sonoita Creek after Larcena, the third oldest child, became ill.

Over the next 13 years, they would make a go at a life in the new territory, living in Tubac, Tucson, along the Mexico border, Calabasas and the then-abandoned Sopori Ranch between 1866 and 1868. Their house on the ranch is described as fortress-like, situated on an upthrust of rock, with stone walls all around it. The protection was necessary; their home was along a well-traveled route for Apaches coming and going from Mexico, and Elias was frequently absent freighting goods to earn money.

The family would eventually relocate back to Texas in 1870 after several swift tragedies struck – which is how the grave markers ended up at the Sopori Ranch Cemetery.

It started when 24-year-old Ann Pennington died of malaria in 1867 while at the ranch. The next year, 35-year-old James, the oldest son, met his end while hauling lumber to Tucson from the Santa Ritas. Apaches made off with his oxen while they camped north of San Xavier del Bac. He and two teamsters followed their trail, but only one survived an ambush laid by the Apaches. James was originally buried in Tucson, but when the family left for Texas, his brother Jack had the body moved to Sopori Ranch so Ann would not be alone.

The next year, Elias took his son Green to farm near Sonoita Creek in a notoriously dangerous area for white settlers. Several people tried to warn Elias about the threat of Apache attacks in the area. Author Virginia Culin Roberts, who wrote a book about the family called "**With Their Own Blood**," records a neighbor saying "Goodbye, Mr. Pennington, I don't expect to see you alive again."

On June 10, 1869, Elias was at his plow – a rifle resting on its handles – when a group of roughly two dozen Apaches attacked from the brush, hitting him with numerous arrows. Green, not realizing his father was already dead, rushed forward to save him, and took three arrows himself. He lived long enough for soldiers from nearby Camp Critterden to arrive. He and his father were buried in the camp's cemetery.

After losing Elias and Green, the family decided to move on to California. They were only 20 miles out of Tucson when 34-year-old Ellen caught a serious case of pneumonia. They returned quickly to Tucson, where she died a mere two days later. At that point, Larcena, the oldest remaining sibling, reached out to Jack, already in Texas, to help move the family.

Only one of the younger daughters, Amanda Jane, would ever see their original destination of California.

Larcena's story

'Larcena, probably the most famous Pennington, is not buried in the cemetery. Shortly after marrying John Page in 1859, Larcena and the young ward of a business associate were captured by Apaches in Madera Canyon. Forced marched through the Santa Ritas, Larcena stumbled down a ridge when she couldn't keep the pace they demanded. The Apaches left her for dead after striking her several times with lances. Larcena would spend two weeks painfully crawling her way off the mountains. She would be the only Pennington to stay in Arizona. She married William Fisher Scott in 1870, her first husband having died several years earlier. She died in 1913, at 76, and is buried in Tucson's Evergreen Cemetery. (much has been written on Larcena and her ordeal)

Pennington Street in the heart of Tucson is named after the family, on the site where they operated a lumber saw pit. (According to Roberts, Josephine Peak and Josephine Canyon in the Santa Ritas are named for the family's youngest daughter.) Josephine Gardner according to ARIZONA NAME PLACES by Will C. Barnes

The grave markers at Sopori Ranch Cemetery were put in place by Robert H. Forbes, a professor at the University of Arizona, and his wife, Georgie, Larcena's daughter. Forbes became fascinated by the Penningtons' woeful tale and chronicled it in a 1919 account published by the Arizona Archaeological and Historical Society. After the last of Elias' living children, Mary Francis, passed away in 1935, Forbes and Georgie were moved to honor the family with the engraved granite that today still warns people to tread softly.'

Source: David Rookhuyzen / www.gvnews.com

"**With Their Own Blood**: A Saga of Southwestern Pioneers" by Virginia Roberts, (accurate dates and places)

Memorials for:

ANN REID PENNINGTON
BIRTH	January 20, 1843, Honey Grove, Texas
DEATH	July 3, 1867, Sopori, Arizona (aged 23-24) Unmarried.

Ann Pennington was born to Elias Green Pennington, Sr. and Julia Ann Hood Pennington around 1843, and died in 1867 of malaria, when she was just twenty-four years old. She was the first of many members of the Pennington family to die on the Arizona frontier.

JAMES "Jim" PENNINGTON
BIRTH	May 8, 1833, Tennessee, unmarried
DEATH	Aug 27, 1868, Pima County, Arizona

In August of 1868 Jim Pennington was camping by the road north of San Xavier, his oxen were stolen by Apaches during the night. Next morning he and his teamster pursued the Indians but were ambushed in the hills west of Tucson and Jim was killed. He was buried first in Tucson, afterward at the Sopori Ranch, where a wooden headboard still marks his grave.

Source: The Penningtons, Pioneers Of Early Arizona: A Historical Sketch (1919) by: Robert Humphrey Forbes

LAURA ELLEN PENNINGTON BARNETT
BIRTH	November 12, 1835, Tennessee
DEATH	December 25, 1869 Pima County, Arizona
	Wife of C. Barnett Underwood, m 25 April 1867

ELIAS GREEN PENNINGTON Sr.
BIRTH	April 16, 1809, South Carolina
DEATH	June 10, 1869 Pima County, Arizona

Pennington Street (in Tucson) is named for an early family that made its permanent home in what is today Arizona.

In **1857**, Pennington and his children joined a wagon train headed for California. When they reached Fort Buchanan near present-day Sonoita, one daughter, Larcena, fell ill, and the family was forced to drop out of the train. For the next two years, they lived near the fort, and they grew hay for the military.

In **1863** the family was in Tucson; in **1864**, it was in Tubac. In both places family members hauled logs from the mountains and whipsawed them, selling the lumber to the military. The Sopori Ranch was their home in **1867 and 1868**. Between **1868 and 1869**, Elias and his two sons - Jim and Green - were killed by Apaches.

What was left of the family, mostly women and children, moved to Tucson and stayed for some years. Jack, the only remaining brother, took his unmarried sisters back to Texas.

Pennington Street, on the south side of the old presidio wall, was originally called Calle del Arroyo and was used by Elias Pennington as a saw pit.

Arizona Daily Star 21 October 2019
David Leighton at streetsmarts@azstarnet.com
Bio Contributed by User Don Stowell

ELIAS GREEN PENNINGTON Jr.
BIRTH	July 27, 1848, Honey Grove, Texas
DEATH	June 17, 1869, Sonoita Valley, Arizona
BURIAL	Sopori Ranch Cemetery

J B CONT
BIRTH	Unknown from Italy
DEATH	4 Feb 1922 (78) Pima County, Arizona
BURIAL	Sopori Ranch Cemetery,

Occupation: Rancher
COD: Senility

JOHN BRISSOT CROLL
BIRTH	13 Dec 1940
DEATH	29 Jun 1999 (aged 58) Arizona
BURIAL	Sopori Ranch Cemetery,

Owner of the Sopori Ranch. (see article about Sopori Ranch Cemetery)

Santa Rita Mountains in the background.

AMADO CEMETERY

By David Rookhuyzen, Green Valley News   Aug 8, 2017

There are not many people around anymore who can talk about Amado's cemetery. But the names and dates on the headstones can tell visitors about who was living and dying in the area while Southern Arizona was still being settled.

The cemetery sits back on private land, to the west of the frontage road, about a mile south of the Cow Palace. Accessing it is difficult and requires getting past a gate and going a half mile up an especially rough and rocky unpaved road. A chain link fence surrounds it, with a metal sign reading "Amado Cemetery" hanging near the entrance.

Most of the graves date back to the first half of the 20th century and show how difficult it was living in the area before many of the modern conveniences. Of the 57 listed interments – there are unmarked graves as well – 19 are for children who were a year old or younger when they died.

A series of gravestones, plus birth and death records, tell the trials of the Rodriguez family. No less than five children of Santiago Rodriguez, originally from Ruby, and Maria Luisa Ahumado (possibly Ahumada) from Arivaca, are buried there. Most died before their first birthday.

Maria Julia was born March 29, 1925, but died Aug 18, succumbing to a fever. Jose Maria also died from a fever in 1929, living only between Nov. 7 and Nov. 21. Mercedes died on April 22, 1934 from pneumonia at the age of 6 months. David was born in 1945 but lived only between February and May. The longest lived child was Miguel, born in 1928, who would live until 1945 when typhoid fever killed him at the age of 17.

Through the ages

The Moreno family graves also record tragedy. Two twins, Jose and Josefa, were delivered still-born on March 15, 1925. Their mother, Rita de Rascon Moreno, passed away the next day at the age of 30, the official cause being listed as pneumonia.

Not that everyone was dying before their time. Francisco Valenzuela was 80 when he passed away in 1947, and his wife Benigna was 70 at the time of her death in 1943. Julia Ahumada, whose grave is topped by a statue of a woman with an armload of flowers, lived from August 1876 to January 1963. Also notable is Louis Figueroa, who was born July 11, 1876 and died Jan. 30, 1954.

One well-kept and recent-looking headstone is for Gertrudes Proctor (Feb. 28, 1897 to Feb. 7, 1934). Gertrudes, born into the Valenzuela family, went by "Tula" and was the wife of Henry Patrick Proctor.

Henry was the son of Vermont native Charles Anthony Proctor, who would be an owner of the Sopori Ranch and the La Tesota Ranch near what was then Sahuarito. When he sold that ranch, he moved to Box Canyon to ranch there.

It was Charles and his family who gave their name to the Proctor Ranch, which in turn is the namesake of Proctor Road at the mouth of Madera Canyon. Like his father, Henry Proctor also ranched in Box Canyon. He married Tula in 1925, but she passed away unexpectedly from a stomach issue in 1934.

Memories live on

Jesse Luna, an 80-year-old Amado resident, said he was a boy when he attended the funeral and burial of Francisco Valenzuela, Tula's father. Valenzuela's death certificate says he died of coronary thrombosis at the age of 80 on Nov. 6, 1947 and was interred in the cemetery two days later. Francisco is buried with his wife, Benigna Bartlett Valenzuela, and one son, Mike, who died in 1926 at the age of 21.

Luna remembers his father had an old Model T or Model A, and they had to lay down wood planks to get the car and the 55-gallon water drum it was carrying up to the cemetery for the occasion.

His father, Jesus, is also interred there, along with a sister, Gloria, and brother, Richard. Richard went into the armed services as a signal operator but died in 1966 at the age of 19 after coming in contact with a live wire.

The cemetery represents the various pioneer families of Amado, Luna said, including the Valenzuelas, Palomares, Ahumadas, Varelas, Valdezes, Rodriguezes and Villas. Members of the Ahumada and Palomares families still visit often, despite having relocated to Tucson, but most of those families are now gone, Luna said.

And with them moving on, the graveyard has slowly fallen out of use. The latest date on any of the gravestones is 1969 and Luna can't recall the last time anyone was put in the ground up there. "There hasn't been anyone buried there in years," he said.

NOTES ON CAUSES OF DEATH: Cholera infantum is an acute noncontagious intestinal disturbance of **infants,** formerly common in congested areas of high humidity and temperature, but now rare. The Monsoon Season was July through September. Check time of year for death. Another common cause of death was listed as teething or stomach problems.

Underground mines are one of the highest risk environments for TB (TUBERCULOSIS) transmission, and miners regularly find living and working conditions make them highly susceptible to contracting the disease

Memorials for:

MANUEL ACOSTA
BIRTH	1920
DEATH	1937 (17 year old) Amado Santa Cruz County, Arizona
BURIAL	Amado Cemetery
	s/o Esequiel Acosta and Emilia Ortiz.
	COD: TB Pulmonary.

ESTELLA AHUMADA
BIRTH	1936
DEATH	1937 Amado, Santa Cruz County, Arizona
BURIAL	Amado Cemetery

GENE D. AHUMADA
BIRTH	August 19, 1937.
DEATH	April 27, 1963, (age 25), Amado, Santa Cruz County, Arizona
BURIAL	Amado Cemetery

JOSE MARIA AHUMADA

BIRTH	1873 Sonora, Mexico
DEATH	10 Mar 1918 (aged 44–45) Arivaca, Pima County, Arizona
BURIAL	Amado Cemetery

s/o Jesus and Agustina Ahumada

Husband of Julia Verdzco Ahumada. COD: Bronchitis.

JULIA PENA VERDZCO AHUMADA

BIRTH	Aug 1876 Amado, Santa Cruz County, Arizona
DEATH	9 Jan 1963 (aged 86) Tucson, Pima County, Arizona
BURIAL	Amado Cemetery

MARY A. AHUMADA RODRIGUEZ

BIRTH	1905
DEATH	1969 (aged 63–64)
BURIAL	Amado Cemetery

RAMON AHUMADA, JR.

BIRTH	Unknown
DEATH	Unknown
BURIAL	Amado Cemetery

WILLIAM PERNELL CHANCE

BIRTH	11 Feb 1915 Claremore, Rogers County, Oklahoma
DEATH	23 Jul 1986 (aged 71) Tucson, Pima County, Arizona
BURIAL	South Lawn Memorial Cemetery

Husband of Margaret Chance.

MARGARET VALENZUELA CHANCE

BIRTH	15 Sep 1907 Patagonia, Santa Cruz County, Arizona
DEATH	26 Jan 2003 (aged 95) Wyoming
BURIAL	Mount Pisgah Cemetery, Gillette, Campbell County, Wyoming

Wife of William Pernell Chance

WILLIE PERNELL CHANCE, JR
BIRTH	18 May 1941 Tucson, Pima County, Arizona
DEATH	26 May 1941 (aged 8 days) Tucson, Pima County, Arizona
BURIAL	Amado Cemetery
	s/o Willie Pernell Chance and Margaret Valenzuela Chance.

MARIA RODRIGUEZ CORTEZ
BIRTH	15 Aug 1900
DEATH	4 Mar 1927 (aged 26)
BURIAL	Amado Cemetery
	Age 27Y Wife of Jose Cortez.
	COD: Childbirth

SENAIDA CHANCE CORTEZ
BIRTH	4 Mar 1927
DEATH	4 Mar 1927
BURIAL	Amado Cemetery
	d/o of Jose Cortez and Maria Rodriquez Chance.
	COD: Stillborn

LOUIS F. FIGUEROA
BIRTH	July 11, 1876
DEATH	Jan. 30, 1954
BURIAL	Amado Cemetery

M. H. FUERTES
BIRTH	Unknown
DEATH	1942
BURIAL	Amado Cemetery

MARTINA GAMBOA
BIRTH	Dec. 16, 1953
DEATH	Aug. 3, 1954
BURIAL	Amado Cemetery
	d/o of . Pedro Gamboa
	Age 7M, COD: Diarrhea, Intestinal,

MIGUEL CASTRO GONZALES
BIRTH	1917
DEATH	Nov. 11, 1942, Age 28Y
BURIAL	Amado Cemetery

s/o Cristobal **Gonzales and** Clara Castro
COD: Crushed Neck - Auto Accident

MIGUEL GONZALES
BIRTH	Mar. 1937
DEATH	Jul. 3, 1937 Age 3M 27D
BURIAL	Amado Cemetery

s/o **Miguel Gonzales and** Dora Apodaca
COD: Gastro Enteritis Acute

MIKE GONZALES
BIRTH	1940
DEATH	1940 8 MO
BURIAL	Amado Cemetery

COD bronchial pneumonia.
s/o **Miguel Gonzales** and Dora Apodaca

FELICIANO JUAREZ
BIRTH	1878
DEATH	1962 (aged 83–84)
BURIAL	Amado Cemetery

Husband of Refugio Plumeda Juarez

REFUGIO PLUMEDA JUAREZ
BIRTH	1896
DEATH	1972 (aged 75–76)
BURIAL	Amado Cemetery

Wife of Feliciano Juarez

MAGDALENA JUAREZ
BIRTH	April 5, 1932
DEATH	April 9, 1932, 4D
BURIAL	Amado Cemetery

d/o Feliciano Juarez and Refugio Plumeda
COD: Fever

GLORIA LUNA
BIRTH	1932
DEATH	1962 (aged 29–30)
BURIAL	Amado Cemetery

JESUS LUNA, SR
BIRTH	19 Apr 1892 in MEXICO
DEATH	**16 Jan 1958**
BURIAL	Amado Cemetery

s/o Martiniano Luna and Ricarda Parra both of Mexico.

PVT RICHARD M. LUNA
BIRTH	1947
DEATH	1966 age 19
BURIAL	Amado Cemetery

COD: Signal operator in the armed services, died after coming in contact with a live wire.

DOLORES MARTINEZ
BIRTH	1882 Guaymas, Sonora, Mexico
DEATH	July 18 1939
BURIAL	Amado Cemetery

d/o Turina Martinez of Sonora, Mexico

JOSE CRUZ MASCARENAS
BIRTH	May. 5, 1925
DEATH	May. 5, 1925
BURIAL	Amado Cemetery

s/o Manuel Mascarenas and Jesus Aros
COD: Stillborn.

ETNIO MORENO
BIRTH	1871
DEATH	May 14, 1934
BURIAL	Amado Cemetery

Husband of Rita De Rascon Moreno

RITA RASCON MORENO
BIRTH	1895
DEATH	1925
BURIAL	Amado Cemetery

Wife of Etnio Moreno
COD: Pneumonia after her twins Jose and Josefa Moreno died.

TOMAS OCHOA
BIRTH	1894 Cocorit, Hermosillo Municipality, Sonora, Mexico
DEATH	23 Jan 1937 (aged 42–43) Tucson, Pima County, Arizona
BURIAL	Amado Cemetery

Occupation: Miner. COD: Miliary tuberculosis (characterized by a wide dissemination into the human body and by the tiny size of the lesions.

ELOISE AMANDA PALOMARES
BIRTH	23 May 1909, Tucson, Pima County, Arizona
DEATH	20 Dec 1940 (aged 31), Tucson, Pima County, Arizona
BURIAL	Amado Cemetery

Daughter of Jose Maria and Julia Verdusco Amanda.
Wife of Reyes Palomares.
COD: Kidney cancer

REYES LEON PALOMARES
BIRTH	February 18, 1900, Sonora, Mexico
DEATH	March 14, 1948, at age 48.
BURIAL	Amado Cemetery

Husband of Eloise Amanda Palomares of Sonora, Mexico

JULIA PALOMARES
BIRTH	Sep 1894, Guaymas Municipality, Sonora, Mexico
DEATH	26 May 1940 (aged 45) Tucson, Pima County, Arizona
BURIAL	Amado Cemetery

ANTONIO S. PRECIADO
BIRTH	4 Jan 1884 Greaterville, Pima County, Arizona
DEATH	17 Oct 1966 (aged 82) Tucson, Pima County, Arizona
BURIAL	Holy Hope Cemetery and Mausoleum, Tucson

Husband of Rosaura Martinez Preciado

ROSAURA MARTINEZ PRECIADO
BIRTH	Sep 1894, Guaymas Municipality, Sonora, Mexico
DEATH	26 May 1940 (aged 45) Tucson, Pima County, Arizona
BURIAL	Amado Cemetery

Daughter of Dolores and Josefa Felix Martinez.
Wife of Antonio Preciado. Cause of Death: Surgical shock.

ANTONIO MARTINEZ "Tony" PRECIADO
BIRTH	5 May 1926,
DEATH	8 Jun 2012 (aged 86) Arizona
BURIAL	Holy Hope Cemetery and Mausoleum, Tucson

s/o Antonio and Rosaura Martinez Preciado
Inscription, PFC US ARMY, WORLD WAR II

ALFREDO PRECIADO
BIRTH	4 Jun 1929, Tucson, Pima County, Arizona
DEATH	20 Apr 1937 (aged 7), Tucson, Pima County, Arizona
BURIAL	Amado Cemetery

s/o Antonio and Rosaura Martinez Preciado

CARLOS MARTINEZ "Kita" PRECIADO
BIRTH	28 Jan 1931, Tucson, Pima County, Arizona
DEATH	3 Mar 1990 (aged 59)
BURIAL	Holy Hope Cemetery and Mausoleum, Tucson

s/o Antonio and Rosaura Martinez Preciado

FRANCISCO P. VALENZUELA
BIRTH	7 Sep 1867, Atil, Atil Municipality, Sonora, Mexico
DEATH	6 Nov 1947 (aged 80), Tucson, Pima County, Arizona
BURIAL	Amado Cemetery

Son of Diego and Carmen Pasos Valenzuela. Husband of Benigna Bartlett.

BENIGNA BARTLETT VALENZUELA
BIRTH	19 Apr 1873, Oro Blanco, Santa Cruz County, Arizona
DEATH	20 Feb 1943 (aged 69), Nogales, Santa Cruz County, Arizona
BURIAL	Amado Cemetery

d/o John Bartlett and Gertrudis Marquez. Wife of Francisco Valenzuela

GERTRUDES VALENZUELA PROCTOR
BIRTH	28 Feb 1897, Oro Blanco, Santa Cruz County, Arizona
DEATH	7 Feb 1934 (aged 36), Tucson, Pima County, Arizona
BURIAL	Amado Cemetery

Daughter of Francisco and Benina Bartlett Valenzuela.
Wife of Henry P Proctor. COD: Peritonitis

DIEGO BARTLETT VALENZUELA
BIRTH	27 Apr 1900, Arizona
DEATH	15 Sep 1953 (aged 53), Tucson, Pima County, Arizona
BURIAL	Holy Hope Cemetery and Mausoleum, Tucson

s/o Francisco and Benigna Bartlett Valenzuela.
Worked as a boilermaker for the Southern Pacific Railroad.

MIKE VALENZUELA
BIRTH	1905
DEATH	1926 (aged 20–21)
BURIAL	Amado Cemetery

s/o Francisco and Benigna Bartlett Valenzuela.

EVANGELINE RIBERA
BIRTH	1929
DEATH	1931, Age 2Y 3M
BURIAL	Amado Cemetery

d/o Juan Ribera and Dolores Rascon.
COD: Pneumonia.

JESUS ROBLES
BIRTH	1880
DEATH	1937
BURIAL	Amado Cemetery

No less than five children of **Santiago Rodriguez**, originally from Ruby, and **Maria Luisa Ahumado** (possibly **Ahumada**) from Arivaca are buried in Amado.

MARIA JULIA RODRIGUEZ
BIRTH	March 29, 1925-
DEATH	Aug 18, Age 5M 10D,
BURIAL	Amado Cemetery

d/o Santiago Rodriguez and Maria Luisa Ahumado
COD: Fever.

MIGUEL RODRIGUEZ
BIRTH 1928-
DEATH 1945, Age 17Y,
BURIAL Amado Cemetery
  s/o Santiago Rodriguez and Maria Luisa Ahumado
  COD: Typhoid Fever.

JOSE MARIA RODRIGUEZ
BIRTH Nov. 7, 1929
DEATH Nov. 21, 1929, Age 25D
BURIAL Amado Cemetery
  s/o Santiago Rodriguez and Maria Luisa Ahumado
  COD: Fever.

MERCEDES RODRIGUEZ
BIRTH 1933
DEATH April 22, 1934   Age 6M 28D
BURIAL Amado Cemetery
  d/o Santiago Rodriguez and Maria Luisa Ahumado
  COD: Pneumonia

DAVID RODRIGUEZ
BIRTH February 1945
DEATH May 1945, Age 3M 8D
BURIAL Amado Cemetery
  s/o Santiago Rodriguez and Maria Luisa Ahumado
  COD: Summer diarrhea. Rickets

JOSEFINA RODRIGUEZ
BIRTH Unknown
DEATH Unknown
BURIAL Amado Cemetery
  Creche with Madonna at grave.

ISIDRO RIVERA SANDOVAL
BIRTH 1887
DEATH 1926 Arizona
BURIAL Amado Cemetery
  s/o Eugenio Sandoval and Marselina Rivero

CLARA DE VALDEZ
BIRTH	1885-
DEATH	1953, Age 84Y
BURIAL	Amado Cemetery

d/o Pilar Castro and Juana Lonez.
Clara de Valdez's grave is written entirely in Spanish.
COD: Carcinorna of uterua.

ERNESTO JIMENEZ VALDEZ
BIRTH	1945-
DEATH	1945 Baby
BURIAL	Amado Cemetery

s/o, Arnulfo Valdez and Maria Jimenez.
COD: Enterocolitis

ARNULFO C. VALDEZ
Birth	DEC. 8,1926
DEATH	FEB. 11, 2014,
BURIAL	Amado Cemetery

EMILIA ORTIZ VARELA
BIRTH	1900
DEATH	1965 (aged 64–65)
BURIAL	Amado Cemetery

ANTONIA VARELA
BIRTH	14 Aug 1934
DEATH	9 Oct 1934 (Age 3M)
BURIAL	Amado Cemetery

Infant of Antonio Varela and Emilia Ortiz
COD: Intestinal Fever

ANTONIO CANEZ VASQUES
BIRTH	December 1933.
DEATH	November 1945, at age 11.
BURIAL	Amado Cemetery

s/o Manuel Vasquez and Laura Canez.

MARIA VERDUGO PENA VERDUSCO
BIRTH	1841, Caborca, Caborca Municipality, Sonora, Mexico
DEATH	10 Aug 1931, Amado, Santa Cruz County, Arizona
BURIAL	Amado Cemetery

d/o Manuel Pena and Susana Verdugo
COD: Acute Enteritis Age 90

MANELITA VERDUSCO
BIRTH	1920-
DEATH	1921 Age 1Y 3M 8D,
BURIAL	Amado Cemetery

d/o Rasolino Verdusco and Conception Verdugo
COD: Stomach Fever

FILEBERTO DIEGO VERDUSCO
BIRTH	Nov. 1921-
DEATH	1921 Age 1Y 3M 8D
BURIAL	Amado Cemetery

s/o Rosalino Verdusco and Encarnacion Verdusco both of Mexico

MARIA LEONINA VERDUSCO
BIRTH	Apr. 1927
DEATH	Sep. 28, 1928
BURIAL	Amado Cemetery

d/o Rosalino Verdusco and Encarnacion Verdusco both of Mexico
COD: Teething,

ROSALINA VERDUSCO
BIRTH	Jan. 13, 1929
DEATH	Feb. 20, 1929, Age 1M 7D
BURIAL	Amado Cemetery

d/o Rosalia Verdusco and Maria Jesus Sanchez
COD: Pneumonia

ANSOLMO VERDUZCO
BIRTH Jan. 10, 1931
DEATH Jan. 18, 1931
BURIAL Amado Cemetery
s/o Rosalino Verduzco and Maria Pena
COD: Gangrenal navel,

LUCIA PENA VERDUZCO
BIRTH 1933
DEATH 21 May 1950 (aged 16–17), Amado, Santa Cruz County, Arizona
BURIAL Amado Cemetery
d/o Rosalino Verduzco and Maria Pena
COD: General Debility

FRANK R. VILLA
BIRTH 1894-
DEATH 1966
BURIAL Amado Cemetery

MISSION LOS SANTOS ANGELES DE GUEVAVI

Memorials for:

CAPTAIN JUAN BAUTISTA DE ANSSA 1ST.
BIRTH: June 29, 1693, Hernani, Gipuzkoa, Basque Country, Spain
DEATH: May 9, 1740 (aged 48), Santa María Suamca - Terrenate Presidio
BURIAL Mission Los Santos Angeles de Guevavi (Defunct)
Father of :Col. Juan Bautista de Anza Bezerra Nieto Lord Governor of Nuevo Spain, July 1736 - December 19, 1788.

Explorer. Juan Bautista de Anza Sassoetta was a Spanish Basque, and an explorer of a great part of the Sonora state and the southwest region of the United States. At the age of nineteen, in 1712, he migrated to New Spain, going first to Culiacán, Sinaloa, where his mother had relatives already established. However, Anza did not stay there long, and was soon involved in silver mining in Álamos, Sonora. From there he became involved in the discovery and exploitation of two important silver mining camps, or boomtowns, between 1716 and 1720, at Aguaje southeast of present-day Hermosillo, Sonora and at Tetuachi, south of Arizpe. He bought other mining properties, such as the Real de San Jose de Basochuca, Sonora, east of Arizpe and by early 1721 he had become a lieutenant in the Sonora militia.

Shortly after that, on August 2, 1721, he joined the regular cavalry as an alférez, or second lieutenant, at the Janos Presidio, under Captain Antonio Bezerra Nieto. Soon after beginning his military career at Janos, about the year 1722, he married the Captain's daughter, Maria Rosa Bezerra Nieto, and quickly rose to the rank of first lieutenant. In November of 1726, he was promoted to captain and assigned to take the place of Captain Gregorio Álvarez Tuñón y Quirós at Fronteras, who had been at odds with the citizens of Sonora for years and had just been removed from office and ordered to Mexico City to stand trial for fraud and misuse of the king's resources. Anza quickly set about whipping the Caballería de las Fronteras (Cavalry of the Frontier) into shape and providing protection to the communities of Sonora from the Apaches. He assigned soldiers to the San Luis and upper Santa Cruz River Valleys in the Pimería Alta, and settlers began to move into the area. He, himself, established the Guevavi, San Mateo, Sicurisuta, and Sópori Ranches, the first livestock operations in what is today southern Arizona.

At the time of the fabulous silver discovery near the Arizona Ranch in 1736, he was not only the captain of the sole presidio in Sonora, but he was justicia mayor, or chief justice, of Sonora as well. Thus, it fell to him to decide what course to take in establishing legalities at the new site. Because of his impounding of all the silver while Mexico City made the determination of to whom it belonged, and because of his using the house of Bernardo de Urrea, his good friend and deputy chief justice, at the Arizona Ranch as a base of operations, he inadvertently elevated the name Arizona into prominence. Thus, he and his escribano, or scribe, Manuel José de Sosa, who wrote all the documents pertaining to the silver, were indirectly responsible for the forty-eighth state of the United States having the name Arizona. Anza continued as a soldier and statesman for the next few years, petitioning the viceroy for permission to discover and establish a route between Sonora and Alta California. Unfortunately for him, however, his dreams were cut short following a routine supply trip to Suamca, Guevavi, Tumacácori, and San Xavier del Bac. Returning home from that expedition on May 9, 1740, he evidently rode a little too far in front of his soldiers and was ambushed and killed by Apaches somewhere between Santa María Suamca and the ranch that would become the Terrenate Presidio. It would be left to the next generation of soldiers and his own son, Juan Bautista de Anza, of the same name to discover the route between Sonora and California.

Bio by: Ola K Ase

MARIA RAFAELA BEZERRA NIETO DE ANSSA

BIRTH	September 1700 in Janos, Chihuahua
DEATH	October 14, 1760, in Tubac, Sonora, Mexico. In present day Arizona.
BURIAL	Mission Los Santos Angeles de Guevavi (Defunct)

Beneath the steps leading up to the altar.
d/o Antonio Bezerra Nieto and Gregoria Catrina Gomez De Silva.
Antonio Bezerra Nieto was the most famous and successful cavalry commander of the Janos Presidio in northern Chihuahua.
Wife of Captain Juan Bautista de Anssa 1ST
Mother of Col. Juan Bautista de Anza Bezerra Nieto Lord Governor of Nuevo Spain.

Maria married Juan Bautista De (Anza) Ansaa 1st, Abt. 1722 in Janos, Chihuahua, Mexico, son of Antonio De Anza and Lucia De Sassoeta. He was Cavalry Captain in command of the Presidio of Fronteras, located some twenty miles south of Douglas, Arizona.

Children of Maria Rosa Bezerra Nietto and Juan Bautista De Anssa are:

1. Francisco Antonio De Ansa,
    b. January 17, 1724/25, Janos, Chihuahua, New Spain (Mexico)
    d. June 10, 1785, Santa Fe, New Mexico.
        buried at The Royal Presidio, Santa Fe, New Mexico

2. Maria Margarita de Anza,
    b. June 29, 1727, Janos, Chihuahua, Mexico.

3. Josefa Gregoria Juachina de Ansa,
    b. March 30, 1732, Fronteras, Sonara, Mexico.
    d. May 03, 1800, Villaro, Bizkaia, Spain.

4. **Juan Bautista De Anza**, (see bio)
    b. July 07, 1736, "Lord Governer General" Cuquiarachi, Sonora, Mexico.
    d. December 19, 1788, Arizpe, Sonora, Mexico.

MARIA RAFAELA BEZERRA NIETO DE ANSSA, was a "criolla," or American-born child of Spanish parents. She was born at the Presidio of Janos, sometime between 1695 and 1700, to Antonio Bezerra Nieto, the presidial captain, and Gregoria Catalina Gómez de Silva. she lived at one of the northernmost frontier outposts on the northern Spanish Frontier. It was subject to near continuous attacks and raids by marauding Apaches and other belligerent native tribes.

About 1722 she married a young widower, the newly recruited, chestnut haired cavalry soldier, whom her father had recently appointed "alférez," or second lieutenant of the Presidio, Juan Bautista de Anza. She immediately became stepmother to his two daughters, María Manuela and María Gertrudis.

Rosa and Juan's first recorded child, Francisco Antonio de Anza was born at Janos in January of 1725. As her husband progressed from alférez to full lieutenant in 1726, Rosa became pregnant with their second child. By the time little María Margarita was born, however, her husband had been appointed captain at Fronteras, or Santa Rosa de Corodéguachi as it was then known. It was after Margarita was born that Rosa moved to Fronteras to be with her husband.

At Fronteras, Rosa again had the distinction of living at the furthest northern outpost on the frontier. Living there with the constant danger of Apache attacks and her husband always off pursuing his duties as commander – as far south as Guaymas, as far east as present-day New Mexico, west to the Gulf of California and Tiburón Island, and continually north into the forbidding Chiricahuas, life was different than anything we can imagine today. It was while at Fronteras, living in the imposing captain's adobe house at the point of the presidio promintory, that the couples' last two children were born: Josefa Gregoria in 1732 at the Presidio, and Juan Bautista, the second, in 1736 at the nearby Opata mission of Cuquiárachi.

It was that same year of 1736 that enormous slabs of nearly pure silver were discovered southwest of present-day Nogales. Rosa's husband, as "justicia mayor" and military captain of Sonora rode over to the site to take control of what had become, practically overnight, a lawless free-for-all. After surveying the site and putting a military guard over it, he rode down the canyon to the ranch of his deputy, Bernardo de Urrea, a place called then and now, "Arizona." It was there that the now-famous silver documents were signed and dated. Eight or ten years prior to the discovery, however, Anza had established the Guevavi Ranch northwest of Nogales. Following in succession he had established the Sicurisuta Ranch, which was probably somewhere near present-day Peña Blanca Lake, and the Sópori Ranch.

But, in 1740, he was killed by Apaches between Santa María Suamca and Terrenate, somewhere near the present-day town of Santa Cruz Sonora, and Rosa was left to care for, not only their children, but the family's ranch and mine holdings. She would do it with resolve and determination and the true grit of a frontier lady.

Having to leave the captain's house at Fronteras, she moved her young family first to the family mine at Basochuca, Sonora. A few years later she and her eldest son, Francisco, and a newly acquired son-in-law, Manuel Tato, acquired the Divasadero Land Grant from the Romo de Vivar family and the Anzas moved there where the Santa Cruz River makes its sweeping turn to the south and flows back into what is today the United States. From the Divasadero she ran it and the other three previously mentioned ranches with the expertise of a college educated businesswoman, although she probably never attended a day of school in her life. No signature executed by her has ever been found, so she probably did not know how to read and write.

She also purchased the Santa Barbara Ranch between the Divasadero and Guevavi, making the family holdings into, not only the northernmost, but one of the largest ranching operations in the Pimería Alta. She hired numerous Yaqui, Pima and Opata vaqueros and maintained foremen on each of the properties. It would be impossible to calculate the number of families she hired to work on her ranches or in the family mines at Basochuca, Tetuachi, and Aguaje, further south in Sonora.

It was not until her youngest son was appointed captain of the Presidio of Tubac that she left the Divasadero. It was probably in January of 1760 that she took up residence with her soon to be famous on the frontier son, Juan Bautista de Anza – again at the captain's house, again at the northernmost and most dangerous outpost on all the frontier. Her trials at that settlement, however, were not to be long and drawn out. She died barely ten months later on October 4, 1760.

Her body was taken south to the Mission at Guevavi where this devout Catholic lady, who had attended church there regularly since 1744, was laid to rest beneath the steps leading up to the altar.

A magnificent lady of the Frontier, Rosa Bezerra Nieto.

Kino Missions:

Los Santos Angeles de Guevavi

NOTE: Ralph Wingfield, a local rancher, donated the ruins to the New Mexico Archaeological Conservancy which, in turn, donated it to the National Park Service. today has hundreds of descendants living in Sonora, Arizona, California, New Mexico, and other areas of the United States, Mexico, and Spain.

COL. JUAN BAUTISTA DE ANZA 2ND

BIRTH July 07, 1736, Cuquiarachi, Sonora, Mexico

DEATH December 19, 1788, Arizpe, Sonora, Mexico

BURIAL Templo de Nuestra Señora de la Asunción
Arizpe, Arizpe Municipality, Sonora, Mexico
at the altar of the Church

s/o Captain Juan Bautista de Anza/Anssa and Maria Rafaela Bezerra Nieto.

m.1761 Ana Maria Regina Perez Serrano de Anza, 1741-1800

Col. Juan Bautista de Anza Bezerra Nieto Lord Governor of Nuevo Spain was born July 1736 and died December 19, 1788. He was a Novo-Spanish explorer for the Spanish Empire.

Juan Bautista de Anza 2nd was born in Fronteras, Sonora (near Arizpe)(Arizona) into a military family on the northern frontier of New Spain. He was the son of Captain Juan Bautista de Anza/Anssa who was killed by Apaches and Maria Rafaela Bezerra Nieto.

Maria Rafaela Bezerra Nieto's father was Captain Antonio Bezerra Nieto, Soldado de Janos - Capitán de la compañia, married Marido de Gregoria Gómez de Silva. The Nieto family were major mine owners as well as connected to the Church.

In 1752 Juan Bautista de Anza 2nd enlisted in the army at the Presidio of Fronteras. Became captain by 1760. He married in 1761 the daughter of Spanish mine owner Perez de Serrano. They had no children. His military duties consisted of forays against hostile native Apache Indian's. He explored much of what is now Arizona.

In 1772 he proposed an expedition to Alta California (A dream of his father) to the Viceroy of New Spain. This was approved by the King of Spain.

Anza paid for the expedition and on January 8, 1774, with 3 padres, 20 soldiers, 11 servants, 35 mules, 65 cattle, and 140 horses he set forth from Tubac south of present day Tucson, Arizona. The expedition took a southern route along the Rio Altar (Sonora y Sinaloa, New Spain) then paralleled the modern Mexico/California border and crossed the Colorado River at its confluence with the Gila River in the domain of the Yuma tribe with which he established good relations.

He reached Mission San Gabriel Arcangel, (San Gabrial, Los Angeles County, California) near the California coast (70 miles) on March 22, 1774 and Monterey, California, Alta California's Capital April 19th.

He returned to Tubac (Arizona) by late May 1774. This expedition was closely watched by Viceroy and King and on October 2, 1774 he was promoted to the rank of lieutenant-colonel and ordered to lead a group of colonists to Alta California.

The expedition got under way in October 1775 and arrived at Mission San Gabriel in January 1776 the colonists having suffered greatly from the winter weather on route. He continued on to Monterey,

California with the colonists; then fulfilling his mission from the Viceroy he continued on with a small party exploring north and located the sites for the Presidio of San Francisco and Mission San Francisco de Asis in present day San Francisco, California on March 28, 1776, which was established later by José Joaquín Moraga. While returning to Monterey, Anza located the original sites for Mission Santa Clara de Asis and the town of San José de Guadalupe (modern day San Jose, CA), but again did not establish either settlement.

On his return from this successful expedition he journeyed to Mexico City with the chief of the Quechan (Yuma) tribe who requested the establishment of a mission. Shortly thereafter, on August 24, 1777, Anza was appointed Governor of the Province of New Mexico, including today's Arizona, New Mexico, California, Colorado etc.

Anza led a punitive expedition against the Comanche who had been repeatedly raiding Taos (New Mexico) in 1779. With his Ute and Apache allies and about 800 soldiers he went north through the San Luis Valley, entering the plains at what is now Manitou Springs, Colorado. He surprised a small force of Comanche near present day Colorado Springs. He found the main body of Comanche, returning from a raid on New Mexico, on Greenhorn Creek and inflicted a decisive defeat. Severely weakened, the Comanche ceased their raids and moved to the southeast into what is now Oklahoma and Texas.

In late 1779, Anza and his party found a route from Santa Fe to Sonora. His various local military expeditions against hostile tribes were successful, but the Yuma tribe which he had establish peace with rebelled and he fell out of favor with the military commander of the northern frontier, the frontier-general. In 1783 Anza lead a campaign against the Comanche on the eastern plains and by 1784 they were suing for peace. The last Comanche chiefs acceded and a formal treaty was concluded in 1786. This paved the way for traders and the development of the Comanchero trade.

Anza 2nd stayed on as governor of New Mexico until 1787 when he returned to Sonora. He was appointed commander of the Presidio of Tucson in 1788 but died before he could take office. Anza was buried in the Church of Nuestra Señora de la Asunción de Arispe. In 1963 he was disinterred and reburied in a marble mausoleum with the participation of delegations from the University of California and San Francisco.

Source: *Legacy*

Col. Juan Bautista de Anza is remembered in California being named for numerous towns, cities, parks, schools, buildings, streets.

TRIVIA:

Nogales High School boasts of the APACHE for a mascot. Anza Trails School in Sahuarita boasts of the "DONS" for their mascot. My nephew was in a high school band wearing dark costumes during a Green Valley parade in hot weather, my sister and I suffered for all the students while passing out cold water bottles. ("Don" is similar to using Mr and Mrs, or Senor and Senora. However "Don" and "Dona" are used to show respect before the person's first name, not used before the last name. It is also used when addressing Spanish senior citizens.)

VICTORIA CARRASCO DE ANZA

BIRTH   Unknown

DEATH   2 Oct 1763, San Luis Valley, Santa Cruz County.

BURIAL   <u>Mission Los Santos Angeles de Guevavi</u>, Santa Cruz County, Arizona
Misión San José de Tumacácori, Santa Cruz Church Records 2 de Octubre de 1763, murió en Buena Vista D. Victoria Carrasco, casada con Dn. Franco (Francisco) Anza, vecino de Tubac, recibidos los Ss. Sacramentos, se enterró en la Iglesia de Guevavi. Custodio Ximeno.

October 2, 1763, died in Buena Vista D. Victoria Carrasco, wife of Don Franco (Francisco) Anza, neighbor in Tubac, received holy Sacraments, was buried in the Church of Guevavi. Custodio Ximeno.

GREGORIA ALVAREZ BENEDICT CHAMBERLAIN

BIRTH   1844 Santa Ana, Hermosillo Municipality, Sonora, Mexico

DEATH   26 Apr 1884 (aged 39–40) Arizona

BURIAL   <u>Mission Los Santos Angeles de Guevavi</u>, Santa Cruz County, Arizona
Husbands:
1. Albert Case Benedict
2. Edward Atherton Chamberlain
She is buried in an unmarked grave at this old deserted and run down mission. All that is left is some adobe walls, that are badly deteriorated.

WILLIAM R. CHAMBERLAIN

BIRTH   11 Mar 1882, Santa Cruz County, Arizona

DEATH   21 Dec 1912 (aged 30) Nogales, Santa Cruz County, Arizona

BURIAL   <u>Mission Los Santos Angeles de Guevavi</u>, Santa Cruz County, Arizona
s/o Gregoria Alvarez Benedict Chamberlain

Photo by the Jones-Marcum Family

OTERO CEMETERY
Rio Rico, Arizona

Memorials for:

JOSEFINA BEJARANO
BIRTH	1906
DEATH	1908 (aged 1–2) Otero, Santa Cruz County, Arizona
BURIAL	Otero Cemetery,

RAMON BEJARANO
BIRTH	1913
DEATH	1913 (13 days) Otero, Santa Cruz County, Arizona
BURIAL	Otero Cemetery

Photo by Jones-Marcum Family

SALERO RANCH CEMETERY

Memorials for:

HORACE CHIPMAN GROSVENOR I
BIRTH	17 Apr 1820, Granville, Licking County, Ohio
DEATH	25 Apr 1861 (aged 41), Tubac, Santa Cruz County, Arizona
BURIAL	Salero Ranch Cemetery
	Superintendent of the Santa Rita Silver Mine. Was scalped by Apache Indians near the Santa Rita Silver Mine on the road to Tubac. Buried at the Hacienda at Santa Rita.

JAMES THOMAS McGREW
BIRTH	4 Mar 1925, Leitchfield, Grayson County, Kentucky
DEATH	14 Oct 1982 (aged 57), Santa Cruz County, Arizona
BURIAL	Salero Ranch Cemetery
	Cowboy and husband of Norma Jean McGrew.

Hello!
I am Thomas Eugene McGrew. My Father was James Thomas McGrew. He came west at a young age and cowboy'd. I was born in Prescott, AZ. He was murdered on a Ranch in the early 1980's. His father was John Robert McGrew. His father was Thomas McGrew (I do not know for certain if it was his first name.) All lived in Grayson County Kentucky, my father was born near Leitchfield -Grayson County, Kentucky. I do not know for certain if my grandfather/great grandfather were.

Should anyone care to comment on a probable line of descent; I would welcome the information. I must warn you that I do not know much more and I am not likely to go much deeper than reading/thanking you for your response.

As always,
Tom/ McGrew Family Line of Descent - Genealogy.com

NORMA EUGENE McDONALD McGREW

BIRTH	4 Jul 1926, Springfield, Sangamon County, Illinois
DEATH	2 Jun 1994 (aged 67), Santa Cruz County, Arizona
BURIAL	Salero Ranch Cemetery, Tubac, Santa Cruz County, Arizona
	Wife of cowboy James T. McGrew.

BY MARINE 69-71 - OWN WORK, CC BY-SA 4.0,
HTTPS://COMMONS.WIKIMEDIA.ORG/W/INDEX.PHP?CURID=94341728

TELLOS-RAMOS-ESPINOSA-LOPEZ BURIAL SITE
Villa Campestre Calabasas, Santa Cruz County, Arizona

Arizona citizen., August 31, 1872

Four Men Murdered by Apaches above Calabasas. We are indebted to Andres Montiel of Santa Cruz, for the following particulars of the death of four more victims by the Apaches. Their names are Ysidoro Telles, Manuel Ramos, Felipe Espinosa and Martin Lopez.

They had been at work for Thomas Gardner in Sonoita valley, and were on their way to Santa Cruz, where their families live. They were attacked about ten miles above Calabasas on the Santa Cruz river, evidently by Apaches in ambush, and all instantly killed; they were stripped of all their clothing and left where killed. Mr. Montiel assisted in burying them at the place where they were murdered.

A GRAVE ON THE SANTA CRUZ ROAD/ SKETCH BY RAPHAEL PUMPELLY

TUBAC CEMETERY

The 2-acre graveyard in the town, which began under Spanish rule in the 1700's, has the oldest legible headstone dating to 1893. Only people with blood relatives already buried in the cemetery are eligible to be buried there. There are 681 internments not listed in this writing.

If interested, please read online about individual burials:

Tubac Cemetery in Tubac, Arizona - Find A Grave Cemetery

Source: Old Tubac cemetery draws visitors tracing their roots.
By Brenna Goth – Jul. 20, 2012, Green Valley News

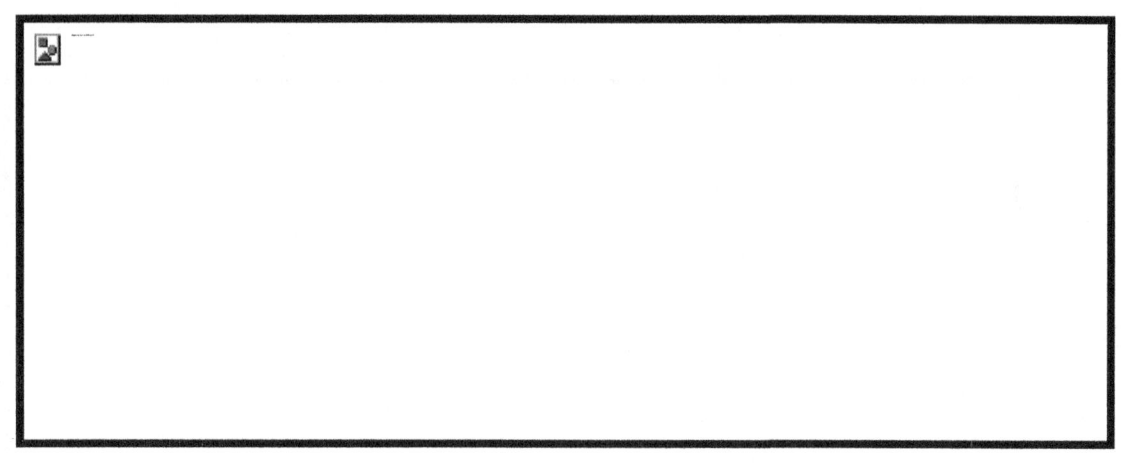

Mission San José de Tumacácori, profile of the church and the granary.
Photo by Ammodramus. Wikimedia Commons.

SAINT JOSEPHS CEMETERY
Tumacacori, Arizona

Originally located on the east side of the Santa Cruz River, the mission moved, following the Pima Revolt in 1751, to its present location on the west side of the river. The mission was then rechristened San José de Tumacácori. By 1757, the community had built a small adobe church. Tumacácori National Historical Park, a unit of the National Park System is located 45 miles south of Tucson, AZ off EXIT 29 on I-19.

Memorials for:

FRANCISCA M ALDAY
BIRTH	1910
DEATH	1969
BURIAL	Saint Joseph's Cemetery

REFUGIO V ALDAY
BIRTH	5 Jun 1915
DEATH	4 Apr 1958 (aged 42)
BURIAL	Saint Joseph's Cemetery

DELORES M ALEGRIA
BIRTH	1885
DEATH	1963 (aged 77–78)
BURIAL	Saint Joseph's Cemetery

ISABEL T ALEGRIA
BIRTH	1898
DEATH	1993
BURIAL	Saint Joseph's Cemetery

JAUNITA T ALEGRIA
BIRTH	1915
DEATH	1916 (aged 0–1)
BURIAL	Tumacacori Mission Cemetery

MANUEL O ALEGRIA
BIRTH	1897
DEATH	6 Feb 1977, AGE 80
BURIAL	Saint Joseph's Cemetery

MARIA A O DE ALEGRIA
BIRTH	unknown
DEATH	1946
BURIAL	Saint Joseph's Cemetery

PADRO MICHAEL ALEGRIA, SR
BIRTH	1918
DEATH	1971
BURIAL	Saint Joseph's Cemetery

PAUL T ALEGRIA
BIRTH	October 14, 1926
DEATH	January 5, 2005
BURIAL	Saint Joseph's Cemetery

RAMONA L ALEGRIA
BIRTH	2 Jan 1921
DEATH	16 Feb 2006 (aged 85)
BURIAL	Saint Joseph's Cemetery

ROMULO OCANA ALEGRIA
BIRTH	17 Feb 1889, **Caborca, Sonora**
DEATH	11 Jul 1965 (aged 76), Nogales, Santa Cruz County, Arizona
BURIAL	Saint Joseph's Cemetery

Parents were Hipolito Alegria, born 1848 in **Sahuarita,** Died **6 May 1924** in **Tumacacori,** and Maria Mercedes Ocana, born 1862 in Los Angeles, California.

MARGARITA ALVEREZ
BIRTH	1918
DEATH	2001
BURIAL	Saint Joseph's Cemetery,

ANGELA CHAVARRIA
BIRTH	1915
DEATH	1986 (aged 70–71)
BURIAL	Saint Joseph's Cemetery

JOAQUIN CHAVARRIA
BIRTH	1904
DEATH	1953
BURIAL	Saint Joseph's Cemetery

JUAN G CHAVARRIA
BIRTH	25 Jun 1918
DEATH	23 Jun 2001 (aged 82)
BURIAL	Saint Joseph's Cemetery

MANUEL G CHAVARRIA
BIRTH	unknown
DEATH	unknown
BURIAL	Saint Joseph's Cemetery

TIBURCIA CHAVARRIA
BIRTH	1914
DEATH	1996
BURIAL	Saint Joseph's Cemetery

IGNACIO FLORES
BIRTH 1875
DEATH 1965
BURIAL Saint Joseph's Cemetery

MANUEL FLORES
BIRTH 1908
DEATH 1930
BURIAL Saint Joseph's Cemetery

MARTHA E KANE
BIRTH 1961
DEATH 1965 AGE 4
BURIAL Saint Joseph's Cemetery

JOSEPH KING
BIRTH 29 Feb 1828, Azores Region, Portugal
DEATH 8 Dec 1912 (aged 84), Santa Cruz County, Arizona
BURIAL Saint Joseph's Cemetery
Husband of Trinidad Ramirez King of Sonora Mexico.
A native of Portugal but had been long an American citizen. When he came to the Santa Cruz region he located upon the land that has been his home since that time, and ever since has followed continuously farming as a calling. Manuel, Jose and Santiago King, all of whom lived with him on the home place.

TRINIDAD RAMIREZ KING
BIRTH Sep 1860, Sonora, Mexico
DEATH 3 Jun 1925 (aged 64) Nogales, Santa Cruz County, Arizona
BURIAL Saint Joseph's Cemetery
d/o: Manuel Ramirez and Concepcion Urias Ramirez both of Sonora Mexico

MARGARITA ANDRADE KING
BIRTH 1874
DEATH 1914
BURIAL Saint Joseph's Cemetery

ERNESTINE R. MARTINEZ
BIRTH	1904
DEATH	1953 (aged 48–49)
BURIAL	Saint Joseph's Cemetery

MANUEL C. MARTINEZ
BIRTH	1906
DEATH	1953
BURIAL	Saint Joseph's Cemetery

RITA MARTINEZ MEJIAS
BIRTH	1889
DEATH	1961
BURIAL	Saint Joseph's Cemetery

CATALINA / CATARINA B MENDEZ
BIRTH	unknown
DEATH	unknown
BURIAL	Saint Joseph's Cemetery (see below)

DON CARMEN MENDEZ
BIRTH	1848 Mexico
DEATH	unknown
BURIAL	Saint Joseph's Cemetery (see below)

In **1899 Carmen Mendez** filed homestead application to a portion of the grant which included the old Tumacacori mission church and grounds. By this time there were numerous homesteaders in the district. On June 30, **1908**, Mendez relinquished to the federal government his rights to 10 acres of this, which included the mission and most of the site of the abandoned Indian village. By this time, a great many people from various parts of the country were taking an interest in the historic old church, and there was much desire that it be set aside and protected against the elements and vandalism.

On September 15, **1908**, President Theodore Roosevelt proclaimed the Mendez relinquishment as Tumacacori National Monument. However, it developed that title to the lands was to be complicated by a historic controversy over what became known as Baca Float No. 3. (Long story shorten. "In **1917** homesteaders on the Float were ordered evicted.")

Source: Tumacacori's Yesterdays (And Dust to Dust) (nps.gov)

In **2005**, the remains of the Mendez Homestead were excavated and the mission's adobe firing kiln and the remains of a possible Cavalry camp were located. Artifacts include a metal sword scabbard, bullets, metal artifacts and charred Pima corn that may have been used to feed Cavalry horses. The scabbard has been dated to the 1840s.

Source: NPS Archeology Program: Research in the Parks

Another of the dispossessed was Carmen Mendez. Mendez moved his young family to Mission Tumacácori in **1884** when he was thirty-six years old. Fashioning bricks from local mud, or scavenging them from the mission's convento, he built a small adobe home for his eighteen-year-old wife Catarina and their baby, Ramón. A stone's throw to the north, the ruins of the mission church slowly crumbled into desert soil.

Mendez was a citizen of Mexico when he arrived, but the international border meant little to anyone in the region except lawyers and politicians then. While Catarina gave birth to a baby every two years, Mendez cleared thirty acres of land, sunk a well, dug irrigation ditches, and planted crops except for two or three years of "drouth." In **1896**, he filed a Declaration of Intention to become a citizen of the United States. In **1899**, he applied for a homestead of 160 acres after the U.S. Supreme Court wiped the Tumacácori land grant off the map. Nine years later, Mendez submitted his final proof. He and four witnesses testified to the improvements he had made and to his continuous occupation of the land.

That same year, Mendez deeded ten acres of his homestead to the United States. Those ten acres embraced the heart of Mission Tumacácori, which was being gutted by treasure hunters and defaced by vandals who scrawled their names on its walls and knocked off pieces of interior frescos for souvenirs. The Arizona Pioneers' Historical Society appealed to the newly created Forest Service to save the site. The Forest Service conducted a survey and Secretary of Agriculture James Wilson attested to its historical importance. On September 15, **1908**, under the provisions of the fledgling American Antiquities Act, President Theodore Roosevelt proclaimed Mission Tumacácori a National Monument (National Park Service 1977).

Then the ratification of Baca Float No. 3 erased both Mendez's homestead and the monument. Mendez lost his land and had to move on like most of the other homesteaders, but James Bouldin and his wife deeded ten acres of Mission Tumacácori back to the United States in 1917. After control passed from the Forest Service to the newly created National Park Service, Frank Pinkley, the superintendent of Casa Grande National Monument, wrested $400 from the government to begin stabilizing the church. That stabilization proceeded in fits and starts, cement patchwork here, adobe patchwork there. Tumacácori National Monument was a slowly emerging vision, not-a-master plan.

Source: Tumacacori NHP:Historic Resource Study (Chapter 8) (nps.gov)

DONA TIBURCIA MENDEZ
BIRTH   1800
DEATH   1915 Tumacacori, Santa Cruz County, Arizona
BURIAL   Saint Joseph's Cemetery

ROSALIA V MERCHANT
BIRTH   1909
DEATH   1985 Tumacacori, Santa Cruz County, Arizona
BURIAL   Saint Joseph's Cemetery

DAVID MONTOYA
BIRTH   1972
DEATH   1973 Tumacacori, Santa Cruz County, Arizona
BURIAL   Saint Joseph's Cemetery

ALEXANDER MICHAEL PEACHEY
BIRTH   July 17,1913
DEATH   Sep. 20,1998 Tumacacori, Santa Cruz County, Arizona
BURIAL   Saint Joseph's Cemetery

ALICE T PEACHEY
BIRTH   1914
DEATH   2007 Tumacacori, Santa Cruz County, Arizona
BURIAL   Saint Joseph's Cemetery

DON RAMON RAMIREZ
BIRTH   unknown
DEATH   Unknown Tumacacori, Santa Cruz County, Arizona
BURIAL   Saint Joseph's Cemetery

KATITA TRUJILLO
BIRTH   1960 Santa Cruz County, Arizona
DEATH   1961 Tumacacori, Santa Cruz County, Arizona
BURIAL   Saint Joseph's Cemetery

LUZ M VALENZUELA
BIRTH	unknown
DEATH	Unknown Tumacacori, Santa Cruz County, Arizona
BURIAL	Saint Joseph's Cemetery

CARLOS VEGA
BIRTH	11 Feb 1948
DEATH	17 Jul 1948 (aged 5 months)
BURIAL	Saint Joseph's Cemetery and Tubac Cemetery
	Carlos is listed in two cemeteries.

CARMEN H VEGA
BIRTH	1915
DEATH	1995 Tumacacori, Santa Cruz County, Arizona
BURIAL	Saint Joseph's Cemetery

IRMA VEGA
BIRTH	1974
DEATH	1989 Tumacacori, Santa Cruz County, Arizona
BURIAL	Saint Joseph's Cemetery

JOSE C VEGA
BIRTH	1943
DEATH	2000 Tumacacori, Santa Cruz County, Arizona
BURIAL	Saint Joseph's Cemetery

RAFAELA M VEGA
BIRTH	1891
DEATH	1971 Tumacacori, Santa Cruz County, Arizona
BURIAL	Saint Joseph's Cemetery

RAMON ALEGREA VEGA
BIRTH	1939
DEATH	1989 Tumacacori, Santa Cruz County, Arizona
BURIAL	Saint Joseph's Cemetery

RAMON M VEGA

BIRTH	3 Jul 1911
DEATH	20 Jan 1968 (aged 56) Tumacacori, Santa Cruz County, Arizona
BURIAL	Saint Joseph's Cemetery

RUBEN M VEGA

BIRTH	1966
DEATH	1989 Tumacacori, Santa Cruz County, Arizona
BURIAL	Saint Joseph's Cemetery

SALLY VEGA

BIRTH	unknown
DEATH	1973 Tumacacori, Santa Cruz County, Arizona
BURIAL	Saint Joseph's Cemetery

TUMACACORI MISSION CEMETERY

This cemetery was in use during the early **1800s**, when the community was under the management of Franciscan friars. The first burial recorded here was by Father Ramon Líberos on October 1, 1822.

After the last residents left the mission in **1848**, travelers used the cemetery as a holding pen for horses and cattle. Livestock and treasure hunters disturbed the land, scattering any evidence of mission-era graves. The graves that you see today probably date to the late 1800s through the early 1900s. The last burial, of little Juanita Alegria in **1916**, is marked by a small monument. The redwood cross between the mortuary chapel and the church, marked "Soto," was placed by the National Park Service in **1980** after members of the Soto family told park staff that they had buried family members there. Records kept by mission priests tell us that at least 680 people are buried at Tumacácori. The majority of these burials are under the floor of the Jesuit-era church and in its cemetery.

Source: www.nps.gov/tuma/learn/historyculture/cemetery.htm

Memorials for:

CASTULA ALEGRIA
BIRTH	3 Dec 1925, Tumacacori, Santa Cruz County, Arizona
DEATH	12 Dec 1925 (aged 9 days), Tubac, Santa Cruz County, Arizona
BURIAL	Tumacacori Mission Cemetery
	d/o Tomas Alegria of Sonora, Mexico and Dolores Mendez of Tumacacori

JUANITA T ALEGRIA
BIRTH	1915
DEATH	1916 (aged 0–1)
BURIAL	Tumacacori Mission Cemetery

LUIS GUILLEN
BIRTH	28 Apr 1887, Mexico
DEATH	12 Apr 1961 (aged 73), Tumacacori, Santa Cruz County, Arizona
BURIAL	Tumacacori Mission Cemetery
	Husband of Manuela Occupation: Ranch Laborer

JUAN "Juanito" MARTINEZ
BIRTH	25 Aug 1946, Tumacacori, Santa Cruz County, Arizona
DEATH	21 Apr 1948 (aged 1), Tumacacori, Santa Cruz County, Arizona
BURIAL	April 22, 1948, Tumacacori Mission Cemetery
	s/o Benigno Martinez, of Mexico and Leonor Cardenas, of Tumacacori. COD: infantile convulsions, rickets.

DOMINGO ALEGRIA
BIRTH	25 Mar 1928, Tumacacori, Santa Cruz County, Arizona
DEATH	25 Mar 1928, Tubac, Santa Cruz County, Arizona
BURIAL	Tumacacori Mission Cemetery
	s/o Tomas Alegria, of Santana, Sonora, Mexico and Dolores Mendez, of Tumacacori, Arizona. COD: Child's Birth.

LORETO AMEZQUITA
BIRTH	1735
DEATH	7 Feb 1780 (aged 44–45)
BURIAL	Tumacacori Mission Cemetery

Mission records reveal that Trooper Loreto Amezquita died on 7 February 1780, apparently while on detached guard duty at Tubac. Amezquita left a widow, María Phelipa de León.

Friar Pedro Antonio de Arriquibar presided over his burial in the cemetery of Tumacacori Mission the following day. Spanish Colonial Tucson

GREGORIO CHAVARRIA
BIRTH	1908, Arizona
DEATH	10 Nov 1949 (aged 40–41), Patagonia, Santa Cruz County, Arizona
BURIAL	Tumacacori Mission Cemetery

Gregorio Chavarria lived in Patagonia, Arizona
s/o Manuel Chavarria Mexico and Carmen Guereno New Mexico
He was a miner and got blown up by dynamite explosion....he worked in the Flux mine.   Gregorio was 41 years old and married.

RAMON CHAVARRIA
BIRTH	12 Aug 1938, Tubac, Santa Cruz County, Arizona
DEATH	12 Feb 1939 (aged 6 months), Tubac, Santa Cruz County, Arizona
BURIAL	February 13, 1939 Tumacacori Mission Cemetery

s/o Joaquin Chavarria, of Huevavi, Arizona and Angelita Madril, of Tumacacori, Arizona.   COD: fever.

CARLOS FIGUEROA
BIRTH	17 Jun 1913
DEATH	31 Oct 1913 (aged 4 months)
BURIAL	Tumacacori Mission Cemetery,

s/o Carlos Figueroa of Rayon, Sonora, Mexico and Rita Acuna of Tubac, Arizona. COD: "unknown"

MIKE C. JAUREGUI
BIRTH	25 Mar 1947, Tumacacori, Santa Cruz County, Arizona
DEATH	2 Jan 1948 (aged 9 months) Tumacacori, Santa Cruz County, Arizona
BURIAL	Tumacacori Mission Cemetery

s/o Felipe C. Jauregui, (Basque name) born in Arizona and Angel Alegria, born Tumacacori, Arizona. COD: malnutrition.

ANGEL MACASAN

BIRTH	18 Nov 1934, Tumacacori, Santa Cruz County, Arizona
DEATH	27 Dec 1934 (aged 1 month) Nogales, Santa Cruz County, Arizona
BURIAL	December 27, 1934, Tumacacori Mission Cemetery

s/o Conrado Moccasin, born Magdalina, Sonora, Mexico and Isabel Tapia, born Calabasas, Arizona

ENCARNACION HORANTEZ

BIRTH	c. 1902, La Paz Municipality, Baja California Sur, Mexico
DEATH	April 29, 1930, Tubac, Santa Cruz County, Arizona
BURIAL	April 30, 1930, Tumacacori Mission Cemetery

s/o Aquiles Horantez, born La Paz, Lower California and Lucia de Horantez, born La Paz Lower California. Husband of Gimona ? de Horantez. Age 60 years.
COD: Paralysis and complication.

JACK POWERS (JOHN A. POWERS)

BIRTH	1827, Ireland
DEATH	26 Oct 1860 (aged 32–33), murdered at his ranch at Calabasas, Arizona
BURIAL	Tumacacori Mission Cemetery, Tumacacori, Santa Cruz County, Arizona

Outlaw, Folk Figure. Jack Powers, whose real name was John A. Power, was an Irish-born migrant taken to New York as a child, a New York volunteer soldier in the Mexican American War, serving in the garrison of Santa Barbara, California. During the California Gold Rush, he was a well-known professional gambler and a famed horseman, in the gold camps, San Francisco, Santa Barbara and Los Angeles. He had two brushes with the law. Once being tried as a member of 'The Hounds,' in San Francisco in 1849, and once in a dispute over land ownership of a ranch in Santa Barbara County in 1853.

In 1856, at Santa Barbara, Powers had protected a fugitive from the vigilantes of San Francisco and helped him to escape. After his role was revealed the following year, he had difficulties with the vigilantes at Los Angeles, who accused him of being the leader of a criminal gang there.

Long known for his skills as a horseman, on May 2, 1858, his skills were demonstrated in a record-breaking 150-mile time over distance race. Soon after this race, he was accused by San Luis Obispo vigilantes of complicity in the 1857 murder of two men, and of being the head of the bandit gang that plagued the southern central coastal region of California, along the El Camino Real with robberies and murders in San Luis Obispo County and Santa Barbara County between 1853 and 1858. This gang was later named the 'Jack Powers Gang' in 1883, by Jesse D. Mason in his History of Santa Barbara County California.

Escaping the vigilantes, by fleeing to Sonora, Powers attempted to return to California in 1860, but was murdered and robbed by his vaqueros at Calabasas just inside Arizona Territory.

Bio by: Ola K Ase

(Many tales in California, Mexico and New Mexico Territory about Powers.)

Unknown SOTO
BIRTH	unknown
DEATH	unknown
BURIAL	Tumacacori Mission Cemetery

AHBRAM TRUJILLO
BIRTH	2 Oct 1904, Calabasas, Santa Cruz County, Arizona
DEATH	11 Aug 1928 (aged 23), Nogales, Santa Cruz County, Arizona
BURIAL	August 13, 1928. Tumacacori Mission Cemetery

s/o: Jose Juan Trujillo, of Ures, Sonora, Mexico and Juana Alton, of Ures, Sonora, Mexico. His residence: Tumacacori, Santa Cruz, Arizona.
Occupation: rancher, cattle grower.
COD: gangrenous appendix.
The Informant for the Certificate was Tirso Trujillo of Tumacacori, Arizona

WHITEHOUSE GRAVESITE MADERA CANYON

Madera Canyon was originally called White House Canyon after the adobe structure said to have been built by a sheep man named Walden in the late 1870s or early 1880s. 1879 records report 78,500 sheep in Pima County, by 1894 there were 1,620. The Santa Rita Mountains were noted for sheep raising. 1882, the White House was being used by Theodore Welisch as a vacation retreat for his family to escape the summer heat. Welisch owned the White House Mercantile Company in Tucson.

MORALES FAMILY CEMETERY

About 1909, the house had been expanded to three rooms and was occupied by Alcario Morales and his family. Morales, a Mayo Indian from Hermosillo, Sonora, Mexico kept burros, mules and horses, made and sold cheese, the family also sold fruit and small trees from an orchard nearby. The White House was abandoned in 1940 upon the death of Alcario Morales at the age of 90. The author's son found a mature rosemary bush near the campground in 2011, we wondered how it got there.

Summarized from **The Nature of Madera Canyon** by Douglas Moore.

Memorials for:

BENITA ARMENTA MORALES

BIRTH	1887
DEATH	1921 (aged 33–34) Pima County, Arizona
BURIAL	Morales Family Cemetery, Madera Canyon, Pima County, Arizona

Married 1911 to Alcario Morales in Tucson, AZ Courthouse
COD: Died in childbirth.

MANUEL A MORALES

BIRTH	1921 Madera Canyon, Pima County, Arizona
DEATH	1921 (aged less-than 1 year) Madera Canyon
BURIAL	Morales Family Cemetery, Madera Canyon, Pima County, Arizona

Alarcio Morales, husband of Benita Armenta Morales and son of Florencio and Ramona Siqueiros Morales, born June 1845 in Hermosillo, Sonora, Mexico died Aug 9, 1941, and is buried in Tucson. The eldest son, Florencio Armenta Morales born in 1919 and died in 2011 is buried in Tucson at Evergreen Memorial Park.

CONCLUSION

May there never be a conclusion to this remarkable history; more will be unearthed and studied to expand knowledge of the Santa Cruz Valley here in Arizona. Many books have been written about the same pioneer people and the same events, copy of a copy, of a copy. May this writing fill in current knowledge with texture and rhythm.

Along the dusty path of researching THE ORPHANED ARIZONA STATE Rt 89, I was 'way laid' by the things I learned, even mentally held 'hostage' by names and events. One small booklet about geology, soil subsistence and how it would affect residents of Green Valley was composed; ONCE THERE WAS A GREEN VALLEY 2016.

When researching another local location and not finding the usual: WHO, WHAT, WHEN or WHY raised curiosity. These questions are primary to writing as time and place is to Law. It seemed that the WHERE was conclusive, but it proved to be just a "cover" that was exciting to tease out. People from the East went West for gold, they were disillusioned and sought another way to get rich. Young men got caught up in questionable circumstances with lawless men. How would anyone have a clue about young men gone wrong unless they wrote about their adventures in their retirement years. Why was someone's name removed from documents? Was this a cover up or a slip up? Has the mystery been solved? How will this news affect descendants in later generations?

Time has finally arrived to put this writing 'to bed' and to wake up a 'sleeping dog'. The SONOITA MURDERS has been gnawing at my sleep at night and is begging for attention. To where this information leads its reader, there may never be a conclusion to the adventures of the Santa Cruz Valley.

INDEX

A
Aguirre, Pedro   42
Amado, Antonio Ferrer   101
Amadoville   41
Anza   11, 57, 76, 174-180
Apache   3, 30, 50, 61, 63, 70, 75, 93,
Arivaca   40-44, 62, 99
Arizona State Museum   62, 129, 130

B
Benedict, Albert C   79, 83
Brevoort, Elias   44, 85-88
Brown, James Kilroy   15, 89-90
Browne, John Ross   44, 45, 126
Burials / Funeraries   131
Bull, James B   23, 90
Butterfield Stage   11, 50

C
Calabasas   12, 27, 44, 52, 59, 60, 68, 70, 79, 84, 113, 117, 197
Camp Continental   25
Camps and Fortifications   58
Canada   3
Canoa   39, 40, 91, 95, 99, 127
Carmen   106-109
Cemeteries   131, 133
Central Arizona Project / CAP   9, 21
Chavez Siding Road   49
Continental   2, 21, 25-27, 37, 90-92
Coyote   53, 55
Crook, George General   65-66

D
Davis Monthan Air Field   17
Duval Mine Road   22, 33, 131

E
Empire Mountains   11, 19, 138

F
Felix   12
FICO   21-22
Forts   58
Franciscan   57, 58, 194

G
Gadsden Purchase   1, 12, 27, 30, 45, 59, 60
Geronimo, "Goyahkla"   63-66, 102
Granger, Stewart   118-119
Green Valley   7, 9, 21-27, 32-34, 39-39
Green Valley Recreation / GVR   38
Grosvenor, H C   117, 182

H
Hacienda del Santa Rita   117
Hartt, William A   23
Heliograph Stations   63
Helvetia   19-20
Hohokam, Ancient Ones   2, 14, 29, 34
Hopkins, Gilbert A   36, 117

I
Isaacson, Jacob   67-68, 72-73

J

Jeffords, Thomas Jefferson   19, 55, 56

Jesuit   8, 56-58, 75, 103, 195

Josephine Peak   36, 157

K

Kitchen, Peter   41, 67, 83, 121-125

Kinsley, Ortho   42

Kino   8, 11, 56, 75-76

L

La Posada   28-29

Los Reales   131-134

M

Madera Canyon   27, 31, 62, 92, 198

Malaria   27, 59, 62, 119, 156

Maps   4, 68, 76

Martinez Hill   9, 77

Mason, Camp, Fort   59, 60-62

McCleary, William B   36

McGrew, James Thomas   182-183

McKee   60

MGM   46

Mileage   4

Missions   10, 72, 75, 177

Mission Road   22, 33

Mowry, Sylvester   45, 88, 112

N

National Park Service / NPS   58-59, 177, 191, 194

Nequilla Mine   132

New Spain   1, 174-178

Nogales   67-72

O

Old Nogales Highway   4, 10, 13, 25-29, 42, 50,

One Stop   15-16

Otero   45, 77, 99, 102-105, 113, 119, 181

P

Pajarito Ranch / Shankle   48

Paramount   46

Peck Canyon   52-54

Pena Blanca Lake   53

Pennington   156-159

Pete Mountain   36

Pima people   2, 14

Pima Mine Road   10-11, 14

Potrero Ranch   12, 41, 67, 122-125

Pumpelly, Raphael   99, 117, 128, 184

Q

Quail Creek, Resort   24-25, 92

Queen Wilhelmina   21, 27

Guayule plantation   21, 26-27

R

Railroad   1, 11-15, 27, 40-44, 59, 67, 69, 79, 88, 92, 96, 103, 112-116, 125, 142

Reventon   60, 62, 86, 97-98

Rice, Cyrus S   78-79

Roods / Rhoades, William B   32, 93-95

Ronstadt   45-46

Rosemont   29, 36

Rubber Company   27, 91

S

Saguaro 18, 78, 90, 132

Sahuarita / Sahuarito 7-19, 21-23, 28, 78-85, 89-91, 180

Sahuarita Air Force Range 17

San Xavier del Bac 8, 76-78, 113, 158, 176

Santa Cruz River 7, 9, 14, 27, 43, 55, 60, 75, 119, 131, 184

Santa Rita Experimental Range, SRER 30

Shankle, Clarence E. "Dutch" 48

Smuggling 52

Sopori 40, 44-45, 155-159, 161

Sykes, Col. Charles Patterson 67-70, 110-117

T

Tarbox, Edwin 96

Texas 1, 59, 78, 159, 179

Tohono O'odhom 2, 8, 10, 14, 30, 58, 77, 99-100, 134

Trails 32, 52, 179

Treaty 1, 77, 179

Treaty of Guadalupe de Hidalgo 1, 59

Trujillo, 50, 107

Tubac 9, 41, 58, 64, 76-77, 95, 107, 177-178, 185

Tucson – Nogales Railroad 12

Tumacacori 49-50, 56, 61, 75, 77, 105-108-120, 195-198

Tunnels 55

Twin Buttes 15, 79, 90, 116, 131, 147

U

Union Pacific 11, 69

W

Walden, R. Keith 21-22

Wars,
  Cold 17
  Civil War 58-59, 85, 110
  Mexican War 122-125
  War, Revolutionary, 1812 156

Wayne, John 50, 118

Whipple Observatory 31

Wrightson 27, 31, 36, 117

Y

Yaqui 3, 8, 30, 67, 177, 208

Yerba Buena Ranch 118-119

Z

Zepeda, Carmen Celaya 106-109

CEMETARIES / FUNARIES

Aguilar Ranch Cemetery 137

Amado Cemetery 160

Guevavi, Mission 174- 177

Los Reales Cemetery 136

Helvetia Cemetery 138

Morales Family Cemetery 199

Otero Cemetery 181

Saint Joseph's Cemetery 186

Salero Ranch Cemetery 182

Sopori Ranch Cemetery 155

Tellos-Ramos-Espinosa-Lopez Burial Site   184
Tubac Cemetery   185
Tumacacori Mission Cemetery   194
Twin Buttes Cemetery   142
Whitehouse Gravesite Madera Canyon   198

BURIALS BY NAME

A
Acosta   162
Acuna   150, 152-153, 195
Aguilar   137, 145, 152
Ahumada   161-163, 169
Alday   186
Alegria   186-188, 195, 186
Altamira   143
Altamirano   131, 134
Alverez   188
Arguelles, Francisco, Chico   143
Armijo, Rosalina   143

B
Beltran / Veltran   154
Bejarano   144, 181
Bianchetti, Bert   144
Bonilla, Artemisa   144
Borquez   144
Bracamonte   138
Burrola, Nasario   144

C
Cabrera   144
Cardenas   145, 195
Carbajal   138

Castillo, Francisco Servantes   145
Castro   134, 145, 153, 165, 171
Chacon,   144
Chamberlain   180
Chance   163-164
Chavarria   188, 196, 199
Chavez, Lito   145
"Chico Pancho"   147
"Chu"   148
Cont / Conte, JB   159
Croll, John Brissot   156, 159
Contreras   134
Cortez   137, 164

D
Diaz   137, 151
Donahue   138
Duarte   147

E
"El Diablito"   153
Espinosa   184
Estrada, Rafael   146
Escalante   134, 138
Eulalia   155

F
Felix   137-138, 140, 168
Figueroa   145, 161, 194, 196
Flores   189
Florez   139
Frederico   134-136
Franco   139
Fuentes   147

G

Gamboa	164
Gandy	139
Garcia	138, 146, 149, 154
Garrison	139
Gastelo	141
Gonzales	165
Granillo, Maria Trejo	136
Gray	139
Grijalva, Jose Ramon	147
Grosvenor	182
Guillen	195

H

Horantez	197

J

Jauregui	196
Juarez	165
Johnson	147

K

Kane	189
King	189

L

Lauterio, Juan	147
Lopez	137-140, 147, 184, 141
Luna	161, 166

M

Macasan	197
Maldonado	135, 137
Martinez	104, 139-140, 144-145, 149, 166-168, 190, 194-195
Mascarenas	166
McGrew	182-183
Mejias	190
Mendez	148, 190-192, 195
Mendibles	148
Mendoza	149-141
Merchant	192
Montano,	109, 149
Montoya	192
Morales	154, 199
Moreno	161, 166, 167

N

Nevarro/ Navarro	140
Noriega, Jose	149
Nunez	147, 150-152

O

Ochoa	167
Olivas	132, 134, 138, 140, 150-151
Otero	104

P

Padilla	151
Palomares	167
Parker	143, 151, 153
Peachey	192
Pennington	156-159
Powers	197
Preciado	167-168
Proctor	161, 169

Q

Quiroz, Carmen Q. Contreras	134

R

Ramirez	135, 189, 192
Ramos	184
Revello	143, 153
Ribera/Rivera	169

Robles	169	Verdusco	167, 172
Rodda	140	Vidal	146, 154
Rodriquez	164	Villa	173
Romero	135, 137-139, 147	Villegas, Martina	137
Ruelas	140	Vindola, (Vindiola) Cruz Rubio	55
Ruiz	140-141		

Y

Yanez, Rosendo	155
Yubeta, Jesus Y. Sanchez	152

S

Salcido	152
Samms	143, 152
Sanchez	135, 141, 152, 172
Sandoval	170
Sanders	153, 145
Santa Cruz	138
Sawyer	141
Servantes,	145
Siliceo, infant of Henry Duarte	153
Soto	136, 146, 198
Stinnett	143, 151, 153
Suares	153

T

Tellos	184
Torres	135, 139
Trejo	135-136
Trujillo	192, 198

V

Valencia	141
Valenzuela	136, 154, 161, 163-164, 168-169
Valdez	171
Varela	171
Vasques	171
Vega	137, 150, 193, 194

Made in the USA
Monee, IL
20 May 2023